I0584422

Alexander Campbell Fraser

Philosophy of Theism

Being, The Gifford Lectures

Alexander Campbell Fraser

Philosophy of Theism
Being, The Gifford Lectures

ISBN/EAN: 9783337071578

Printed in Europe, USA, Canada, Australia, Japan

Cover: Foto ©ninafisch / pixelio.de

More available books at **www.hansebooks.com**

PHILOSOPHY OF THEISM

BEING

THE GIFFORD LECTURES

DELIVERED BEFORE THE UNIVERSITY
OF EDINBURGH IN 1894-95

FIRST SERIES

BY

ALEXANDER CAMPBELL FRASER, LL.D.

HON. D.C.L. OXFORD

EMERITUS PROFESSOR OF LOGIC AND METAPHYSICS
IN THE UNIVERSITY OF EDINBURGH

WILLIAM BLACKWOOD AND SONS
EDINBURGH AND LONDON
MDCCCXCV

CONTENTS.

PHILOSOPHY OF THEISM.

LECTURE I.

THE FINAL PROBLEM.

My first words must give expression to the emotion Personal. which I feel on finding myself once more admitted to speak officially within the walls of this ancient university, with which, as student, graduate, and professor, I have been connected for sixty years. For it is sixty years in this November since I first cast eyes of wonder on the academic walls which now carry so many memories in my mind, and which to-day are associated with an extraordinary responsibility. In the evening of life, in reluctant response to the unexpected invitation of the patrons of the Gifford Trust, I find myself, in the presence of my countrymen, called to say honestly the best that may be in me concerning the supreme problem of human life, our relation to which at last determines the answers to all questions which

A

can engage the mind of man. No words that I can
find are sufficient to represent my sense of the honour
thus conferred, or the responsibility thus imposed, upon
one who believed that he had bid a final farewell to
appearances in public of this sort, in order to wind up
his account with this mysterious life of sense.

The final
problem
and
Simonides.

It is an appalling problem which confronts me, and,
indeed, confronts us all, for all must dispose of it in
the conduct of life; and I am now required to handle
it intellectually. One may not be ready to say with
Pliny, that all religions are the offspring of human
weakness and fear; and that what God is, if indeed God be anything distinct from the world in
which we find ourselves, it is beyond man's understanding to know. Yet even the boldest thinker,
when confronted by the ultimate problem of existence, may well desire to imitate the philosophic
caution of Simonides, when he was asked, What God
was?—in first demanding a day to think about the
answer, then two days more, and after that continuously doubling the required time, when the time
already granted had come to an end; but without
ever finding that he was able to produce the required answer;—rather becoming more apt to suspect
that the answer carried him beyond the range of
human intelligence. Often in the course of these last
months I have wished that I could indulge in this
prudent procrastination, taking not more days only
but more years to ponder this infinite problem. But .

after the threescore years and ten, this is a forbidden
alternative, if I am to speak in this place at all. I
see now near at hand

> " The shadow cloak'd from head to foot,
> Who keeps the keys of all the creeds."

It is the ultimate problem about the universe that
is at the heart of a philosophical Theism. The ideal
of this Theology is "the true intellectual system of the
universe," as Cudworth puts it. It virtually asks what
this illimitable aggregate of ever-changing things and
persons really means, if indeed it means anything.
What is the deepest and truest interpretation that
can be put by man upon the immeasurable actuality
in which I found myself participating when I became
percipient, and with which I have been in contact and
collision ever since I began to be conscious? This is,
surely, the most universally human question that can
be raised: no man can escape from giving some sort of
response to it, consciously or unconsciously, in his life
if not in speculative thought. "In what sort of environment, and for what purpose, do I exist?" might
be taken as the form in which the final question about
the universe of reality expresses itself, when it is looked
at on its human side. What finally is this universe,
to a dim perception of which I awoke when I became
conscious, and in which I am now struggling? It
seems to be for ever changing the appearances it
presents to me. What may be the origin and outcome

Forms in which the final problem of the universe may be expressed.

of this endless flux ? Is the principle which finally determines all events reasonable, trustworthy, divine ? or is the universe, on the whole and in the end, chaotic and misleading, with a transitory semblance of physical order only ? or must I remain for ever ignorant about this, and therefore unable to adopt either of those alternatives ? And if I adopt one of them, do I thus get any light shed upon my present duties, or upon my final destiny, as myself a part of the mysterious Whole ?

The ultimate problem disturbs modern thought.

It is this problem of the ultimate meaning and purpose of the universe, or whether indeed there is any purpose or meaning in it, human or other, that, as I have said, lies at the heart of the subject that has been handed over to Gifford lecturers, for free but always reverential discussion. It is a many-sided problem, which each lecturer is expected to discuss at his own point of view, with the advantage to truth of its being thus looked at on many sides—a problem, too, that is surely more than usually disturbing thought and faith in this outspeaking era of European and American civilisation.

Lord Gifford's instructions for dealing with it.

When I engaged in this work, I turned to Lord Gifford's Deed of Bequest, in the hope that it might contain articulate directions with regard to the object-matter to be investigated, the intended method of investigation, and the chief end of the proposed inquiry. I found, under each of these three heads, particular instructions, but more or less ambiguous.

It may be convenient to consider them in this opening lecture, as an introduction to the present course. It is a form of introduction that is perhaps not uncalled for by popular misconceptions about what we have got to do, and about the method of doing it, which criticism of former Gifford lecturers has brought to light.

As regards the matter of inquiry, it is an object absolutely unique that is put before us. Indeed, in the ordinary sense of the term, it cannot well be spoken of as an "object" at all; for it cannot be made visible and tangible; nor is it finite, as all objects studied in the natural sciences must be, and as the word *object* itself seems to imply. This unique object, if object it may be called, is thus spoken of in the Deed of Foundation: — "God, the Infinite, the All, the First and Only Cause, the One and the Sole Substance, the Sole Being, the Sole Reality, and the Sole Existence"; more particularly, "the nature and attributes of God," and "the relations which men and the whole universe bear to God." "Science" of all this is "Natural Theology in the widest sense of the term." Such at least is Lord Gifford's definition of this sort of Natural Theology.

It is the Infinite Being, and so an absolutely unique object, that we have to inquire about.

Next I am told something about the method of procedure in conducting this unique investigation concerning the Infinite Reality. For it is strict scientific method that is enjoined, according to the analogy of the natural sciences, unrestrained except by evidence,

The Infinite Being is to be inquired about in scientific method and spirit.

with consequent obligation to follow facts, in pursuit of whatever is found on the whole to be true or reasonable. As thus:—"I wish the lecturers to treat their subject as a strictly natural science, the greatest of all possible sciences, in one sense the only science —that of INFINITE BEING; without reference to, or reliance upon, any supposed special, exceptional, or so-called miraculous revelation. I wish it to be considered as astronomy or chemistry is. . . . The lecturers shall be under no restraint whatever in their treatment of their theme. For example, they may freely discuss (and it may be well to do so) all questions about man's conceptions of God or the Infinite; their origin, nature, and truth; whether man can have any such conceptions; whether God is under any or what limitations; and so on,—as I am persuaded that nothing but good can result from free discussion. . . . The lecturers appointed shall accordingly be subjected to no test of any kind, and shall not be required to take an oath, or to make any promise of any kind; they may be of any denomination whatever, or of no denomination at all (and many earnest and high-minded men prefer to belong to no ecclesiastical denomination); they may be of any religion or way of thinking, or, as it is sometimes said, they may be of no religion; or they may be called sceptics, agnostics, or free-thinkers, . . . it being desirable that the subject be promoted and illustrated by different minds." So much for the temper in which the study of Infinite

Being, or the final interrogation of the Universe, is expected to be pursued by Gifford lecturers.

Finally, our code of directions suggests that a broad social purpose of utility, using the word "utility" in its highest sense, is to be kept in view throughout the inquiry. This is indeed the chief end, in the intention of the founder, of the existence of those lectureships, concerned with what, as above defined, he calls "Natural Theology in the widest sense of the term." It is a human and practical more than a purely speculative or intellectual purpose. For we find as follows:—"I having been for many years deeply and firmly convinced that the true knowledge of God — that is, of the Being, Nature, and Attributes of the Infinite, of the All, of the First and only Cause, the one only Substance and Being; and the true and felt Knowledge (not mere nominal Knowledge) of the relations of Man and of the Universe to Him—being, I say, convinced that *this* knowledge, when felt and acted on, is the means of man's highest wellbeing, and the security of his upward progress,—I have therefore resolved to institute and found, in connection if possible with the Scottish universities, lectureships, for the promotion of the study of the said subjects, and for the teaching and diffusion of sound views regarding them, among the whole population of Scotland." This means that a man's faith or doubt about the final realities shows what he really is, and makes him what he really is.

The inquiry may be made the means of man's highest wellbeing and upward progress.

Let us face facts fully.

It is, accordingly, with this deeply human purpose in view, and in the scientific spirit which seeks for truth, truth only, and truth all, that we ought now to address ourselves to the ultimate problem of the universe, involving as it does Infinite Being, and constituting "Natural Theology in the widest sense of the term." We are in quest of the wisest and truest answer available for a being such as man is to the one supreme human question—In what sort of universe, and for what final purpose, am I existing? Am I able, and indeed obliged in reason by the facts and conditions of the case, to put a religious or theistic interpretation upon the universe, as truer and more comprehensive than any merely physical or material interpretation; or, on the contrary, do the facts, interpreted according to the conditions of reason, forbid me to recognise a final conception higher than the physical, or that which is now apt to be called exclusively the "scientific" conception? Either way I must follow as facts and reason oblige me to go. "Things are what they are," as Bishop Butler says, "and the consequences of them will be what they will be; why, then, should we desire to be deceived?" Let us face facts, seeking only to know what they are, and, as far as we can, what they really mean.

Recognition of the ultimate mystery of the

I. Look first at the Infinite Reality with which the final problem of existence is concerned. The mystery of his own existence, and of the universe in which he finds himself, seems to be a mystery only to man, among known sentient beings; and it is a conscious mystery only to a few men. "With the exception of man," as Schopenhauer says, "no being *wonders* at its own existence and surroundings." To the brute, if destitute of self-consciousness, the world and its own life are *felt*, naturally and uninquiringly felt, as a matter of course. But with man at least life becomes a thought in which even the most degraded may be moved to feel an interest. Men show themselves dimly conscious of the thought in the rudest forms of religion. A sense of the ever-abiding presence of the enigma of existence—shown in the form of wonder as to what we are ourselves, what our surroundings mean, why we are what we are, why we are so surrounded, and what we are destined to become—is more consciously the motive to intellectual philosophy in the minds of the thinking few. But it is the awe involved in the vague sense of man's final dependence, amidst the Immensities and Eternities, and the more precise sense of moral responsibility for the way we conduct our lives, that gives rise to religion, so that religion more readily than purely intellectual curiosity finds a response in human sentiment.

universe characteristically human.

It is the virtual presence of the Infinite that gives distinctive character alike to philosophy and to religion. It is in their common concern with Infinite Reality that both are distinguished from ordinary knowledge and special science. We are accustomed

A merely physical solution of the mystery seems self-contradictory.

in the sciences of the material world to a feeling of
intellectual satisfaction, when we are able to refer unexpected events in nature to preceding sense-presented
phenomena, on which they are believed naturally to
depend, and by which, as their finite and perceptible
causes, they are at least provisionally explained. But
it is something deeper than this provisional satisfaction
that moves philosophical curiosity, and that is latent
in religious reverence or worship. For the complete
or final meaning of the infinite universe of reality cannot be discovered by referring *its* illimitable reality to
other universes, in the way material phenomena are
referred to their natural causes. There can really be
only one universe. The desired science of its supreme
meaning would be therefore absolutely unique science.
The universe, when regarded in its divine principle,
cannot be treated as if it were only a finite term in
a causal succession. It is not like a visible event in
one of the physical sciences, as to which when a place
has been found for it in some sequence that is believed to be part of the customary order of events,
physically scientific interest is then satisfied, and the
phenomenon, so explained, ceases to perplex. But
in asking for an explanation of the totality of existence presentable in time, we are not trying to find
a phenomenon to explain another phenomenon—the
already experienced to explain the newly presented.
Philosophic wonder and religious reverence are states
of mind which seem to call us out of this experience

altogether, and require us to deal intellectually with the infinite reality, with which narrow and ephemeral human experience is mysteriously charged. To try to reach out beyond the natural evolution of the visible universe itself, and to treat the entire evolution as if it were only a finite effect in an ordinary causal succession, when one considers the attempt, seems to imply that one can have experience of *universes;* and this surely involves a contradiction. For the universe, including its supreme principle, must be all-comprehensive; yet it seems as if I must get outside of it, and out of myself as a part of it, in order to speculate about it, and solve the problem of its origin, meaning, and purpose. At the most it is only an infinitesimally small part of what exists that can be presented to each man's senses, or even to the race of mankind; and during an infinitesimally short time too, in the case of each person, or even to all men. Surely Omniscience is the only form of science in which the final reality can be met, one is ready to say.

This cardinal difficulty in dealing scientifically with the final problem perplexed David Hume, the most intrepid theological and philosophical thinker that Scotland has produced. For it seems to me that the logical dimension of the problem of " Natural Theology in the widest sense of the term " was realised by an Edinburgh citizen of last century more fully than by any preceding modern thinker, unless perhaps Spinoza. This is how David Hume makes Philo

David Hume's suggested difficulty about this.

speak, as an interlocutor, in the "Dialogues on Natural Religion:"—"If we see a house," Philo argues, "we conclude with the greatest certainty that *it* had an architect or builder; because this is precisely the species of finite effect which we have experienced to proceed from that species of [finite] cause." As to this familiar argument itself, let me interpolate the remark, that even here the reasoner takes for granted, without scientific proof, that man *does* know enough about the universe and its ultimate principle to be certain that it *is* a universe in which like sorts of natural effects must proceed from like sorts of natural causes —that the natural procession of events must be always orderly, and therefore intelligible—that the universe must be physically trustworthy. Waiving this, however, Philo thus proceeds,—"Surely you will not affirm that the *universe* bears such a resemblance to a *house* that we can with the same certainty infer a cause, or that the analogy is here entire and perfect. Can you think, Cleanthes, that your usual phlegm and philosophy have been preserved in so wide a step as you have taken, when you have compared the universe to houses, ships, furniture, machines; and from their similarity in some circumstances inferred a similarity in their causes." This suggests in short that it does not follow that because you can infer the finite or *caused* cause of a house, a ship, a piece of furniture, or a machine, you can also, and in like manner, infer the *absolute* cause or principle of the universe.

"Thought, design, intelligence," he continues, "such as we discover in men and other animals, is no more than *one* of the innumerable springs and principles in the universe, which as well as a hundred others, such as heat and cold, attraction and repulsion, fall under daily observation. It is a [natural] cause by which some particular parts of nature, we find, produce alterations on other parts. But can a conclusion with any propriety be transferred from [finite] parts to the [infinite] whole. Does not the great [infinite] disproportion bar all comparison or inference. . . . But, allowing that we are to take the operations of one part of nature upon another part, for the foundation of our judgment concerning the origin [and purpose] of the whole (which never can be admitted), yet why select so minute, so weak, so bounded a principle as the reason and design of animals living upon this planet is found to be? What peculiar privilege has this little agitation of the brain which we call thought [consciousness] that we must thus make *it* the model of the whole universe? So far from admitting that the operations of a part can afford us any just conclusion concerning the [infinite] whole, I will not allow any one part to form a rule for another part, if the latter be very remote from [unlike] the former. . . . And if *thought*, as we may well suppose, be confined merely to this narrow corner, and has even here so limited a sphere of action, with what propriety can we assign *it* for the original cause [absolute prin-

who makes his domestic economy the rule for the
government of kingdoms, is in comparison a pardonable
sophism. But were we ever so much assured that a
thought or reason, resembling the human, were to be
found [to-day] throughout the whole universe, and
were *its* activity elsewhere vastly greater than it [now]
appears on this globe; yet I cannot see why the
operations of a world now constituted, arranged, ad-
justed, can, with any propriety, be extended to a world
which was in its embryo state, and only advancing
towards that constitution and arrangement. Nature,
we find, from our limited experience, possesses an
infinite number of springs and principles which in-
cessantly discover themselves on every change in her
position and situation. And what new and unknown
principles would actuate her in so new and unknown
a situation as that of the [original] formation of a universe, we cannot, without the utmost temerity, pretend
to determine." So far David Hume.

The pres-
ence of evil
and of
death in
the uni-
verse in-
tensify
human in-
terest in
its final
problem.

Notwithstanding this obstacle to our getting into
relation with the final principle of the universe, there
are facts in experience that intensify, if they do not
give rise to intense longing for at least a practical
explanation of what the whole thing means for us, and
what it is finally to issue in for us. What probably
most quickens this inquiry, and rouses men out of the
sensuous indifference that is confirmed by the mere
custom of living, is, in the first place, the seeming

chaos of suffering and sin that is mixed up with life; and, in the next place, the vanity that appears to be stamped upon each person's share in the whole transaction, through the fact that every human being is confronted by his own approaching death. The presence of evil and of death in the universe excites painful wonder, and excites also a sense of absolute dependence. Evil and death are chief difficulties, moreover, in the way of a solution of the final problem. If this conscious life of ours—in which we become individually, for a time at least, part of the actual reality, without being able to avoid our fate—if this were an endless and a perfect life, the interest man could take in the ultimate problem of things would be more speculative. The gaunt spectre of Evil would not then disturb the harmony of experience and of our ideals. Neither should we be confronted by the mystery of our own prospective disappearance from this visible scene—

> " To die,—to sleep ;—
> To sleep ! perchance to dream : ay, there's the rub ;
> For in that sleep of death what dreams may come,
> When we have shuffled off this mortal coil,
> Must give us pause."

Philosophy has been described as a meditation upon death. It is in this light an expansion of what the gentle and religious English essayist represented according to popular conceptions in the "Vision of Mirza." But the common faith in immortality seems incredible to those who are accustomed to take the postulates of

The mystery of an endless individual conscious life.

mechanical materialism for regulating their final interpretation of reality. Their world is found to be in
constant change, in which all that is individual seems
naturally to be transitory. Is it not contrary to all
the analogies of present experience, we are asked, to
suppose that I who lately began to be shall never cease
to be, or that I shall not be refunded into unconscious
existence as in the centuries before I was born ? Whatever is generable must surely be perishable. My soul
if immortal must have existed before my birth, and if
its existence then noways concerns me now, as little will
its existence after death. Our unconsciousness before
the natural organisation of our bodies seems, according
to analogy, a sufficient proof of a similar unconsciousness when the organisation naturally dissolves. What
arguments can justify prevision of a sort of existence
which no human being ever saw, or which no way
resembles what any member of the human race has
ever experienced ? In man as in all other animals the
sentient principle and the body seem to have all in
common, and should we not conclude for this reason
that, in all that is animated, sentiency depends upon the
visible organism ? " When it is asked," says the sceptic,
" whether Agamemnon, Thersites, Hannibal, Varro, and
every stupid clown that ever existed, in Italy, Scythia,
Bactria, or Guinea, are now alive,—can any man think
that a scrutiny of nature will furnish arguments strong
enough to answer so strange a question in the affirmative ? " Then how can this infinite personal existence

be reconciled with any sense of personal identity, or with memory of its immeasurable past in the eternal future? If it is difficult for a grown man to identify himself with the new-born babe which once he was, how is this difficulty increased when the person has become millions of years old? What practical identity can there be between Plato at Athens and Plato a hundred millions of years hence? And, above all, what means a personal consciousness that is endless or infinite, thus transcending time? Is not an infinite succession, whether of conscious states or of events of any sort, an impossible supposition? What scientific verification of a conclusion so stupendous is conceivably possible? Even the crucial instance of a man who has died and been restored to life telling his experience of what follows death fails, for he could not have had experience of the endlessness of his life, which of course is infinitely more than its continuance for a time, after his body dies. It is questions of this sort that the mystery of physical death is apt to suggest to those who are accustomed to assume that the natural interpretation of the world is its deepest interpretation. The infinite conception is alien to their universe. In abstract idealism, on the other hand, an escape from the hypothesis of absolute annihilation is sought, by substituting the immortality of abstract reason for the immortality of the individual man, as, in like manner, an abstract existence of God is substituted for the only sort of divine existence that is practically interesting to men.

Plato's allegory of the Cave illustrates this life of sense.

Man's position in relation to that final mystery of the world, which gives rise to philosophy, and which evokes religious faith and hope and worship, may be taken as represented in Plato's famous parable of the Cave. Which things are an allegory, for in them the philosophic Greek figures the contrast between the infinite realities of existence and the constant succession of changes in our transitory life of sense. So that, with respect to what exists absolutely, men in this mortal state are not unlike those who are getting educated in the Cave, looking on shadows, with their eyes turned away from the light which reveals the final reality.

An atheistic universe.

A man's interest in a final settlement of the problem of life seems to be connected by Schopenhauer too exclusively with a vague desire for "some kind" of existence after the man's physical death. "We find," he says, "that the interest which philosophies and religions inspire has always its strongest hold in the dogma of some kind of existence after death; and although the most recent systems seem to make the existence of God the main point, and defend this most zealously, yet in reality this is because they have connected their faith in a future life with God's existence, and regard the one as inseparable from the other. Only on account of this supposed future life is the existence of God practically important to man. For if one could sustain belief in one's own unending existence in some other way than by faith in God's existence, then zeal for the existence of God would at once cool; and if conversely the absolute impossibility of immortality for man were proved, the zeal would give place to complete theological indifference. Also, if we could prove that our continued existence after death is absolutely inconsistent with the existence of God, men would soon sacrifice God to their own immortality, and become zealous for atheism, in order to retain their hope of a future life." Does not all this proceed upon a wrong idea of what ought to be sought for, in seeking to assure ourselves of the " existence of God "? Does it not involve a misconception of what ought to be meant by the word God ? A universe without God is really a universe without meaning, law, or order; without reason—either supremely immanent in it, or supreme and external to it—and therefore even physically uninterpretable ; without purpose, and therefore without moral reason at the root of its thus ultimately chaotic evolutions. It is a universe which, for aught we can with reason believe, may be charged in future with purposeless misery to us all, and to all other sentient beings, transcending the most terrible woes which the most wretched human beings have experienced in the past. It is a universe without reasonable hope ; and on the supposition that each conscious life in it must be endless, it may become to all a hell of endless suffering, from which there is no escape into unconsciousness. Without the divine or perfect principle of order at its centre, man would be in a worse condition than that of the unhappy inquirer whose thoughts are paraphrased by Pascal. Who has sent me into this scene of existence in which I now find myself living, I know not; what the true meaning of my surroundings may be, I know not; what I really am myself, I know not. I am in a bewildering and terrifying ignorance of all things, and know not how to interpret any of the experience through which I pass. Encompassed by the fathomless and frightful abysses of Immensity and Eternity, I find myself chained to one little corner of their boundless extent; without understanding why I am here rather than there, now rather than then; with infinity and unknown powers all around, which may at any moment cause me to disappear like a shadow. The sum of my knowledge, after the utmost experience that I can have of the infinite reality in which I am living, is, that I must in a short time die; my highest wisdom seems to consist in nothing better than a fruitless meditation upon the insoluble mystery of death. Faith in the absolute supremacy of active moral Reason— that is, faith in God—is the only unconditional satisfaction in this perplexity.

A universe in which the divine principle of order is wanting must be an insane universe.

It is told of Bishop Butler that in conversation with his friend Dean Tucker he one day startled his companion by asking, Whether nations and other societies of men, as well as individual men, might not occasionally be liable to fits of insanity? "I thought little at the time of that odd conceit of the Bishop," the Dean remarks; "but I own I could not avoid thinking of it afterwards, and applying it to many cases of nations and their rulers." Butler's "odd conceit" is apt to suggest, in the train of thought I am now following, a question not unlike his, with regard, not to nations only, but to the ever-changing world, with which we are all continually in contact and collision in the real experience of life. May not the supposed cosmos, to a dim perception of which we all awake in the first exercise of our senses, be really the manifestation of an unknown Power that is, or at least that may become, the source of an irrational and infinitely cruel human experience. We have no absolute guarantee against this virtual insanity, when we lose active moral Reason as the Supreme Principle, with the consequent disappearance, sooner or later, of natural as well as moral law in the procession of events. Under such conditions, can we even justify the vulgar faith, which, alike in daily life and in the previsions and verifications of science, takes for granted, without logical proof, that man knows enough of his surroundings and of himself to be able safely to assume that he is living in an intelligible unity, in an actuality the evolutions of which are fit to be reasoned about. For it may then be that, after all, one is living in what may turn out at last a physical and moral Chaos instead of a physical and moral Cosmos? May not the dogma of order in nature — reason or law immanent in things — be a mistake for purposeless unreason, so that all our applied logical and ethical conclusions shall, either in this or in some future life, be baffled by capricious unreason at the heart of the whole ?

Contemporary philosophical idealism.

Much of the philosophical and religious thought of the past is, unconsciously if not consciously on the part of the thinkers, the issue of endeavours to find the best form of answers to questions like those now suggested. Reflecting men have been moved to the final inquiry because they wanted to find reasonable security that the commonly supposed Cosmos is not finally Chaos, so that the world may be trusted in, as for all human purposes sufficiently interpretable, and that its phenomena are to some extent truly interpreted by man. This in its own fashion is the dominant note of contemporary Idealism, which in its own way seeks to *show* that experience is coherent in the organic unity of reason, so that no rightly exercised human being can be put to permanent confusion by the irrationality or the immorality of the Supreme Principle. To do *this* is really to try to show that God, or Perfect Moral Reason, is constantly immanent at the heart of things and their infinite contingencies.

The question which " Natural Theology in the widest meaning of the term " has got to consider.

Is this theistic solution of the problem of the universe the truly philosophical one—the most reasonable that is open to man, and sufficient for human nature ? Is the immeasurable reality in which I find myself living and moving and having my being rooted in Active Moral Reason, and therefore absolutely worthy of faith ; or is it hollow and hopeless, because at last without meaning? According to the answer practically given to this question, our surroundings and our future are viewed with an ineradicable expectation and hope, or with literally unutterable doubt and despair. It is this question that "Natural Theology in the widest sense of the term" has to determine.

II. Think next about the Method of procedure we are desired to follow when we are trying to find whether, and if so, on what grounds, it is determinable. Lord Gifford's Deed of Foundation, as we saw, recommends one way of dealing with the final problem of existence, while it particularly warns us against another and favourite' way of doing so, as inconsistent with genuine inquiry and honest thought. In dealing with the ultimate principle of the universe—the problem of Infinite Being—it is to be disposed of, we are told, according to the "strictly natural" method of "science"; according to methods as strictly natural as those adopted in the sciences of astronomy and chemistry, which are expressly mentioned as examples of the use of the right method. This is one instruction. The other condition is that we must pursue the inquiry "without reference to, or reliance upon, any supposed special, exceptional, or so-called miraculous revelation." *What is meant by the "strictly natural method of science"?*

Each of these conditions, when so stated, seems to involve ambiguity. *Ambiguity.*

In the first place, it seems plain, even from what has already been said, that this absolutely unique "science *Natural theology is not "nat-*

ural" in
the way
astronomy
and chem-
istry are.

of Infinite Being," or science of the universe of things
and persons in their ultimate relation to their divine
principle, cannot be a science of "nature," or of finite
causes, in the same way as astronomy and chemistry
are natural sciences.   For these two, and others like
them, are special sciences; that is to say, they are
sciences of finite portions of external nature, their
facts receive their full natural explanation in inductively ascertained sequences of physical causation, in
which the inferred cause is imaginable, presentable
in sense, and fit to be experimented on and used.   But
Infinite Being—the final Principle of the universe—
that in virtue of which the universe is a universe,
and which keeps it a universe—*this* cannot be treated
as merely a portion of nature.   For that would be to
divest it at the outset of its absolutely unique character—to reduce "Infinite Being" to the level of the
finite phenomena in which the astronomer and the
chemist see illustrations of outward natural law.   Indeed this very uniqueness is expressly presupposed in
those words of the Foundation Deed which speak of
"Natural Theology in the widest sense of the term,"
as being properly "the only science"—"the one universal science"—thus distinguishing it from, and even
contrasting it with, special sciences of portions of
nature, like astronomy and chemistry.   Theology, as
Aristotle saw, is truly that in which all philosophy
culminates: for theology deals with the universe in its
absolute totality (if the word totality may be so ap-

plied) or infinity: the other two are concerned, one with the finite orbs of heaven that occupy immensity, the other with the elements, or kinds of matter, that enter into their constitution. The first is infinite in its scope: the second and third concentrate themselves upon their selected portions of what is finite.

Therefore, when a theology is (somewhat misleadingly) called " natural," and when Gifford lecturers are enjoined to treat this subject as " a strictly natural science," I am obliged to infer that the important adjective " natural " does not mean that the Infinite Being, the object of study and inquiry, is to be included in nature—unless this ambiguous word is used in an all-comprehensive meaning—not as a synonym for things presentable in space and time, which are supposed to be connected by physical causation. It is the visible " agents " within this causal system which natural sciences, such as astronomy and chemistry, are employed in seeking for, and in interpreting through their connections with other finite terms in the same causal system—connections of which so-called natural causes are virtually the signs. In the ordinary meaning of the words " nature " and " natural," the Infinite Being of natural theology is supernatural; and theology is concerned with what is supernatural or metaphysical. The implied analogy between the theology that is called " natural," and special sciences like astronomy and chemistry, must, therefore, mean something different from their being all three concerned with causes that

The ordinary meaning of "nature."

are presentable to the senses, and representable in imagination.

The dogmatic assumption that there is a supernatural revelation disallowed.

I conclude, accordingly, that the intended meaning of " natural," in Lord Gifford's deed, is found more fully in the next injunction :—" I wish the lecturers to treat their subject . . . without reference to, or reliance upon, any supposed special, exceptional, or so-called miraculous revelation." That means, I suppose, that, just as " astronomy and chemistry "—the two named examples of " natural " sciences — are bound to be formed by man's own methodical observation of events in nature, and his own freely formed inferences, founded on calculation of events—so, the theology which is " natural " must be all through the issue of a human interpretation of human experience of the really existing universe of things and persons ; determined by principles of reason, known to be ultimately true in their own light ; independently of words that are dogmatically assumed, only on the authority of living men, or of a book in which they appear, to express infallibly some of the reason or purpose that is latent in the universe. We know that there is no similar claim blindly accepted as authority for a supernatural and therefore infallible astronomy, or a supernatural and therefore infallible chemistry, which would supersede rational investigation.   In like manner, blind reliance on a dogmatically supposed source of infallibility in matters of religious thought must be put aside by the Gifford lecturer ; so that all the three sciences—the two special ones now named, and the unique science of Infinite Being—must alike make their final appeal to reason in experience, and not merely to traditional authority as such, which can never be the final court of appeal for a reasonable being, on any question, natural or supernatural. So what is meant, perhaps, is, that instead of deprecating reason, or a reasoned experience, in theology, reasonableness must finally direct us, in this as in everything else, if we are reasonable beings. But this of course need not imply that conformity of the individual judgment to external authority must in all cases be unreasonable, or that it may not in some cases be the only human way of getting to truth.

So I do not interpret the terms of this Foundation as putting an arbitrary restraint upon reason, by withdrawing from its regard a part of what is reported to have happened in the history of the world,—including those signal examples of religious experience, in Palestine and elsewhere, which claim to be the issue of what is called " supernatural interposition," and of which so much Hebrew literature is the record. Whether natural or supernatural, in any of the several meanings of those ambiguous terms, this human experience is a portion of the world's history, and therefore a portion of that revelation of the final meaning and purpose of things which is to be sought for in the facts of history. " God," as Locke says, " if He makes the prophet, does not unmake the man." He leaves him to judge, as a reasonable being, of the so-called inspirations, whether

But supposed supernatural revelations are at least part of the history of mankind.

they be divine, and therefore finally authoritative, or
not.   Man's assent to the truth or divinity of any proposition, on any subject, must of course be justifiable
either by the ordinary conditions of scientific proof ; or
if it is something that transcends this proof, it must
still be finally sustained by something, whether called
natural or supernatural insight, that can be recognised
by reason as reasonable—in the form, it may be, of faith
or trust, which seems to be the highest form that
reason takes in man.   Consult reason we must, when
we go to the root of any matter, and with its leave
determine whether the so-called "exceptional" revelation is really divine.   And if reason finds, either intui-
tively or by reasoning, that it is reasonable to regard a
so-called supernatural revelation as divine, reason itself
then declares for it, and makes the "supernatural"
revelation one of its own dictates.

Reason and
faith.
It is still the office of reason to judge under what
conditions it is reasonable to accept personal authority
as revelation of divine meaning and purpose, and also to
interpret the meaning of the words in which the revelation is presented by the person who delivers it.   Whatever God, who is immanent reason, really has revealed is certainly true ; we are obliged in reason to
accept that, for in doing so we are accepting reason
itself.   But that this which claims to be divine *is*
really divine cannot be ultimately determined blindly :
reason must judge whether on the whole it is reasonable to transform it into one of its own dictates.   Now

reason can never permit the mind to reject a greater evidence, in order to embrace what is less evident, nor allow us to entertain probability in opposition to absolute certainty. No evidence that any authoritative revelation is divine can be so clear and so certain as are the universal and necessary principles of reason; and therefore nothing that is *absolutely inconsistent* with what is self-evidently reasonable has a right to be received as a matter of faith. Whatever *is* divine revelation ought to rule all our opinions, and can claim assent in the name of reason. "Such a submission as this of our reason to faith," as Locke says, "takes not away the landmarks of knowledge; this shakes not the foundations of reason, but leaves us that use of our faculties for which they were given us." But it must be remembered that what Locke here means by "reason" seems to be discursive thought or reasoning, measured by nature, in the narrow meaning of nature. Reason, in the wider meaning of the term, becomes at last faith, in a finite experience of the universe; and its own ultimate constitution, mostly latent or dimly conscious in men, may be regarded as really a divine or supernatural revelation, to which reason in its narrower meaning, or the understanding that judges according to external nature, is necessarily subordinate.

One feels the need for some Socratic questioning when the words "natural" and "supernatural" are employed, and opposed to one another, or when they are placed in relation to reason. What conception

What is meant by "supernatural"?

of " nature " and " reason " is taken, when theology is
called natural or rational, and only as such admitted
to academical treatment; as the " one only science," or
queen among the sciences ?   Is there a difference in
kind between what usually happens in " nature " and
any event in nature, however extraordinary, that can
be supposed to occur in the history of an ultimately
reasonable universe—a difference such that, on account
of it, certain events may be called supernatural and
miraculous ?   Must not all that can enter into the
·history of the universe be regarded by the theist as
natural, in the higher meaning of " nature " ? and must
not all possible events, whether called natural or supernatural, be consistent with the perfect rational ideal—
the intellectual system of the universe ?   Nay, is not
supernaturalness, in another view, the characteristic of
man, so far as he is a moral agent, and to that extent
independent of physical nature ?   Is not " miracle "—
when the term is applied to any physical event, *e.g.*,
the resurrection of a dead man—a relative term, dependent on the limitations of human experience and
human intellectual grasp ; so that, in proportion as
intelligence and experience are widened, events called
supernatural or miraculous would be seen by the eye
of reason to take their places in the perfect order of
the Divine intellectual system ;—but still at a point
of view transcending that share of the reason that is
latent in experience in which a human being can
consciously participate ?   In the view of Perfect Intel-

ligence can any event, even the actual resurrection of
a dead man, or any other not less extraordinary, seem
miraculous or wonderful, and not rather in natural conformity with the perfect reason and purpose immanent
in things? Looked at from the *centre* of things, either
nothing should be called supernatural, or all should be
called supernatural. Supposed events or experiences
are called miraculous by men, because they are of a sort
which transcends those processes in the universe to which
men are accustomed, and to the aggregate of which the
term "nature" is commonly confined. I suppose that
a dim idea of this sort may have been in Bishop
Butler's mind, when he suggested that there can be
no "absurdity in supposing that there may be beings
in the universe whose capacities and knowledge may
be so extensive as that the whole Christian dispensa-
tion [commonly called supernatural or miraculous] may
to them appear natural, . . . as natural as the visible
course of things appears to us." If all that happens, or
that can happen, in "external nature" is the immediate
issue and expression of supreme active reason, immanent in all, the distinction between natural and supernatural in the end disappears; but not therefore the
distinction between what is physical or sensuous and
what is spiritual; nor is the rational possibility shut
out of uncommon, and by man incalculable, events
actually occurring, because involved, in a way unap-
proachable through his conceptions, in the perfect
order which final reason in nature presupposes :

whether they have actually occurred or not is of course a question of fact and historical evidence. But it is premature to raise these questions: they must be met later on.

Are not events "natural" and "supernatural" relatively to the intelligence of the percipient?

In the meantime I would ask you to consider, whether any "special" revelation of God that is possible must not be regarded as in itself an expression of reason, and therefore natural, when "nature" is taken in its high meaning, as comprehending all that happens, conceived according to the final intellectual system of the universe. This may be unimaginable; but, if the universe is in its ultimate principle divine, it cannot contradict reason. Also, must not everything, however natural, at last become *for man* infinite or mysterious, so that in this high meaning of "nature" all theology must be "natural" theology? This recognition of rationality, we are learning to see, is an indispensable presupposition of human intercourse with the realities. "Upon the first establishment of Christianity," Cleanthes remarks, in Hume's Dialogue, "nothing was more common than declamations against reason. All the [sceptical] topics of the ancient Academics were adopted by the Fathers of the Church. The Reformers embraced the same principles of reasoning, or rather declamation; and all panegyrics on the excellency of faith were sure to be interlarded with some severe strokes of satire against natural reason. Locke," he adds, "seems to have been the first Christian who ventured openly to assert that *faith* was nothing but a

species of *reason;* that religion [intellectually consid-
ered] was a branch of philosophy; and that a chain of
arguments similar to that which established any truth,
e.g., in morals, politics, or physics, was always employed in discovering all the principles of theology,
natural and revéaled. It is now avowed by all pre-
tenders to reasoning and philosophy that atheist and
[universal] sceptic are almost synonymous. And as
it is certain that no man is in earnest when he professes
the latter principle, I would fain hope that there are as
few who seriously maintain the former." This suggests
that immanence of rational order, not irrational and
capricious interference with order by the Supreme
Power—which would involve final scepticism—must be
presupposed as the foundation of all "revelations" of
the meaning and purpose of the universe, and of our
chief end in it, whether the revelations are called
natural or supernatural.

And it is not inconsistent with the principle on
which Goethe objected to Hegel for "bringing the
Christian religion into philosophy, although philosophy has really nothing to do with it"; inasmuch as
" Christianity is found in experience to have a might
of its own, by which dejected, suffering humanity is
re-elevated from time to time." Nor is it inconsistent
with the fact, that when we, on the ground of this
experience, recognise its divinity, we see that it is
raised above abstract philosophy, and that it needs no
further support therefrom. For in this, which after

[sidenote: Experiential faith in the rationality or divinity of Christianity.]

C

all is argumentative appeal to "experience," the tried
spiritual efficacy of Christianity, proved by the consequences of its admission into the world, is taken
by reason as what renders it acceptable in its sight,
so that this religion is thus found to be practical
reason, or reason in the highest form that can enter
into human experience.

Illustra-
tions of
the depen-
dence of
human
conduct
upon our
final inter-
pretation
of exist-
ence.

III. Further, Lord Gifford's Deed, as I have said,
gives the motive for his encouragement of this "natural
science" of "Infinite Being." It was because he thought
he saw in the best solution of the final problem of existence the means of man's highest welfare, and security for his upward progress; and he also saw that this
knowledge could be thus valuable only when it was genuine conviction, "really felt and acted on," not merely
speculated about, in abstraction from human life and
social regard.   And I think it may be granted, that
the conception of the final meaning and purpose of life
that is (consciously or unconsciously) adopted in fact
by each man, mainly determines what that man is
and what he does.   Thus if one supposes himself
to be only passive in the necessitated process of
nature, in his ultimate conception of the universe,
then morality and immorality become meaningless
words, and Fatalism, as the logical, is apt to become
the practical issue.   So, too, our behaviour to ourselves and to other men, and our judgments of human
actions, should differ widely as the materialistic or

the spiritualistic, the pessimist or the optimist, conception of existence is adopted, and made to govern our lives. Also, unless we presuppose that active moral Reason is latent in the universal evolution, we can justify no interpretation put upon any event, and that whether, according to the analogies of experience, the event is common or extraordinary: it is all physical chaos, under a present illusive semblance of cosmos; deceptive moral chaos, with only a semblance of moral order in the form of harmony with the illusion of conscience of man—so that the possibility of the universe containing divine revelation, call it natural or supernatural, is foreclosed.

It must surely be with a sense of weighty issues that we address ourselves to the consideration of the final and universal problem which in faint outline I have now put before you. In the treatment of it, either of two objects may be kept mainly in view. We may concern ourselves either with the history of the gradual development of the religions of the world, or we may examine the philosophic basis of the adopted solution, negative or constructive, of the final problem. I may investigate either the gradual outcome in history of religious hopes and fears, the consequent modifications of religious thought or belief, and the customs and rules of conduct in which these feelings and thoughts have expressed themselves; or I may inquire into the ultimate relation to reason

We may inquire either, How men have dealt with the final problem, or Whether men are at all entitled to dispose of it religiously.

of all religious hopes and fears, thoughts and convictions, ritual and conduct.   The one inquiry is
exemplified in Hume's 'Natural History of Religion,'
the pioneer of that historical science of comparative religion which is characteristic of the nineteenth century; the other is the subject of Hume's
'Dialogues concerning Natural Religion,' in which
we are brought face to face with the ultimate questions which underlie all religious phenomena.

Is the
theological
conception
of the uni-
verse an
anachron-
ism and
absurd?

Lecturers on the Gifford Foundation, in this and the
other Scottish Universities, have hitherto, I think,
mostly inclined to the historical treatment of their
high problem.   Deeply interesting as that is, it leaves
in the background the supreme human question—Are
religious beliefs, or any of them, *true?*   Is religious
worship and faith and hope the transitory illusion of
certain stages in history, or is all this a permanent attitude of feeling and will, consistent with reason; and if
so, by what criteria may its reasonableness, and its best
intellectual form in human consciousness, be determined?   Is truth in such matters, and if not in any
other matter, capable of being, either naturally or
supernaturally, realised in the mind of man?   Is the
religious conception of the universe an illusion, explicable indeed as a physical effect that is characteristic
of certain stages of human development, but becoming
an anachronism in a civilisation like that of modern
Europe and America, which is apt to see the only
criteria of what is true in verified previsions of events

naturally evolved, under the merely physical or mechanical conception of existence?

I wish to take the second of these two points of view in the treatment of the universal problem. I proceed accordingly to inquire about the philosophical foundations of the different final interpretations of existence —all religious, if religion means vague recognition by man of a power or powers in the universe superior to his own; but not all theistic, or properly religious. The Philosophy of Theism, not the Natural History of the religious phenomena presented by mankind, is our appropriated subject—but with the history taken in occasionally, in verification or illustration of philosophical conclusions. The moral interest of the facts revealed in the history lies in the intellectual validity and worth of the faith and thought by which they are inspired. Religion, in its monotheistic form, presupposes that human experience of what is real admits of a deeper interpretation than that offered in the mechanical causalities of material science. Theistic faith claims for man a right to recognise the universe . of the Real as supremely a moral or spiritual unity, incompletely comprehensible, that may reasonably be rested in and reverenced. Religious phenomena may be found, by one who does full justice to his humanity, to be insufficiently treated, when regarded only as physical growth or evolution, the scientific ordering of which, for the satisfaction of scientific curiosity, is taken for our whole concern with them. One still

The second of these inquiries prominent in this Course.

longs to be satisfied regarding their absolute and eternal value for man.. He wants to know whether he is duly submitting to the reasonable limitations of human experience, when he is putting a religious meaning upon experience, and treating this as its final and highest meaning. Is religion, or the idea of absolute dependence on, and móral responsibility to, the Supreme Power of which the changing universe is a revelation, an intellectually legitimate state of mind, the expression of man's deepest relation to the realities of existence? Is the faith, hope, and love which it involves, in its progressive development, the practical solution for man of his final problem?

Aids to reflection on the Philosophy of Theism. In what follows I will try at least to supply some incitement to reflection suggested by questions of this sort, frankly facing difficulties apt to arise in the minds of thoughtful persons, always seeking to keep the reality of things in view, and satisfied to make the best of glimpses of truth that may be within our reach.

LECTURE II.

THE FINAL PROBLEM ARTICULATED : EGO, MATTER, AND GOD.

THE ultimate problem of existence, in the vague form
in which it was presented in last lecture, may seem
to evade the intellectual grasp. It must be further
articulated before it can be even taken hold of, for
orderly meditation and investigation. An advance
towards this is made when we recognise that the
actual reality of which we are part, into which we
are all born, and the meaning and purpose of which
philosophy and religion are especially concerned with,
finally presupposes three existences, as it is presented
in the common consciousness of men. Each of these
existences men seem to be mentally obliged to recognise, with innumerable differences in their individual
conceptions of each, and also of the mutual relations
of the three. All the three make their appearance
without premeditation and as matter of course, in the
very words of Lord Gifford's Deed which define the

Ultimate
articula-
tion of
existence
τὸ πᾶν in
common
belief.

province of "Natural Theology, in the widest meaning
of the term." For the words lead us to think of it
as comprehending "the knowledge of God's nature and
attributes;" also knowledge of "the relations which men
bear to God;" and "knowledge of the relations which
the whole [remaining part] of the universe bears to
God." Here we have "men" — exemplified by each
man for himself, in his own invisible self-consciousness; then "the world of visible things, outside each
ego;" and lastly "God," the Infinite Being, the harmony
of the whole. The three are supposed to be in some
sense distinguishable, in the final analysis of the universal reality—το πᾶν, which we begin to have to
do with, intellectually and otherwise, when we begin
to perceive things in sense.

The three
postulated
existences
of com-
mon belief
differently
conceived
by different
minds.
But although these three existences are commonly
postulated, each as real and distinguishable from the
other, it is not to be supposed that the terms "existence," "substance," and "reality" are applied to each
of the three in the same meaning, by all men in all
stages of their spiritual development. All men do not
think the same meaning when they employ the personal
pronoun "I,"—a pronoun often uttered or implied, yet
withal so mysterious. Not less do they differ in their
final conceptions when they speak of "external matter,"
as they find when they proceed to define the words
"matter" and "external." Most of all does difference
appear when they try to conceive "God" or Infinite
Being. Each of the three ideas is found to be differ-

ent when it is traced through human minds, now and
in the history of mankind; and the changes are connected with the experience persons who employ the
words pass through, and their natural and acquired
power of interpreting it. Moreover, some one of the
three postulated final existences is apt to be conceived
as more truly entitled to have existence and substantiality and power affirmed of it than either of the other
two. In the view of one man, his own invisible self-
conscious personality is so borne in upon him as to
usurp the supreme place: the existence of things outside in space and the existence of God are taken as
secondary, because reached through states of his own
personal consciousness—there being no other consciousness than his own of which he can avail himself. To
another the things around him — things that can be
seen and handled—form his ideal of reality and substance, compared with which the spiritual ego and God
look pale and shadowy and chimerical. Again, in the
mind of the "God-intoxicated" Spinoza, or of the religious mystic, the Divine Being seems to exhaust the
universe of reality, and to absorb the other two factors.
In fact, Lord Gifford's own Deed, in the clause which
goes before the words last quoted, appears to claim "real
existence" for God alone; for it asserts that God is
"the One and the Sole Substance, the Sole Being,
the Sole Reality, and the Sole Existence," implying
that if anything else really existed, anything in which
God was not the sole substance and power, then there

would be two gods, neither of them infinite, and therefore neither of them God.

Accordingly, Natural Theology, in its concern with the final problem of existence, has to inquire whether, and if so, in what sense, each of the three presupposed existences, or factors of experience, may truly be called real, and what their final relations to one another are. But, as we have seen, the terms of the foundation of this lectureship seem tacitly to attribute to the common sense or common consciousness of man, at least in its modern European stage of development, some sort of recognition by each man of his own individual existence; the existence of a world of finite things and persons outside his own private or personal consciousness; and the existence of the Divine Being, fixed, eternal, and as such more real than either of the two finite and changing realities—namely, one's own ego, and the collective aggregate of things around one, present in space, and commonly called the external world.

What "Natural Theology," in the widest meaning of the term," has to do in regard to the three postulated existences.

The relations of the individual ego, the outward world, and God to one another, form the principal part of the Philosophy of Theism. The present course is arranged throughout with reference to the three postulated existences. This lecture, therefore, may be usefully devoted to some account of them as they are found in the common consciousness; the commonly accepted tests of the reality of each; and the enigmas with which each is charged, which philosophy

Consequences of any one of the three being over-emphasised.

tries in various ways to resolve, in different *monist* conceptions of existence—universal materialism, pan-egoism, and impersonalism or pantheism—that have been proposed, for resolving the three into one; also in polytheism and monotheism—all which have to be thought out critically in the sequel. Anterior to and independent of philosophy, however, a spontaneous faith in self, in external nature, and in God, seems to pervade human experience; mixing, often unconsciously, with the lives of all; never perfectly defined, but in its fundamental ideas always and necessarily incomplete; latent often intellectually, yet never without a threefold influence in human life. We may even say that unbalanced recognition of one of the three over the other two, in thought, feeling, and action, is the chief source of error and moral disorder; and that life is good and happy in proportion to the due practical acknowledgment of all the three. Unintelligent faith in the three postulated existences is at any rate an inexhaustible source of two extremes—superstition and scepticism.

Take Locke's account of the philosophical foundation of certainty as to the ego, the material world, and God. It is given expressly in three chapters of the fourth book of his 'Essay'; but, indeed, the whole 'Essay' may be made to converge and rest finally upon what Locke calls "man's threefold knowledge of existence." I select Locke among the philosophers for this purpose because he gives expression more than most of them to

The three presuppositions of existence as articulated by Locke.

the uncriticised convictions of the common mind, and at a time when natural science and theological ideas were unmodified either by the scientific conception of universal physical evolution, or by the criticism of Kant and the dialectic of Hegel. What I want now to do is to incite to reflection upon Locke's articulation of the ultimate problem of the universe, as a preparation for the consideration of more pretentious philosophical speculations, in which the three supposed realities are resolved into one of the three. Locke expresses the common convictions of his age. This is how he puts the case in the ninth chapter of the fourth book of the 'Essay': "Let us proceed now to inquire concerning our knowledge of the existence of things, and how we come by it." Let us, that is to say, inquire what the realities of existence ultimately resolve themselves into; and also how we come to know each, and that there are so many, neither more nor fewer. He finds elsewhere that " we have the ideas of but three sorts of substances "—" namely, God, finite intelligences, and bodies. First, God is without beginning, eternal, unalterable, and everywhere. Secondly, finite spirits having had each its determinate time and place of beginning to exist, the relation to that time and place will always determine to each of them its identity, as long as it exists. Thirdly, the same will hold good of any particle of matter, to which no addition or subtraction of matter being made, it continues the same. Though these three sorts of *substances,* as we term them, do not exclude *one another* out of the same *place*, yet we cannot conceive but that they must necessarily each of them exclude any of the same kind out of the same place; else there could be no such distinctions of substances [as that of those three sorts], or of anything else, one from another." This argument seems to imply that all the "three sorts of substances," or factors of experience, are alike contained in and conditioned by space, which although assumed by many in their uncritical presupposition of the outward world, self, and God, seems to be without warrant in reason. One cannot but regard God as unworthily conceived, when described as an outward being, needing place in space for His reception, even though it is allowed to be a place which does not exclude from it either material things or finite spirits. When "personality" is assumed of God, why should this be supposed to mean that God could not exist, and exist as a person too, unless "space were ready for His reception"? But of this in the sequel.

Look next at the question, how men come to think the realities of existence in this threefold fashion. See what Locke has to say about the basis of man's knowledge of each of the three postulated existences. Is the knowledge in each case a conclusion of reasoning, which may be tested by logical conditions of proof; or does it form itself spontaneously without logical proof, in response to a human necessity, and with increasing distinctness of intelligence as civilisa-

How, according to Locke, knowledge of the three postulated existences enters human consciousness.

tion advances?   Locke puts our knowledge of the
ego, and our knowledge of outward things, in this last
category, while he finds knowledge of the existence of
God, or Eternal Mind, at last resolving into a conclusion, founded on a demonstration "as evident as any
conclusion in mathematics," and thus virtually self-
evident. We have our knowledge of our own existence, he says, " by intuition "; our knowledge of the
existence of outward things that exist independently
of ourselves, " by sensation," or sense-perception; and
our knowledge of the existence of God " by demonstration."   Consider each of these positions, as preparation
for what is to follow in a course of lectures arranged in
relation to the three supposed final realities.

How the
presup-
position
of our own
existence
arises in
conscious-
ness.

The most obvious of the three certainties about existence, in Locke's view, is, the assurance one finds he
has of his own existence, when he recognises *himself* to
be somehow more than merely a succession of isolated
conscious states—rather as the invisible personal centre
to which exclusively a portion of the conscious experience that is in process in the universe must be referred,
as being his own private and continuous conscious life.
" As for our own existence," he says, " we perceive it
so plainly and so certainly that it neither needs nor
is capable of any proof. For nothing can be more
evident to me than *my own existence:* I think, I
reason, I feel pleasure and pain; can any of these
[successive states of consciousness] be more evident to

me than my own existence [in which they are all somehow connected as *mine*]? If I doubt of all other things, that very doubt makes me perceive my own existence. Experience then convinces us that we have an intuitive knowledge of our own existence, an internal, infallible perception that we are:" This he thinks neither needs nor allows mediate proof.

In all this Locke supposes that he is simply giving expression to the uncritical common-sense of the human mind. The enigmas that underlie the fact are left to the speculating philosopher to disinter. Many such emerge when we proceed to rake Locke's foundation. For further reflection is provoked to ask,—What is meant by one's own existence as a separate person, —by that *something more* than a series of isolated conscious states, which is supposed to be distinctively signified by the pronoun "I"? This is the riddle of personality. The personal pronoun, in so far as it means this "something more," must mean what cannot be presented, either to the senses or in imagination. Must it therefore be discharged from language, as a meaningless word, an empty sound? This is 'the way the ego has been sometimes treated. David Hume, for example, supposing himself to be under an intellectual obligation to regard all terms as jargon to which no imaginable meaning could be attached, found himself obliged, on this principle, to dispense with the personal pronoun, if it pretends to express this consequently impossible meaning. For, on trying the mental experi-

The enigma of separate personality.

ment, he found that he could never light upon anything perceptible or imaginable, corresponding to ego, except the isolated and transitory conscious states of successive moments; so he concluded that if any one professed to think that *he* was something more than the single perception or conscious feeling of the moment, it was "impossible to reason with him." If any one perceives something simple and continued which he calls "himself," I am certain, he argues, that there is no such perception of continuous existence in me: the personal pronoun must not be made to mean nothing, as it is thus made to do. But this negative certainty of Hume is confronted by the difficulty that if the personal pronoun really signifies nothing more than an isolated momentary perception, there must be as many persons or egos as there are momentary perceptions; each momentary perception in what is popularly called one's "mind" constituting a separate person, whose life lasts only as long as the indivisible momentary consciousness lasts. It is further confronted by the fact that the mysterious *ego* inevitably reappears by implication in the words and actions even of the sceptical philosopher, who thus shows that he is obliged in fact to acknowledge as real more than can be presented in sense or pictured in sensuous imagination. As for Locke, he does not, in the words quoted, expressly say whether, when he recognises his own existence, he means to claim for himself only an existence that lasts while each momentary consciousness lasts, or an existence which takes in also all that is given to him in his memory; thus acknowledging that, through memory, the present consciousness becomes somehow continuous with an imperfectly remembered personal history that existed in the past. But the context of the 'Essay' shows that the continuity opened up by memory is meant to be included in the meaning of the personal pronoun "I." For Locke says elsewhere that each person remembers certainly that *he* has existed for a time, longer or shorter. We each know, too, that we have not existed always: we each know that our individual existence had a beginning somewhere in the past; we have all had our birthdays. And, as we shall see, on this fact is founded Locke's "mathematically certain proof" that God exists.

Other enigmas involved in the idea of our own existence, that lie more on the surface than the one now suggested, readily occur when one reflects. Thus the origin, evolution, and final destiny of this invisible and continuous ego; the relations of the invisible ego of consciousness to its present visible organism; the necessity or not of its connection with that or any other visible or invisible organised body,—are among the questions suggested by the meaning of the personal pronoun "I" which modern thought presses. Locke, as an exponent of ordinary practical convictions, is satisfied with giving emphatic expression to his consciousness of his own existence, without criticism. *Si non rogas, intelligo.*

Other enigmas involved in the idea of our own existence.

D

The belief
that indi-
vidual
things ex-
ist outside
the indi-
vidual
person.

He deals more analytically with perception of outward things actually present to the senses—the second of the three postulates. Contact and collision with outward things is found to be the occasion of our awaking to the last mentioned conviction of our personality, continuous in memory. That conviction involves a recognition of something outside and independent of each ego, to which the personal states are found to be related in innumerable ways. For every act even of sensuous perception " gives us," Locke says, " an equal view of both parts of Nature—the corporeal and the spiritual. Whilst I know, by seeing and hearing, that there is some corporeal being without me, the object of that sensation, I do more certainly know also that there is some spiritual being within me that sees and hears that object." So he finds that each human ego becomes spontaneously possessed of an " irresistible assurance " of the outside existence of things visible and tangible ; things which cannot be appropriated by the ego as conscious states of its own, in the way that the past and present feelings and thoughts, which one can call " his own " feelings and thoughts, are appropriated. But it is important to remark that it is an " outward existence " that is very limited both in space and duration which is supposed by Locke to be thus immediately perceived— that is to say, perceived without the need or possibility of reasoned proof, over and above the spontaneity of the sensuous perception itself, and the certainty which

this is taken to involve. The object is limited because the world of " outward things " is found in a
constant flux. The ever fluctuating objects are felt to
be certainly real—with the perfect certainty that each
really is what it is perceived to be — only (Locke
assumes) during the brief period in which each particular outward thing, " by actually operating upon our
senses " in a manner *forces* us to perceive that it is
then and there existing. Accordingly, when an outward object is withdrawn to a distance from one's
organs of sense—separated by space, or by an interval
of time, from his senses—Locke supposes that he can
have no absolutely certain knowledge of its *continued*
actual existence. Its absent existence, at least in the
form it had when presented, can then only be inferred,
and that with a variously conditioned probability, according to the circumstances in each case. Thus, when
one is actually looking at the sun, he must have perfect
assurance that the sun is *then* really existing: this is the
spontaneous certainty of actual perception. But when
at night he is only *imagining* the sun, and then naturally
expecting its reappearance in the morning, this *expectation* is nothing more than a conditional certainty, or
probable conviction, of the continued actual existence
of the absent sun : the solar system, Locke would say,
might conceivably be dissolved, and there is no unconditional guarantee that this may not actually happen.

Innumerable enigmas underlie Locke's infallibly cer- The enig-
tain sensuous perception of what is outward—certain mas involved in

the pre-
supposi-
tion of
things
existing
outwardly.

only while actually felt in fluctuating sense. They seem to be scarcely apprehended by him, especially in the forms in which some of them now appear in scientific and religious thought. Take an example. He tells us that we have an "irresistible assurance" of the present corporeal reality of all things that are "actually operating" upon "our senses"—especially the sense of sight, and, above all, touch—as long as they persist in "actually operating" upon our senses. Here a question of deep and far-reaching significance arises, which Locke touches only incidentally. In what meaning of the ambiguous words "power," "operation," and "cause" may things of sense be said to "operate," either on one another or on me? Have I reason for saying that any atom or mass of *matter*—my own body, or any thing external to it—can be rightly called an *agent;* although in common and also in scientific language bodies are commonly so spoken of, nay, are sometimes even supposed to be the only agents in the changes which are constantly going on in the world? Locke himself hesitates to include "active power" in the complex idea that men are justified by reason in forming of material substance; although he falls into the popular mode of expression when he speaks of bodies "operating" on our senses. "Material substances," he suggests, with characteristic caution — in a part of the 'Essay' where the "powers of substances" are expressly treated of—"material substances are not so entirely active powers or agents as our hasty thoughts are apt to represent them." And again, "Whether matter be not wholly destitute of active power . . . may be worth consideration." But if that be so, the solid and movable things by which we are surrounded can be only the natural occasions, not the originative causes, of our perceptions of them. And we must, in that case, look elsewhere than to things visible and tangible themselves, for the active power that directs the changes which the physical and natural sciences are gradually learning to explain. It is only order of procedure or laws of change, not originative causation, that those sciences are concerned with, under this conception. Natural science is in that case only an articulate expression of our faith that in nature the future will so far resemble the past as that we, through the past, may, with practical safety, anticipate the future. But our anticipations are often mistaken, when tested by the issue; and even in those cases in which they are verified by experiment, it is only probable verification of hypothesis, not unconditional knowledge, that one is landed in. The concrete past can never make the concrete future known, in the way abstract premisses make known an abstract conclusion, in a pure mathematical demonstration. We can reach no absolute certainty as to what all the powers in the universe of existence are which may determine a particular change; nor that the possible causes which determine impending change must be what physical science assumes that they are. Accordingly, we can-

not be said to *know absolutely* even that the sun will
rise to-morrow.   An "accident," as we in our ignorance
would call it, may have occurred to the solar system in
the interval, so that there may be no " to-morrow " in the
ordinary meaning.   All physical "science" of outward
things is thus sustained in an undemonstrable faith.

The duality of the finite universe.   Nevertheless—with mysteries like these wrapped up
in each of its finite factors—this duality of the conscious
self, and unconscious things external to, and in a way
independent of, each individual consciousness, may be
taken as tacitly presupposed, in the common sense
of men living in the *si non rogas, intelligo* state of
mind.   So one may say that he has a natural assurance of his own existence, as a separate self-conscious
ego ; and also of the existence of things outside, things
that are actually seen and touched, or otherwise present
to his senses.   He finds when he acts that he cannot
rid himself of either of these working convictions, and
he finds too that each of them is the correlative of the
other.

Incompleteness of the finite duality, and the presupposition of Infinite Being.   Still this dual universe of existence in which I thus
find myself is felt, or seen with the eye of reason,
to be somehow *incomplete*, when one thinks of it as
consisting *only* of his own self-conscious ego, and
the outside world of solid and extended things in a
state of flux—the occasion to the ego of innumerable
pains and pleasures.   Locke expresses the common
sense of this incompleteness, dim though the consciousness of it may be in many persons, when he says that

he finds himself unable to think of his own existence
without also recognising the existence of Something
Eternal or Infinite — more and other than his own
finite self—more and other than the outer world of
finite individual things. He finds himself as certain
of the eternal reality of this Something—as certain
too that this Eternal Something must be Eternal Mind,
and that therefore a Mind exists that cannot be said
to be his own, because his own, he is sure, had a beginning;—he is as certain of all this, he says, as he
is certain of any conclusion in pure mathematics. He
finds himself surer that an Eternal Mind really exists
than he is sure that anything else " outside of himself "
really exists; and he believes that every other human
being, who makes the trial deliberately, must find that
this is so in his own case too. " It is as certain in
reason," he says, " that there is a God as it is certain
that the opposite angles made by the intersection of two
straight lines are equal, or as that the three angles of a
triangle are equal to two right angles." Yet while the
existence of the Infinite Being, the supreme factor of
experience, is thus forced into conscious certainty in all
who reflect, the certainty, Locke grants, does need reflection to awaken it in the individual mind. Without
due reflection a man may remain as ignorant of this
reality as an entire stranger to geometry may remain
all his life ignorant of any of the demonstrable propositions, or even the axioms, of Euclid, which lie
latent in the minds of millions. Even so, individuals,

and whole nations too, may never have the rational necessity for the existence of the Eternal Mind awakened in their conscious experience. But it must also be remembered that the other two ideas and presuppositions—that of their own existence, and that of the existence of the outside things of sense—are also only obscurely recognised in thought by many, although all in a way acknowledge them, in feeling and action.

Locke's account of how we come to suppose Infinite Being as an Eternal Mind.

But how does the idea and conviction of the real existence of Eternal Mind at first enter a human mind? The Eternal Mind cannot, of course, be presented to any of our senses, nor, indeed, can any other ego than my own be present to me as my own ego is; and I cannot be conscious of Eternal Mind in the way I am conscious of my own existence in memory. Here is how Locke explains its presence; on the grounds of standing reason, he would say, which make atheism and agnosticism logically impossible, however much unreflecting persons may suppose that they are atheists or agnostics. "I cannot want a clear proof that God exists," so Locke argues, "as long as I carry *myself* about with me. For each man knows that he individually exists;" and he also knows "that he has not existed always. It is therefore inevitable to him, as a rational being, to conclude that Something [more than his own individual self] must have existed from eternity, . . . this being of all absurdities the greatest in the eye of reason—to imagine that pure Nothing, the perfect negation and absence of all beings, should ever produce any real existence. I cannot myself be this Eternal Something, seeing that my own existence, as I know, had a beginning; and whatever had a beginning must have been produced by something else; and it must have got all that belongs to its existence [*i.e.*, all my so-called "powers" and "attributes"] from that other being. Further, I find that I am a thinking being: therefore this Something, the original source of my existence, must be a thinking being too; it being as impossible that what is wholly void of knowledge, and operating blindly and without any perception [consciousness], should produce a knowing being, such as I am, as it is impossible that a triangle should make itself three angles bigger than two right ones." This argument, afterwards elaborated by Samuel Clarke, is in substance as old as Aristotle.

This mathematical certainty of the actual existence of Eternal Mind thus virtually resolves itself into an absolute necessity in reason for a *sufficient* cause of whatever now exists. The theological conception of the universe is, in short, only the final application of the universal principle of causality, when that principle is understood to mean that whatever is found in the effect must be found in the originative power into which the effect is refunded. Here conscious and percipient mind, found in me, must be refunded into the Eternal and Infinite Something.

The intellectual need for a sufficient cause of my own existence.

Nevertheless, "Mind," when recognised by Locke as the Eternal Something, is so regarded with an im-

Can Infinite Being be regarded as Mind?

portant qualification, of which more must be said afterwards, when speculations like those of Spinoza and
Hume come into view. Am I obliged in reason, or
even permitted by reason, to think of the Eternal
Something as Mind, if I mean the sort of mind I find
in myself—mind as it manifests itself in self-conscious
life ?   Is the Eternal Mind conscious mind, or is the
term " consciousness " in any way applicable to the
Eternal Something ?   Are we obliged to suppose an
individual conscious life in what is called God, in
which subject and object are distinguished—the distinction essential to human consciousness; and must
we think of this Eternal Mind as an individual or
separate conscious life, won and continually passing
through conscious changes; and if so obliged, what is
the ground in reason for the obligation to think this ?
How do we know that the Eternal Something is an
ever operative conscious life, in present fact, and that
it must be so eternally ?   As to this Locke shows
his characteristic caution.   The Eternal or Infinite
Something, he suggests, may be thought about as
Eternal Mind, because it is so far related to me in
experience in the way one person may be related to
another person—" so far," that is to say, " as is necessary to the true end of my being, and the great
concernment of my happiness."   But then he adds,
" though for this reason I call it mind, I must not "—
because I thus apply this *name* to the Eternal Something, in common with myself—" I must not equal

what I call mind in myself to the Eternal and Incomprehensible Being, which, for want of right and distinct conceptions, is also called Mind, or the Eternal Mind." This even suggests that what is called " mind " may in the Supreme Power be supra-conscious, in some inconceivable and ineffable sort of existence.

The words I have quoted—"the Being which, for want of right and distinct conceptions, I call the Eternal Mind "—show some sense of the mystery involved in all human ideas of the divine reality. They touch what is really at the root of the theological embarrassment of the present day—the question, What does the word " God " mean ?   And as to the "mathematically certain " proof of the existence of the so explained "Eternal Mind," it may well be considered inadequate.   To conclude that there must be Mind Eternal and Infinite, because I am now conscious, and only lately began to be conscious, is surely an eminent example of circular reasoning, in which the stupendous conclusion is really presupposed in order to be proved. " My own existence " means the existence of a finite being ; and unless infinity is presupposed in the datum of the argument, the conclusion fails.   Infinite Being cannot be concluded from one finite being : God is not in this sort of way logically involved in me.   When I take data of experience—in this case my own short-lived existence revealed in memory — as the sole material of the premisses, this single finite fact *per se* cannot yield Infinite Being in the conclusion.

The enigmas involved in the third belief.

Finite data only yield a finite conclusion, and to conclude a finite mind or god, how inconceivably great
and long-lived soever, sends the craving for absolute
finality still in quest of a deeper foundation. A finite
god leaves unsatisfied the religious sense of absolute
dependence, and the demand for a final basis for science
and human life.   In truth, if the word God means the
Infinite Being whose existence forecloses all ulterior
inquiry as to the cause of His existence, then the word
is not applicable to any being whose existence is inferred from finite facts only; and which, as finite,
still raises, instead of foreclosing, the previous question,
as to the cause on which *its* existence and nature
depend. The supposed gods of polytheism, and supposed spirits superior to men, are all finite; therefore
dependent, and unfit to satisfy the need for absolute
support, or to meet man's sense of incompleteness in
the finite. The essence of the meaning of the word
God is wanting in them all. When the Infinite Being
is taken to be a conclusion from a finite being, instead
of the presupposition involved in all reasonable interpretation of the finite, then the word "God" is used in
an atheistic meaning; and, as far as this applies to
polytheistic religions, they are in this respect atheistic.
Moreover, if we adopt this philosophy, it may be
argued, as indeed Hume among others argues, that
we know too little about *matter* to be warranted in
denying that *it* may contain in itself the source and
spring of order; so that there may be no more

difficulty in supposing that its several elements, from an internal unknown cause, may fall into order, than there is in the supposition that the ideas which form Eternal Mind, from a like internal and unknown cause, contrive and produce what I call my mind, and also contrive and produce the things which present themselves to my senses. We must not off-hand take the operations of one part of finite nature upon another part, as analogy for the forming an infinite conclusion, and one too that claims to be demonstrable, concerning the origin of the whole. And so it came about that God was habitually thought of, by theists of last century and since, as one among the innumerable "substances," material and spiritual, which among them make up the entire universe of reality, rather than as One in whom all live and have their finite being — incomprehensible under genus or species — incapable of being classed with finite substances.

In Locke's "mathematically certain" proof that the religious conception of the universe must be the true ultimate conception of it, the intellectual necessity of the causal principle is offered as the sufficient reason for concluding that because "I" exist an "Eternal Mind" must also exist. But there can be no analogy between causal sequences in which each of the terms is a finite phenomenon, and this absolutely unique instance in which one of the terms is not finite. The Ultimate Principle of the universe, and of each thing and person, must be *sui generis*, if not supra-generic. Besides, in

Locke's " mathematically certain " proof that God exists.

purely mathematical demonstration, the disturbing element of change, and unknown as well as known active agents, is eliminated ; but outside the mathematical province of abstract quantity, there is no room for unconditionally necessary demonstration. Abstract mathematical truth, not concrete things or concrete persons, is the proper sphere for unconditional demonstrative necessity. As for this semblance of demonstration, about the Power and Purpose that is eternally dominant in the universe, on the narrow basis of the fact that I find myself existing now, and that I only lately began to exist ;—if this professed demonstration is all that can be produced in vindication of the divine postulate, our "line," the sceptic may well say, "is too short to fathom such immense abysses." Locke himself indeed allows that the word "substance," when applied either to individual things which we see and touch in the outward world, or to our own individual personality and that of other finite spirits, is not to be taken in the high meaning which it has when it is applied to God or Eternal Mind. He sees that no finite beings, corporeal or spiritual, are finally self-subsisting and self-contained : they are all dependent on something external to themselves. Locke, however, did not conclude from this, as Spinoza did, that, besides God, no "substance" can exist, or can be conceived to exist ; or that the self-conscious things we call ourselves, and the extended things which surround us, are not in any sense substances, but only transitory modes or affections of the One Substance.

I have suggested some of the mysteries in which we find ourselves involved when we reflect philosophically upon the three postulates of existence, the three factors of living experience, each of which, under one form of conception or another, is, I believe, in fact, if often unconsciously, recognised by all. These difficulties are the theme of Kant's Transcendental Dialectic. If the 'Essay' of Locke, at the end of the seventeenth century—one of the two correlated classics of modern philosophy, in the second stage of its development—is pervaded by the three presuppositions of existence, the 'Kritik of Pure Reason' of Kant,—its complement and corrective,—at the end of the eighteenth century, culminates in an exposition of the difficulties for the understanding which each of the three involves. It suggests the conclusion that the freedom of man, the unconditional necessity of nature, and the existence of God, are alike incapable of scientific proof. *Kant's 'Transcendental Dialectic.'*

The three presupposed existences are severally the occasions of morality, natural science, and religion. My own existence, implied in the recognition of my continuous personality, and in the independent power which I refer exclusively to myself, when I acknowledge personal responsibility for acts of will, calls forth the idea of morality, and affords material for moral judgments. External nature, at least as it is presented *Morality, science, and religion.*

to our senses and in our sensuous experience, is non-moral. Yet without the medium supplied by external things persons seem to have no means of discovering the existence of other persons; still less of receiving from them their ideas, or of communicating ideas to them: so that, but for "outward things," there would be no room for that exercise and evolution of intelligence which interpretation of external nature requires, and on which individual and social progress depends. The material world, non-moral in itself, is the medium of the social intercourse through which individual man becomes part of the moral organism, while it is that through which he is educated as a scientific intelligence and gets part of his moral training. Then, too, without the supremacy of the divine principle of moral and therefore physical order, on which the universe of change is presumed to depend, and on which we repose in faith, as the basis for thought and action, both morality and natural science must be paralysed. In this divine faith religion is rooted, so that secular morality and natural science become at last moral religion. "I ask not," said Goethe, "whether the Supreme Being *has* reason and understanding; for I feel that He *is* Reason and Understanding itself. Therewith are all creatures penetrated; and man has so much of it that he can apprehend the Highest Being in part." Trust even in natural law is faith in God in germ.

Superstition and scepticism are two extremes into

which men are led by not preserving the balance between the three ultimate factors. While no one of the three can be wholly explained away, consistently with sane human life, any one of them may be so exaggerated as to paralyse the moral influence of the others, and to distort the true conception of human life.

Superstition and scepticism issues of misconceptions of the three existences.

Take some examples. At certain stages in man's religious and intellectual development, there is a prevailing disposition to see God only in what is uncommon, unexpected, miraculous, and to refer in the end to what are called "natural" agents or forces all events that are interpreted as instances of customary sequence. According to this assumption, whatever is found to evolve or grow—for evolution seems to be another name for growth—whatever is found to grow, and that gradually and regularly, is referred wholly to supposed "power" in nature, which means only the continuous process of changes through which the issue is reached: God is recognised only when something happens which seems not to appear gradually and regularly, under cognisable natural law, but in what is taken to be a scientifically inexplicable manner. So the realm of natural powers and the realm in which God is supposed to operate are regarded as each excluding the other; with the result in an unconscious polytheism, which makes one god of "nature" and another god of "supernature." It follows that every new scientific discovery of natural modes of procedure is supposed to

Examples of this. God recognised only in uncommon events.

E

exclude God more and more as the operative agent in the universe. God is seen acting only in what science cannot naturally bridge over, and these vacant intervals of course become fewer and fewer with the advance of natural science. The need for a theological interpretation of what happens in the universe seems to diminish with each step onward in natural interpretation: the idea of the universe as being in itself throughout finally interpretable only physically, and therefore foreclosing ulterior theological interpretation, in the end takes the place of the religious idea of the whole. The advance of physical science becomes the paralysis of religious thought, because an orderly system of nature leaves no room for that violation of rational order, in which superstition and confused theological thinking find the only sign of the providential presence and action of God. When superstition is not permitted by science to retain an irregular and capricious universe of this sort, its deity and its religion disappear. The modern appreciation of natural causes, after dissolving the personifications of polytheism, is now destroying the relics of polytheism in an inadequately conceived theism.

The supposition that God may be found there although not here.

This conception of God, mechanical and local and external, appears at the bottom of theological appeals against the presumption of the atheist, who dares to conclude that God does not exist, merely because neither our eyes nor our telescopes reveal His presence, within the comparatively narrow and always

finite space to which our senses, even when arti-
ficially assisted, and our imagination give positive
access.   If not *here*, a God, it is suggested, may possibly be *there;* if not the cause of this which comes
within our experience, a God may possibly be the
cause of something elsewhere that man cannot see.
If man, it is said, does not know every agent in the
wide expanse of the universe, the agent that he is
ignorant of may be a God.   If he cannot assign the
causes of all that he perceives to exist, the unperceived
cause of that unknown remainder may be a God.   If
he does not know how everything has been done in
past ages, some of those doings may have been the
doings of a God.   In short, unless I preclude the possible existence of another god by being omniscient or a
god myself, I cannot know for certain that the Being
whose existence I deny may not exist *somewhere.*
Now a god that can be locally and potentially present,
here but not there, in this event but not in that event;
or that might be detected by a telescope in some
remote part of space, if a powerful enough telescope
could be invented; or detected in extraordinary events,
if they were brought within range of human experience
—spoken of too as "*a* God," not God—is surely not
the God, the unique reality, "in whom we all live and
move and have our being," presupposed tacitly in all
perception and self-consciousness, or else everywhere
and for ever out of relation to human life.   God, as
Bacon says, does not need to work physical miracles

in order to refute atheism.   If the whole natural
course of things does not presuppose God, as the condition of its being even physically interpretable, no
extraordinary local manifestations in nature can in
themselves supply the evidences.   With the presupposition granted of divine Reason latent in the heart
of existence, some events in the history of the universe
may doubtless be more fitted than others are to evoke
into fuller intelligence the divine faith latent in man;
but without the tacit presupposition of God present in
all perception and consciousness, this fuller or richer
intelligence, otherwise naturally evolved by enlarged
experience, seems to have no foundation.

Or might
have been
found then,
although
not now.

Again.   Is it not also an inadequate and inconsequent
theism that is left to depend finally upon historical or
other empirical proof that the cosmical economy of
our little planet, or even of the solar system, had
no natural beginning; because only under the conception of an unnatural beginning, it is assumed, could
there be reason for the supposition of "a God."   If
the economy of the present solar system must first
be shown by historic records to have been formed
unnaturally, or, according to the common expression,
by a special creative act, before faith in God can be
justified, the basis seems too narrow and too precarious
to support the conclusion.   It is not enough to argue
for Eternal Mind, as some have done, on the doubtful
ground that it can be proved historically that the solar

system originated in a Mind, but that there is no historical proof that the Mind in which it originated had also in its turn a beginning, as Hume suggests it too might have had. If we thus make history or finite data of experience reduce questions which lie beyond their sphere, what is the difference in this respect between the solar material system and the possibly dependent mental system it is supposed to prove? They are both treated in these arguments and counter arguments as caused causes in an infinite succession of such. "A mental world, or universe of ideas," as Hume suggests, " requires a cause as much as does a material world or universe of objects. In an abstract view, they are entirely alike; and no difficulty attends the one supposition which is not common to both of them." Is it not only after the ultimate supernaturalness of all physical processes has somehow been presumed that any sort of experience is found to manifest what is divine?

So much in illustration of the perplexities in which thought becomes involved under crude or inadequate conceptions of the three fundamental postulates of existence. We shall meet examples in other connections in the sequel. What is important now is to see how the difficulty of reconciling these postulates with one another, along with the desire awakened in advancing intelligence to think existence in a har-

Panmaterialism, Panegoism, and Pantheism.

monious whole, leads abstract thinkers to philosophical
theories which tend finally to resolve all that exists
into *one only* of the three postulated existences of
ordinary consciousness. Those theories differ according as this or that one of the three obtains exaggerated, and then exclusive recognition. Thus the
outward or material world, which fills the horizon of
sense, has been taken for the one ultimate reality, in
a final conception of existence which makes the universe of reality at last only a universe of molecules
in motion. This is Panmaterialism, which pretends to
find in matter what common consciousness refers to
the ego and to God. On the other hand, those in
whom the introspective habit is strong are apt to
seek for the desired unity of existence in the conception that All is ultimately the ego only, in a
philosophy of Immaterialism or Panegoism : when we
occupy this point of view logically, we become subjective idealists and solipsists. Lastly, dissatisfaction
with a universe of individual consciousness, combined
either with an ideal All seen in the dry light of pure
reason, or with mystical emotion, disposes both the
courageous thinker and the mystic to seek for the
one ultimate reality, neither in outward things with
the Panmaterialist, nor in the inward life with the
Panegoist, but instead in what is supposed to transcend both, because superior alike to individual sense
and to individual consciousness. Hence the various

schemes of Pantheism, Impersonalism, or Acosmism, in which the world and ego are identified with God; instead of God and ego being resolved into molecules in motion, as in Universal Materialism, or the outward world of sense and the Infinite God being reduced to the self-conscious life of the individual, as in Panegoism.

In the four following lectures, I will ask you to occupy with me each of these three Monist points of view in succession; in order to try whether any of them affords a satisfactory ultimate conception. Are we under an intellectual obligation to accept any of them, as the true and final interpretation of all that exists? and if so, which one of them is thus made obligatory by reason? And if supreme regard for reasonableness obliges us to dismiss them all, what other alternatives are open? Must we turn away from the final problem of existence altogether, as one which admits of no solution, not even a working human solution; our utmost knowledge being the negative knowledge, that "the whole is a riddle, an enigma, an inexplicable mystery"; so that at last no judgment formed about anything in man or in nature, in science or in theology, can be regarded as more certain than its contradictory? Or, already expelled from Monism in its three forms, may we return to reason, in the form of faith in the three commonly

Is any of these a sufficient resting-place for man?

postulated existences, through a deeper and truer interpretation ? These are questions which I wish to keep steadily in view to the end. In next lecture I shall ask you provisionally to look at the final problem of existence as the materialist may be supposed to look at it, and to inquire whether Universal or Final Materialism is a coherent conception, or a possible rest for the human spirit.

LECTURE III.

UNIVERSAL MATERIALISM.

In the infancy of philosophical speculation, as in the early years of each man's life, it is the world of solid and extended things—what can be seen and touched—that is apt to be regarded as the one only reality, and as what alone is entitled to be called a substance. So it was that in the pre-Socratic era, among early Hellenic inquirers, the mystery in which we all find ourselves, when we look before and after, seemed to be relieved as soon as some sort of material could be detected, out of which it might plausibly be conjectured that things and persons originally issued. They were satisfied when they thought that they could answer the final question about the universe and man, by resolving the whole into some sort of presentable substance,—into one of the crudely conceived elements of matter— water, air, fire, as it might be. The totality of real existence was thus finally identified with matter; but

Early Hellenic attempts to finally interpret the universe.

without analysis of what matter as perceived in sense means, or a distinct conception of its outwardness in relation to self-conscious mind. The objects of sense were thus tacitly credited with powers which seemed to supersede the other two factors in the three primary postulates. It was among things that appeal to the senses, so conceived, that Thales, Anaximander, and other contemporaries found satisfaction, when their crude experience of existence gave rise to their philosophic wonder. This pre‑Socratic cosmological materialism, latent in the universal flux of Heraclitus, but developed in the atomism of Democritus, was idealised, and may be seen at its best, in the magnificent poem of Lucretius.

Material- ism in the nineteenth century. Our own nineteenth century finds millions trying to get satisfaction in the same sort of way; still turning to what the senses present, for explanation when they are confronted by the mystery of their own existence, or when their desire for intellectual unity rebels against the three traditional postulates, and strives to reduce them to one. Modern materialism, recognising the innumerable useful secrets which the material world holds within it, and which science is disclosing to the increase of our comfort—in gratitude for what matter is now doing for us all—is ready to fall down and worship its benefactor, and to lose human spirit and Divine Purpose in the immensity of outward things, and their eternal evolution. For modern science of outward things, after three centuries of successful ex-

perimental intercourse with the ever-changing world
that is presented to the senses, has much to say for
itself. It is able to say that it has gradually succeeded,
with universal consent, in provisionally interpreting
many things that surround us in space, solid and extended; one kind of thing that we see being found to
explain another kind of thing that can be seen; and
to contrast the universal consent in physical interpretation with the perplexities in which metaphysical
interpretations of the universe seem to be involved.
So trust is generated only in what is outward or can
be measured. What can be made good by sight and
touch, one is ready to say, is bound in reason to carry
it over speculative fancies, which are all that we possess when we pretend to something superior to sense.
I find in fact that I am the sport of illusion whenever
I forsake this one safe sphere: what I see I can also
touch; what I touch I can make experiments upon; I
can repeat the experiments in new circumstances, and
then compare at my leisure in verification the issues of
various well-calculated experiments. In this way I find
that I can foresee physical issues, and anticipate the
natural behaviour of things. For these and other
reasons I am certain that in the data of the senses I
have got hold of existence on its only real side. I find
that I can use tangible and visible experience as the
one undoubted test for interpreting whatever happens
in the universe that is certainly interpretable. While I
keep on this path I can walk with a firm intellectual

step, and can stake my life on the certainty of my inferences. Such is the voice of modern science of external nature, as translated into Universal Materialism. So interpreted, science of natural evolution leads back to what, in naïve and confused fashion, was the assumption of Hellenic cosmologists in the infancy of philosophical questioning. It is supposed to demonstrate the insignificance of man in external nature, and therefore the baselessness and unintelligibility of "the theistic hypothesis," as the last word about the Whole. For dogmatic atheism, or at least theological agnosticism, is the natural philosophy of those who confine experience to external sense, disallowing any deeper experience than this, or any final principle of harmony other than customary succession of sense appearances, supposed to centre in material substance.

The anthropocentric conception of the universe in Hebrew and Hellenic history.

It was not always thus in the long interval which separates Thales and Democritus from the nineteenth century. A teleological conception of existence that might be called *anthropocentric*, instead of the earlier or the later cosmological materialism, pervades in a striking fashion ancient Hebrew literature, as we have it in Genesis and other books of the Pentateuch; intensified into a spiritual anthropomorphism in the Jewish psalmists and prophets, with their deep intuition of the moral relations of man to the vividly conceived personal God. Unique in this intense intuition, teleological, if not an anthropocentric, conception is not exclusively Hebraic, even in the ancient world. Among the Greeks there is the faint recognition by Anaxagoras of active reason as the supreme cosmic principle, superior to blind necessities of molecular motion, and apt to suggest a religious conception of the relations of the Whole. By an emphatic recognition of man rather than outward things as the primary object of intellectual interest, —the moral agent, not the starry heavens—according to the Delphic oracular "know thyself,"—Socrates recalled his followers from exaggerated regard for outward things; he also directed reflection to ends latent in experience, connected with man as their final goal. In Greece the Socratic reaction finds articulate expression in the genius of Plato, and more articulately in Aristotle, while among the Romans the natural theology of Cicero, based on a theological idea of the world, with a recognition of man as conscious and spiritual, sometimes expresses itself in language that might be called anthropomorphic.

But it was the profound personalism of Christianity, in its occasional exaggeration among Christians, that reduced material things to relative insignificance, in the highly elaborated theology or philosophy of the ages of faith. The conception of the supremeness of man in the cosmos found a scientific auxiliary in the accepted Ptolemaic astronomy, and its *geocentric* conception of the material universe, in which all else falls into subordinate relation to a man-inhabited

Above all in Christianity.

Earth. Man thus came to be regarded as even the
final and eternal purpose of the universe; and it was
assumed, in harmony with this, that the Supreme
Principle of the Whole must be a living Spirit,
analogous to the living spirit found incarnate in
man.

Signs of a
narrow
anthropo-
centric
concep-
tion.

A narrowly conceived anthropocentric conception of
this Supreme Principle of the Universe culminated
in the middle ages of European thought. Monastic
separation from the visible world; absolute separation
between what is held in abstraction as secular and
what is held in abstraction as spiritual, or between
state and church; antithesis of nature or natural law
on the one side, and spiritual or supernatural power
on the other, are among its outward symptoms. It
induced indifference to order and science of nature;
warfare with those who try to rule their lives by
the physical idea of natural law; endeavour to live
only in consciousness of supernatural environment;
man at the centre of space, seeing the infinite eternal
economy all directed to his own spiritual government
—man's welfare supposed to be marred by acknowledgment of the potential spirituality of sense and
secular life. Religion, under this ascetic form of religious thought, in medievalism and later too, took
the place that is now claimed for sciences of outward
nature. The atomism of Lucretius was exchanged for
the curious conceits of the 'Divina Commedia,' the
mythology of Milton, the elaborated Christian theology

of Aquinas, and the familiar human analogies of Puritan divines.

Man's imagined place of local supremacy under the Ptolemaic astronomy came in this way to be regarded as necessary to the theological conception of life. A scientific revolution in men's ideas of their own place in the material universe, which reduced human beings to local insignificance, and under which men might form the habit of thinking of themselves as the transitory issue of a natural process, seemed fatal to the supremacy of the religious idea, and an invitation to the atomistic and mechanical one to resume its old place, as the only true interpretation of all that is and happens. The postulate that Reasonable Purpose is at the root of the Whole seemed to be bound up with exploded uniqueness in the local position held by man as an organism in the material world.

Local insignificance of Man.

So modern free search for the caused or natural causes that are perceptible by the senses has been changing the long-established anthropocentric idea— under the belief that causes are only material phenomena, which appear in regular sequences, open to experimental detection. This also accustoms the mind to consider only what is adapted to use under a purely physical view of utility, while the teleological conception that pervades polytheism and monotheism seems barren by contrast. The change finds voice in what Bacon and Spinoza say about the fruitfulness

Bacon and Spinoza on the teleological conception.

of natural causes, as compared with the inutility and inapplicability of final causes. It is as the visible means according to which human purposes in nature may be carried out by men as ministers of nature, but still as means originally established, it may be, by Divine purpose, that Bacon sets a high value on natural or caused causes, and on physical science, which discloses them : in a final cause he found nothing tangible — nothing which man could employ as his instrument, or of which he could be the minister and interpreter : final causes in this respect are unpractical. The inscrutable will and purpose of an external and distant God looks like an asylum for indolent neglect of useful causes; or it is used as a shelter for prejudice, thus withdrawing men from experimental inquiry into the actual texture of the web of nature. So Spinoza urges, in arguing against anthropomorphism. In this he exceeds Bacon, who complains only of the abuse of final causes, when they make us neglect the causes that address our senses, but not denying their value in other aspects. Not so Spinoza, who insists that reason teaches men the futility of the very idea of a final cause in which man is the end; and argues that when once men have satisfied themselves that the laws of nature were not intended for their satisfaction, they would be more likely to see that the reality of things is to be measured only by what is discovered through scientific evidence. Nothing, he says, should be considered true or false because it is or is not in harmony with human interests; and it is a profound mistake to call things or events good or bad, because they happen to be agreeable or repugnant to the insignificance of man. But Bacon, while he presses the need for engaging in the neglected search for the actual causes that may be found by our senses within the visible successions of nature—seeing that with such causes we may more or less co-operate when we discover them—argues also that experimental search among physical phenomena may even confirm and exalt our recognition of divine purpose : he suggests that inductive inquiry into the natural causes that may be found by our senses within the material part of the universe, and which are the established conditions of the changes that go on around us, so far from dissolving faith in dominant providence, should only make those most devoted to scientific investigation see more clearly than others do, that full intellectual satisfaction even is not to be attained without recognition of the invisible providence of God in the natural evolution.

The centuries which have elapsed since Bacon and Spinoza have witnessed a steady reaction against what is called anthropomorphism, in the interest of a secularly fruitful search for the natural causes, visible and tangible, under the laws of which our bodily surroundings are scientifically connected, and our bodies themselves become scientifically interpretable — laws which may be used by men experimentally, as means

Modern reaction against the anthropocentric conception.

for making this a more comfortable planetary abode for themselves. Thus the vast material world, as the only apparent agent of changes, desirable and undesirable, has come to fill the popular imagination: all besides, including that small portion of matter which is appropriated by each person as his own body, is reduced to insignificance in our imagination. The criterion by which a merely physical interpretation of external nature is regulated, with its tacitly supposed, but all undemonstrated, faith in physical order, is next assumed to be the only legitimate sort of evidence, and to open the only way in which reason can be followed. Appeals to other constituents of the faith out of which reason rises, and into which, in an improved form, it seems obliged to return, are disparaged, as appeals only to emotion, imagination, or dogmatic authority, not to what is reasonable, which must, it seems, be always only physically natural. Shall we, then, surrender ourselves to the influence of this intellectual atmosphere, and adopt this essentially materialistic conception of the Whole, as ultimately only molecules in motion? Much appears to recommend the conception to the disciple of fact and reason who comes with those presuppositions, when he presses the conclusion, that the only available solution of the ultimate problem of existence — the problem which concerns these Gifford Lectures—is to be found at the point of view at which the invisible self-conscious ego, and also the invisible God, disappear as superfluous imaginary postulates, added by imagination to the one solid fact—a universe of molecules in motion. Hence a determination to search only among the visible and tangible things that are presented to the senses, when we want to find the final meaning of things and persons. A revolution in the constitutive conception of the universe is the issue of the adoption of this rule, with its implied supremacy of the customary order of visible sequences, and with the strength which issues from ardent faith exclusively in this.

A change in the astronomical conceptions of men led the way in this modern revolution. Copernican astronomy gradually dissolved the old Ptolemaic idea that man's abode was the centre of the material world —the starry hosts dependent on human interests—made for the service of man. Copernicus consigns man to a place that became relatively more and more insignificant locally with each advance in stellar science. Even under the old assumption about the starry heavens, the Hebrew poet was lost in wonder that the Supreme Purpose should have regard to a being so mean and insignificant as man: "When I consider Thy heavens, the work of Thy fingers, the moon and the stars, which Thou hast ordained ; what is man, that thou art mindful of him ? and the son of man, that Thou visitest him ? " But with what deepened emphasis may this question of the unscientific Hebrew be put by the modern astron-

The reaction sustained by astronomical discovery and speculation.

omer ? In the mind of the Jew, the "lights" in the
vault of heaven which cheered this solid earth seemed,
through a wonderful providence, to have been made
because man was made. According to his innocent
conception, God had said, "Let there be lights in the
firmament of heaven to give light upon the earth."
But how can so grand a spectacle as modern astronomy
puts before us be supposed by any reasoning being to
have for its final cause the convenience of short-lived
animals who find their home on this small planet—
transitory in their successive generations, in the Homeric
imagination, as the leaves which yearly appear and disappear on the trees of the forest ?

The starry heavens and man's relative insignificance in space.

The progress of modern astromony has been a run-
ning commentary on the local insignificance of men,
when men are thought of only as parts of the illimitable material system now apparently in possession of
the immensity of space. What is a human organism,
infinitely invisible at the centre of things, in comparison
with the infinite material world ? The Earth itself, instead of being conceived as the solid centre of all that
appears in space, is recognised as only one in a system
of planets, more or less like itself, some immensely
larger, all at present revolving round a central sun, on
which they and all their contents depend. Then this
solar system itself is said to be only one among
innumerable other solar systems, like itself, all it
seems revolving collectively round some undiscovered
centre. And even this enlarged material system now

appears to be only a subordinate part of an inconceivably greater; which again in its turn may be
an appendage to a greater still; and so onwards and
onwards in an unending series of enlargements,—for
why should any boundary be set to the possible material
contents of infinite space?

All this is the commonplace of astronomical science
and astronomical speculation, familiar even to the
schoolboy. Our little planet, with its solar system
added,—on this supposition of an infinite number of
stellar masses suspended in space,—may appear to an
intelligence that is able to comprehend the Infinite, as
less worthy of regard than the few grains of sand in
which a microscope reveals innumerable living beings,
each relatively to them more important than the
animals of our solar system in relation to the universe. So the human organisms, by which the Earth
is occupied, are inferred to be of less value, at the
central point of view, than the most insignificant
and shortest-lived insects on this planet appear to
us. What, indeed, is this human animal—so much
made of in the anthropocentric conception — when
placed beside innumerable conscious organisms which
may occupy the innumerable worlds that are moving
through Immensity? What is man that he should
be regarded at all in a universal Purpose? Above
all, what is man that he should be the supreme
object in that Purpose—as in the Christian economy
of redemption, according to the medieval interpretation

Astronomy and theology.

of it, which so long affected the teleological view of the universe.

The insignificance of man as an organism evolved in time. But if scientific investigation of the contents of *space* reduces the petty organisms which constitute the race of man, from supremacy in the supposed final purpose, to inconceivable insignificance in the universal material system, this reduction is even more difficult to resist when one turns to what modern inquiry has to tell about the continous course of events in *time.* Above all, this is so if we accept a modern conception of the causal process, according to which constant phenomenal evolution of the material universe proceeds in what, for aught man can know, may be an unbeginning and unending series of changes or metamorphoses of its molecular constituents. If modern astronomy, inaugurated by Copernicus and Newton, has revealed the insignificance of man's planet among the illimitable starry hosts, and the infinite insignificance of each ephemeral human organism, when all these are interpreted in terms of space—what shall be said of the revelations of modern geology, and, much more, of modern biology? They seem to show that all the organised bodies on this planet, as well as the planet itself, are transitory issues, in continuous natural processes of integration and disintegration—without beginning and without end, as far as man can tell. Some of the present laws according to which changes occur seem to be discovered, and those who claim to be discoverers have thus put passing pleasures within the reach of those by whom the discoveries may be applied, or have enabled them to escape passing forms of suffering; but no ultimate account of all this can be given. Nor can we tell whether the physical order —presumed to be permanent within the narrow sphere of men's discoveries of natural causes—is really an expression of divine reason, or only an accident in a brief interval within which chaos, in human experience, assumes the semblance of cosmos.

In the light of geological and biological discovery and speculation, one seems to see animal life gradually evolving, in its relative place in the continuous natural succession, in a process according to which lower forms of living matter on this planet are slowly followed by higher and moré complex forms. Each generation in this continuous natural evolution, infinitesimally different from that which preceded it, transmits the infinitesimal difference to its successors; and thus, out of what may have been the common mass of protoplasm at an early stage, animal life becomes gradually differentiated into ever-multiplying species, with the human organism the most notable as yet, among the organisms thus naturally evolved in the history of this planet. The human organisms themselves, at the present stage of the unbeginning and endless procession of changes which the material world presents, are found to be in advance of their remote natural ancestors in intelligence and morality, and with a present prospect, according to the analogies of

The alternations of development and dissolution in organised matter.

nature, of continuing to advance with the process of
the suns.   But human organisms, with their unique
characteristic of self-conscious life, are only part of
the phenomena mysteriously presented, in the unbeginning and unending evolution, which is taken for the
supreme natural process according to which the elements of matter change and grow.   They seem to
rise into life naturally, when the conditioning material
causes occur of which organisms of this sort with
their self-conscious lives are the natural sequence.   But
those physical causes, as well as their consequences, are
all passive subjects of the natural rules of universal
change.   Reasoning by analogy, and under the maxims
of common-sense, all-embracing materialism may accordingly anticipate, in the future history of this planet,
the final extinction of human organisms, in analogy
with preceding extinctions of inferior races, and the
extinction too of the planet itself which they inhabit;
along with all their works—their scientific discoveries
and their whole history—in the general disintegration
of the solar system.   Later still, the whole material
universe may be refunded into the original fire-mist out
of which it was once evolved, or it may all be con-
densed into one stupendous mass of molecules—ready
to resume another prolonged course of natural integration, or, as one might call it, natural creation,—an
integration of new stellar and planetary systems, it
may be; or perhaps of other constructions of matter,
unpredictable, because under physical conditions now

to us unknown, and even by us inconceivable. In the new material universe of that immeasurably remote future, what room is there in retrospective thought for the petty human organisms of an immeasurably remote past, with their ephemeral records of social institutions and social struggles, scientific discoveries, achievements of mechanical art, humanly admired creations of imagination, religions and philosophies,—all dissolved and buried in the dissolution of the vast molecular economy in which, even while they existed, they were as nothing,—for ever forgotten, in the new heavens and new earth into which a universe, essentially of molecules, has then been transformed, in another of its endless metamorphoses?

These are only dreams, for of course they are not, through verification, acknowledged discoveries of natural science; but they are dreams which are in analogy with the universally materialistic conception of existence, which I am asking you to try to realise in imagination. They presuppose a universe of molecules in motion; the perceptible history of which must be a history of the motions of the molecules, separately or in aggregation, and of the changes which would be presented in their customary sequences if the dreams were realised. Materialistic dreams.

Two conditions, which both play an important part in the physical sciences, are presupposed, but not unconditionally demonstrated. The one is the indestructibility of the molecules, or the matter which Indestructibility of matter, and conservation of energy.

consists of them; and the other, the conservation
of what is ambiguously called energy, which matter
is supposed to involve. The indestructibility of
Matter, and the conservation of its energy are, as we
know, hypotheses which dominate modern inferences
about the past and future history of the molecules
which, on the materialistic conception of man, and the
universe of which human organisms are a part, form
the elementary totality of what really exists. Accordingly, as long as the material universe exists, and it
is presumed to be indestructible, it must consist of
exactly the same quantity of matter—the same number of molecules—as now exists;—this through all the
metamorphoses which, in endless duration, these have
undergone, or may yet undergo—in the form of stellar
systems, and living matter, in the various degrees of
life, sentient, intelligent, self-conscious, which, as more
or less elaborately formed, organised matter is found to
manifest; as well as in remote future visible or other
sensible issues which human imagination cannot anticipate. The assumption of the indestructibility of
matter as final forbids an inconceivable transformation of *nothing* suddenly into *something*, as in the old
idea of a special creation, and obliges us always to
suppose and seek for physical causes, presentable to
sense, although not necessarily perceptible by human
senses, when we resolve to account, through its exact
material equivalent, for each new metamorphosis. The
history of the universe is therefore a history of the

natural transformations of what already exists molecularly: the addition of absolutely new molecules, or the absolute extinction of old ones, are unscientific conceptions. Each new appearance in nature implies an equivalent withdrawal of some other appearance, and the whole succession is an endless metamorphosis. Light reappears in equivalent heat: electricity in equivalent magnetism: molecular changes in the living organism, in their equivalent states of conscious life: the births and deaths·of men and other living organisms have their resulting compensation: the births and deaths of planets and suns have deaths and births in something else corresponding to them.

If all that has been, and that can be, must thus be thought of at last in terms of material molecules, the final problem should be solved in the discovery and thoroughgoing application of the ultimate law or laws according to which the innumerable molecular metamorphoses proceed. The search for cause is confined to a search for the perceptible conditions which constantly precede, or constantly accompany, each perceptible change. Causation is nothing more than the *sort* of sequences and coexistences which seem to be customary among material phenomena. It is the sort which is believed to be constant, and which is therefore significant —significant in the perceived causes of their so-called effects, and in the perceived effects of their so-called causes. To explain the universe accordingly would be, to read its endless changes under the principle of causality,

May not any sort of change be in reason the effect of any natural antecedent?

in this its physical or mechanical interpretation.   A
criticised experience of the special sorts of connection
that seem constant, becomes the only criterion for determining the particular causes of particular effects; not
any *a priori* idea of the sufficiency, or insufficiency, of
this agent to be the cause of that sort of change.   Ab-
stractly, or apart from actually finding that *this* is
always in nature followed by *that*, man has no right
to assume that only this sort of cause *can* explain that
sort of effect ; that unorganised atoms can, or that
they cannot, account for the self-conscious life that is
found on this remote little planet, in connection with
human molecular organisms.   For, if experience finds
organised life rising, first out of certain inorganic conditions, and then the self-conscious sort of life rising out
of certain sorts of living organisms, one is bound honestly to accept the facts.   One is told to see in the so
related molecules and their motions the true and only
explanation of the psychical phenomena which appear
in certain organisms — especially in the human, and
which are vulgarly referred to what are called " human
minds,"—the word " mind " a convenient refuge for the
ignorance of those who use it.   For, *a priori*, any
material thing appears equally fit, or equally unfit,
with any other to be the cause, or customary natural
antecedent, of any sort of change.   Causality is thus
only the sort of sequence that is constant, or exemplified in the visible custom of nature ; and as any
event may follow any other, anything may be its in-

variable antecedent or natural cause. The falling of a pebble, to take David Hume's examples, may extinguish the sun, for aught we know *a priori;* or the will of a man may disturb the planets in their orbits. "Were any object presented to us, and were we required to pronounce concerning the effect which will result from it, without consulting past observation, after what manner," Hume asks, "must the mind proceed? It must imagine some event which it ascribes to the object as its effect; and it is plain that this invention must be entirely arbitrary." The mind can never without experience find the sort of effect in the cause, or the sort of cause in the effect, by the most accurate scrutiny of either *per se.* For the effect is totally different from the cause, and consequently can never be discovered in it, nor can the cause in the effect. We fancy that were we brought on a sudden into this world, we could have inferred without trial that one billiard-ball would communicate motion to another upon impulse; and that we needed not have waited to see this event, in order to pronounce with certainty that it would be so. But motion in the second billiard-ball is a distinct event from motion in the first; nor is there anything in the appearance of the one phenomenon to suggest the other. When I see one billiard-ball moving in a straight line towards another, even if motion in the second ball should by accident be suggested to me as the result of their contact, might I not conceive hundreds of other sorts of events as well following from that particular cause. Might not both the balls remain at absolute rest? Might not the first ball return in a straight line, or leap away from the second in any, linear direction? All these suppositions are consistent or conceivable. Why then should we give the preference to one of them, which *a priori* is no more consistent or conceivable than the rest? No *a priori* reasonings will ever be able to show us any unconditional necessity in reason for this preference. The general conclusion from all this would be, that we must turn, for the ultimate ground of our determination, to the evidence of experience, as presented in those sorts of sequence which seem, after calculated experiments, to be in point of fact invariable in the constant succession, or continuous evolution, of molecular change.

The possible issues of a universe of molecules in motion in the infinite succession of changes.

Under this sensuous and imaginable causality or power as the supreme human conception; with survival of the physically fittest as its highest biological illustration; with the indestructibility of matter and the conservation of energy for working hypotheses; and with the speculative postulate of an unbeginning and unending succession of causal integrations and disintegrations of a universe of molecules in perpetual motion—with all this, abundant opportunity seems to be given, in the form of infinite time, for infinite variety in the relations of the molecules to one another, and for all sorts of resulting molecular aggregations; which when they emerge, as far as man can see before trial, may each be a cause of *any* sort of effect. So, under this ultimate conception of the universe, what forbids that in the course of time *one* of the innumerable possible molecular collocations might be that presented by the universe of individual things and persons, as man now finds it, in the transitory economy of which the human organism forms a part, and into which each man so formed has been therefore naturally introduced. The universe of molecules, at this stage of its history, now and here, includes those elaborate molecular organisations which, while they last, are found in experience to be the physical or perceptible causes of different sorts of life; in their more notable elaborations the natural causes of life sentient; and in due time, even of life that is self-conscious or rational. Indeed, the whole universe of molecules in motion may seem fit to be regarded as the universe, or infinite material organism, perpetually in life; life in its lower degrees being identified with molecular motion, and in its higher degrees with those special relations of some of the moving molecules, which form sentient and self-conscious organisms, more or less transitory in their constitution, each subject to growth and decay.

So conceived, the totality of what exists seems to be emptied of those supposed special examples of a divine adaptation of natural means to human ends, in which, under the anthropocentric conception of things, this visible world of ours once seemed to abound; Self-conscious lives a consequence of molecular organisations which naturally

occur in
the infinite
history of
molecules
in motion.

which impressed ordinary minds, when presented by Cicero or Paley; or, earlier still, by the Hebrew poet, to whom the heavens "declared the glory of God; and the firmament" showed "His handywork." Under this Hebrew conception of things, "day unto day" was uttering this higher "speech," and night unto night this higher "knowledge." As the Jew looked at it, "there was no speech nor language" where this Divine Voice was not heard: "their line is gone out through all the earth, and their words to the end of the world." Under the purely molecular final idea of existence, on the contrary, the heavens and the earth, with all their living and intelligent population, declare the supposed potentialities of innumerable material molecules, in the infinity of their possible relations in the constant succession; in any of the sequences, any sort of issue, whether insentient mass or organism, sentient and even self-conscious life, for all we can predict *a priori*, being able to attain its actual but ephemeral existence as naturally as any other. That the motion of one billiard-ball should be the natural sequence to contact with another billiard-ball in motion, is neither less nor more wonderful in itself, than that an elaborate special organisation of molecules, itself the natural issue of the infinite possibilities of the universal motion, should, while the organism lasts, be the prior term in a sequence in which the consequent term should be a state or act of self-conscious life. The self-conscious life may seem to itself to be continuous in what is called memory, and it may thus seem to last a little longer than the visible motion in the impelled billiard-ball; but the sequence could in neither case be predicted without sufficient experience of its constancy: in each case it is equally credible and certain after experience of what is reckoned sufficient. According to the rules which the molecules are somehow exemplifying in their motions, the particular sort of collocation of molecules of which billiard-balls are made up is the issue of comparatively few and simple natural experiments, while the competitive process of survival of the fittest, for example, in the case especially of the curious human organism, must have involved innumerable rejections, with all the involved waste of product, before man, with his self-regarding and his benevolent physical dispositions, gradually made his appearance. With this mechanical difference of elaboration only, the two sorts of sequence, as causal, are analogous, if causality contains only sequence. In neither is there any evidence of external contrivance, as in the phenomena we attribute to the design of a human artist; and, moreover, so-called effects of human contrivance are themselves only examples of natural laws, which issued in the natural evolution of the organism of the individual contriver, with its transitory purposes. The watchmaker, when his organism is making watches, is really only an insignificant part of the great process of universe-making and universal metamorphosis that is constantly going on. The blind " power," which is

G

seen in natural or customary sequence, the particular terms of which are unknown to us till experience reveals what they are,—this—not Purpose, benevolent or malevolent—is the final solvent of the problem of the universe ; and of a universe, too, that is found on this planet to evolve examples both of benevolent and malevolent character, in organisms which enjoy or suffer in their transitory lives as long as the needed correlative organisation of molecules lasts.   Deeper than this the human line cannot go, in the attempt to sound the infinite abyss, when one has to explain the universe under the postulate which Universal Materialism finds sufficient.   The intrepid scientific inquirer, with his universe conceived as ultimately molecules in motion, who can see nothing in experience that is inconsistent with this solution of the final problem, accepts it unappalled, in the true spirit of science.   He is ready to say that " things are what they are, and are not other things "— but this with an eye turned exclusively to phenomena of matter, and only in their relations of coexistence and sequence.

The material organism is the Man in Universal Materialism.

Man and his organism are absolutely identified in this final interpretation of the universe, in which man himself becomes one of its most insignificant items : his self-conscious existence is accordingly measured by the continuance of the visible organism which *is* himself.   Self-conscious lives of men, especially those who have entered into actual existence in this era of the universal history, are the most remarkable manifestations of the psychical phenomena that come within man's experience; but even this highest sort is invariably embodied: our only example of self-conscious life is presented in the human organism, in its little more than momentary existence. Given this organism, the self-conscious life mysteriously springs forth, as Professor Huxley puts it, "like the appearance of the genius when Aladdin rubbed his lamp in the Eastern story," or as any other natural fact which appears in its due season.

It is thus that man is reduced from the fancied height of a moral agent, who must be independent of external physical law to the extent of his moral responsibility: he is identified with those aggregates of atoms in the natural evolution, which differ from the lifeless things of inorganic nature only in the fact of their organic association with pleasurable or painful feeling, and with other automatic states of consciousness, manifested in the course of molecular changes of which the organism and its surroundings are the subjects — invisible states as wholly automatic, and dependent on molecular motions, as the visible changes in the organisms themselves. "Man, physical, intellectual, moral," according to Professor Huxley, "is as much a part of nature, as purely a product of the cosmic process, as the humblest weed." Therefore, men at their best present only this ephemeral and automatic consciousness, caused by the always indifferent, and often practically cruel, natural mechanism

Man thus viewed is only a paltry part of physical nature.

within which, without their leave, they find themselves
inextricably involved. Inconsolatory to the individual
as this discovery of what he is, and in what he is, may
be, it is inexhaustible in resources of physical explanation : it explains, as physical consequences of relations
among molecules which occur in the course of their
history, man's illusion that he can be morally free from
natural law, and his aversion to the conception of
omnipotent physical necessity. For the illusion and
the aversion are both found in invariable sequence to
certain organic states and their surroundings, which
are themselves the present issue of the innumerable
molecular collocations and motions that have occurred
in the past history of the material universe. The
sufferings through which the sentient beings on this
planet pass, and the sins with which men are charged,
are now seen in their infinite insignificance, as phenomena in the eternal succession of natural changes
among the atoms which occupy the immensity of space :
they are not more significant ultimately than the pains
or pleasures of insects too minute to be seen by the
microscope in the summer sunshine now seem to us.
Good and evil, right and wrong, merit and demerit,
self-satisfaction and remorse, are scientifically discovered to be words which have acquired their misleading meaning at the particular era in this world's
history at which it was natural for them to acquire
it; through man's natural ignorance then of his own
insignificance, as only an item in that unbeginning

and unending succession of molecular changes which Universal Materialism assumes to be finally co-extensive with reality.

But in another way of reasoning—if anything may be the cause of anything, because it may be its accompaniment and its successor—might one not refer to the molecules into which the universe is resolved all the attributes of man, and even those that in theism are attributed to God? And if all this may be potentially latent in the molecular universe, is it not only a question of names — as between this omnipotent and omniscient Matter, on the one hand, and the God of pantheism, or even theism, on the other. Where is the universal materialist to stop in what he attributes to matter, if we may refer to it the rational acts and moral axioms of which material organism is the present condition in human experience? What, in short, does he mean by Matter? But of this afterwards.

Deification of matter.

The molecularly constituted deity of Universal Materialism has, it seems, naturally caused at one stage in the conscious life of the human organism what are discovered to be illusions, under the later evolved conceptions to which its natural laws are now automatically conducting scientific men—conceptions, too, which may in their turn be all after this as naturally dissolved. Among those illusory natural products may hereafter come to be included the moral rules which presuppose the importance of the race of man, as compared, say,

The transitory illusion of what is called morality.

with a race of invisible animalcules,—presuppositions from which men infer the need for individual self-sacrifice on behalf of their race, as a duty for the sake of a longer survival of the whole. Conscience begins to appear as an artificial device for the prolongation of the race: it was naturally generated at that particular stage in the physical history of the molecules at which men were naturally made to suppose that some unique dignity and importance belonged to them, different in kind from what belongs to the most loathsome reptile. But scientific disinterestedness, itself a physical sequence, on the occasion of certain molecular motions, comes to see that the man and the reptile are virtually alike insignificant, being both the transitory outcome of universal physical law. To call an "agent" in a distinctive sense "moral" or "spiritual," is to apply a misleading predicate; for the "agency" can be only the physical causality in which a certain condition of the human brain is accompanied by the delusion that love and will and conscience are somehow superior to brain, that is, to the molecules on which they all ultimately depend. It is under a natural law that the organism in man becomes apparently ethical, and as such seems to struggle against nature.

The transitory illusion of a rational consciousness.

More than even this dissolution of morality seems to follow from the premisses which yield a merely molecular solution of the problem of existence;—if indeed any conclusion at all about anything can be consistently drawn in such a universe, where reason itself—

reason to which one is wont to appeal as the supreme tribunal, or as at the root in the nature of things —is transformed into one of innumerable transitory issues of purposeless organic conditions. For what is called intellect, with its product science, as well as what is called conscience, with morality as its product, come to be conceived as only transitory natural outcomes of certain molecular conditions. The very thinking and observing processes themselves, those processes through which the materialist finds that conscious mind, in all its processes, is virtually molecules in motion, are themselves a part of the molecular process. Human intelligence, as well as human conscience, is only one among the many sorts of ephemeral phenomena to which the molecular universe, in its eternal flux of molecules and aggregates of motions, is supposed to be continually giving birth. Its verified inferences, as well as its unproved hypotheses, are all alike transitory; if we are not allowed to presuppose in the primary data more than molecules, accustomed under certain conditions to manifest self-conscious life. And thus even Materialism, this philosophic Monism, itself disappears, along with the phenomenon of self-conscious intelligence by which it was reasoned out, in the abyss of universal Nescience.

Shall we then accept as a solution of the problem of the universe, and of man as a constituent part of it, *this*, which asks us habitually to think of the whole

Is reason an accidental issue of the

molecular motions going on in this corner of the uni- verse ?

as finally purposeless molecular motions, of which intelligence and conscience are transitory issues, but which, in the darkness of Universal Materialism, can, while they last, put in no claim to determine the inter- pretation of the whole ? Can Matter claim this final universality or supremacy ?

What has rational conscious- ness in man to say for itself ?

In next lecture we shall consider what mind, mani- fested in man, has to say for itself, when confronted, in this remote corner, by the conception of a universe of molecules and molecular changes, making a claim to finality.

LECTURE IV.

PANEGOISM.

HUMAN organisms and their self-conscious life appear, The second at the point of view of atomism or moleculism, to be postulated existence only part, and a very insignificant part, of the transitory exagger-ated in natural issue of the universe of molecules in motion. Universal Material-They emerge for a time in a remote and petty corner ism. of immensity, under those particular physical conditions which are found to give rise to self-conscious organism. Mind—the state of matter called consciousness, accord-ing to materialism—is one among innumerable other sorts of manifestation which molecules make of them-selves; not in itself more significant than any one of the many sorts of quantitative differences, in size, shape, or arrangement, of the molecules and molecular masses, on which conscious life, as well as all the other quali-ties of things, are, on this conception of existence, assumed to depend. Just as fire differs from water, and water from gold, ultimately on account of supposed differences in the size, shape, motion, and consistency of their respective constituent molecules,—differences which might be described with precision if one could construct microscopes powerful enough to reveal them,—so, on the same condition, those special characteristics of molecular organisation which give rise to consciousness, when *they* happen to become actual, might in like manner be described in detail. This is the universe of the materialist, which rises in imagination, when the second of the three postulates of existence is exaggerated, and is at last taken as alone sufficient for the explanation of all.

What of the first postulated existence— the ego ?

But has the phenomenon of percipient and self-conscious life by which man is characterised, and which has started up in this remote planetary corner of the material world, nothing more than this to say for itself ? Is this all that it in any way implies ?

The exaggeration of the first postulate occurs later than that of the second.

This question and the answer to it do not so soon force themselves into notice in the way the boundless and endless world of outward things presented to the senses does. The conscious self does not at first obtrude itself upon the unreflecting as exclusively entitled to be called *real.* Our assumed invisible reality seems ready to resolve itself into transitory modes of the solid and extended entities with which the senses are perpetually concerned, and with which we are constantly in contact and collision. Reflex science of life, especially of the sort of life that is conscious, follows in the wake of actual life ; for thought must have material, in the form of spiritual states passed through, before it begins to reflect upon these, and to reduce the life to science.

> " The baby new to earth and sky,
>   What time his tender palm is prest
>   Against the circle of the breast,
> Has never thought that this is ' I.'
>
> But as he grows, he gathers much,
>   And learns the use of ' I ' and ' me,'
>   And finds I am not what I see,
> And other than the things I touch ;
>
> So rounds he to a separate mind,
>   From whence clear memory may begin."

Or again—

> " Dark is the world to thee : thyself art the reason why;
> For is He not all, but thou, that has power to feel ' I am I ?' "

Accordingly the second of the three fundamental postulates of existence—that which assumes outward things—is apt to be exaggerated into the one solitary postulate sooner than the first, which assumes the individual ego. In the earlier stages of one's development he is more ready to suppose that consciousness can be refunded into the universe of outward things, than to suppose that the universe of outward things is dependent on his own self-conscious perceptions. We are all in our childish years more or less materialists. And we find the materialist point of view the favourite one in the childhood of the race of man, as in early Hel-

The outward transformed into the inward.

lenic speculation: so it was in the ancient world to the end, with only a dim apprehension of human individuality and personality. It was with the rise of Christianity that this idea of the individual person unfolded into distinctness. The early Christian theologians found something in a self-conscious person that was foreign to Hellenic and Roman thought in the pre-Christian world. "Great is the power of memory," one finds Augustine exclaiming in his 'Confessions,'—" great is the power of memory, in all its depth and manifold intensity; and this strange thing is my mind; and my mind is myself. Fear and amazement overcome me when I think of this. And yet men go abroad to gaze upon mountains and waves, broad rivers, wide oceans, and the courses of the stars, and overlook *themselves,* the crowning wonder." In the next thousand years after Augustine one finds many utterances in harmony with this. The supreme significance of the ego survives after the rise of the modern reaction against scholastic thought, and a philosophy determined by ecclesiastical authority. When new conceptions of the universe and the ultimate meaning of life were struggling into reflective life in Descartes, the watchword was *Cogito ergo sum—Ego sum cogitans:* my thinking is the essential fact for me. Not atoms but egos, or rather each ego—each person—was taken as the primary element. His own self-conscious life is what is nearest to the person whose individual life it is, and his world is the world which is continually living in his ideas. This was the starting-point and centre of introspective Cartesianism, that first birth of the new philosophic spirit, which so strenuously asserted itself in the seventeenth century. That "nothing can be more evident to us than our own existence," was what we found Locke afterwards acknowledging. "If I doubt all other things, that very doubt makes me perceive my own existence as a conscious being, and will not suffer me to doubt of that." The more this invisible fact of self in which consciousness centres is pondered, the more one seems to see the dependence of the universe on it. So self, conscious and percipient, comes by degrees to absorb all outward things, converting an illusory outwardness into real inwardness. Like Actæon, changed into the stag, and then torn to pieces by his hounds on Mount Cithæron, the once too obtrusive world of molecules is wholly swallowed up in the world of one's own self-conscious personality.

For, when one takes his own living consciousness, reflected on and recognised as the universe of *his* experience, for the philosophical point of view—instead of physical quantities of molecules in space, and the changes in and through which they evolve in time— one finds that his final conception of the universe undergoes a transformation; and the new conception seems to be deeper and truer than the old one. Conscious life in me—conscious life, if there are other egos, whenever it arises—no longer looks like an ephemeral and insignificant accident, that has somehow, through

Conscious life the light of actual existence.

the concourse of molecules, happened to make its appearance on this one planet. I seem at any rate no longer able to suppose that percipient consciousness of man, and conscious intelligence in other phases, in other possible egos, might cease for ever in the universe of existence, and yet that, after its extinction, the huge aggregates of molecules in their molecular masses, with all their properties and other consequences, might continue as they were before its extinction, without any change in their appearance. Percipient life seems now to be able to say for itself, that it is the one paramount necessity, the one indispensable condition of all actual reality, and of all the changes that occur in what actually exists. The introduction of percipient consciousness into existence looks like the introduction of light into a dark room that is distinguished by the beauty and variety of the colours which it presents by day. In the darkness this beautiful variety of form and colour was virtually not in existence, in the sombre and uniform darkness. The brilliant spectacle suddenly becomes actual as soon as the lamp is carried into the dark chamber. If light had never existed, or if it were now to be suddenly and for ever annihilated throughout the universe, the visible glories of earth and sky, as well as of the darkened room, would all cease to be: and if light had never existed, they would never have existed, as we now see them; for they are all virtually created by, because dependent on, the command, "Let there be light." So too with the percipient life introduced into existence by the ego, that "candle of the Lord," which seems to show itself in this way as the unit of the universe. "Let there be a self-conscious ego"—if we could suppose this fiat possible on the hypothesis without a contradiction—"let there be a self-conscious ego," and all becomes the actuality that we perceive. The reflective thinker seems to find this so, when he tries in vain to imagine a material world—a universe of molecules and their aggregates—after all percipient life has been withdrawn. Let this mental experiment be made by one who desires to pass from the exclusive materialism, according to which we were trying to think the universe in last lecture, and who wants to occupy the point of view of egoism, which I am asking you to take provisionally now.

Consider further what becomes of the world revealed in vision and touch, which is the object of daily interest to every human being, which is the means, when scientifically interpreted, of advancing man's comfort, and on which the progress of civilisation depends;— what becomes of this solid and spacious world, of all the physical and natural sciences too, and even of materialism itself as the living philosophy of a self-conscious spirit, when this postulated reality is withdrawn, so that conscious reason, human and divine, is for ever extinct. *The fate of an unperceived material world.*

For one thing, all experience of outward things, including the philosophy which teaches that existence is ultimately outward and molecular—all special sciences and philosophy—*depend on what is inward.* They are contained in consciousness, which is not a molecule nor a mass of molecules. The inward perceptions and inferences, of which living knowledge of external things consists, are indispensable conditions in the construction of that interpretation of existence, as a wholly external and extended natural process, which constitutes the universal materialism or moleculism in which consciousness looks so insignificant. But for the conscious life that it contains, in this little corner of the universe or elsewhere, the world of outward things would be virtually nothing, because all unperceived, in the entire absence of percipient life. If the persons who are percipient of the universe in space, and supposed to be able, by reasoning combined with observation, to discover all that is scientifically affirmed about it, are themselves found, in the progress of their own discoveries, to be in the last resort only transitory issues of unintelligent and unintelligible Matter, this materialistic philosophy of theirs must, like all else that depends upon them, be unworthy of trust, because an outcome of unreason. A merely human science is discredited in the degradation of the beings by whom it is made into accidents of the universal flux. For sciences and materialistic philosophy are then only accidents in the history of certain organisms, which, at this era in the molecular evolution, happen to be formed on this little planet. The supposed discovery that the whole is ultimately only continuous mechanical motion of atoms, without guarantee in a divine-natural order, discredits the discovery itself. Unless there is that in man which is more than physical evolution of matter into organism—if "matter" means only what is given in sense or understanding measured by sense—there can be no valid science, and no valid materialistic philosophy. The testimony given by our human adventurer to the fact that he has been cast up inexplicably in the endless succession of the molecular changes which are the only ultimate reality, and who thinks that he sees scientifically that all conscious life must sooner or later disappear out of existence—this testimony, under such conditions, can neither be vindicated nor refuted. The issue is a literally unutterable scepticism about everything. The key which pretended to open the secrets of reality has been taken away in the very act of using it. Universal moleculism is intellectual suicide.

The larger human life is a continual protest against this. To suppose that conscious intelligence itself is essentially only molecular, is found to be an inadequate, if not a self-contradictory position. The modern science of outward things, of which the race of man is justly proud, as one of the most signal of its glories, is made only one among innumerable other sorts of accidental and temporary modifications of atomic form and movement; culminating in the discovery of the irrelevancy

The conscious ego greater than a universe of unconscious things.

H

and insignificance of the conscious reason that recognises the discoveries. The existence in a living thought, of the great mechanical law of gravitation, or of the still greater biological law of universal natural evolution, including of course the evolution of those very discoveries themselves, surely implies, in the final constitution of the universe, something deeper than an originally unconscious and accidental concurrence of atoms. We are reminded of the familiar sentiment of Pascal. When looked at only as a visible and tangible organism, that occupies an infinitesimal portion of space, during an infinitesimal period of time, *man* seems no more than a reed, even the weakest reed, in external nature: he is nevertheless a thinking or self-conscious reed; with all the tremendous consequences that may be found involved in this one unique fact. Physically, he is a transitory individual organism. When we measure *its* size and duration, and compare *this* with the Immensities and the Eternities, I and all other men are seen to be so insignificant that there is no need for the boundless material world to employ its collective forces in order to compass our destruction. A vapour, or a drop of water, is found to be enough for this purpose. Yet even if the illimitable material world were to have all the molecular forces that are supposed to belong to its atoms exclusively combined for destruction of men, there is still that in man which is greater, and therefore more noble, than this by which the organisms would be destroyed; greater, too, than the organism itself, as a mere portion of the outward world. For the man would be *conscious* of his fate; while the universe of things visible and tangible, in which his organism disappeared, would be *unconscious* of its victory. The true character and standing of man in the universe is to be read, not in the quantity of space that his body is seen to fill, nor in the periods of time during which the physical evolution of which his body is the ephemeral issue has been going on, but in the invisible life, percipient and self-conscious, which at last emerges, and is indeed his very self. Invisible egos are therefore superior to unseen molecules, and also to visible aggregates of molecules, however vast in size they may be. Each of us is greater than all matter abstracted from all percipient life can be— the ego is greater than any objects presented through the senses; because the ego is conscious and active, while things presented to our senses are only passive and unconscious appearances.

The Panegoist looks into a question which material- What ism always overlooks. He asks what the word *matter* should we mean when should ultimately mean, when the word is rightly used. the real What is meant by the real existence of a molecule, of matter or an aggregate of molecules, or by the existence of cules? molecules in motion? What is meant by an outward thing, or by the external existence of anything? Let us by this kind of reflection try to bring more fully into light the second postulated existence, — instead of leaving it in the vague form of an uncriticised

faith.   When we do this, at our new point of view, in
obedience to that exclusive supremacy of the first of
the three postulated realities, we begin to see that there
is more mystery than we had supposed in the fact of
conscious perception of things that are assumed to be
not conscious,—and that are yet held to be things upon
which perception and all else that is called "mind"
absolutely depends.   There is here a chasm, which the
history of philosophical inquiry suggests the difficulty
of bridging over,—a chasm between, on the one hand,
those living perceptions of things that are referred to
myself—to the mind of the individual person who is
conscious of them—and which succeed one another in
the absolute privacy of one's own conscious life, and,
on the other hand, solid and extended things, molecules and masses of molecules, supposed to exist, and
to continue to exist, just as one actually sees them
and touches them, whether or not there exists a percipient who is seeing or touching or otherwise having
sentient experience.   The things once called "outward,"
and believed to be quite independent of any inward
percipient life, seem now to lose their so-called qualities one by one.   These begin to disappear as empty
abstractions, when percipient life is supposed to be
withdrawn from the universe; so that one is obliged
to ask whether a molecule, or an aggregate of molecules, *could* exist externally—if to exist externally
means to exist, in the way it now appears to the
senses to do, after the extinction of all mind in the

universe. When I say that outward things are, have been, and will continue to be, can this really mean more than that I or some percipient is, has been, and continues to be conscious of the mental states called seeing and touching? in the faith, it may be, that those seeings and feelings, and the pleasures and pains which accompany them, are part of the universal order; which faith, however, being only another expression for faith in God, is an unexplained addition to a purely individual egoism.

Again. One begins to see that, when one speaks of external things, he must include among them the minute organism which he calls his own body—that organism which, for the materialist, is really the whole man, —an organism, the visible insignificance of which, among the other contents of infinite space and duration, and its arbitrary unintelligible connection with their molecular evolution and physical constitution, signified to the materialistic imagination the insignificance of self-conscious life, as an item in the immeasurable universe. For one's own body is a part of the material world. Even though it is called "living matter," it is still external, like all other visible things, to the private and invisible self, or proper ego. When it is seen in this light, the thought occurs that no sufficient reason can be produced to show that the conscious life is necessarily embodied, although it is now embodied. Is that an *a priori* reason which forbids the supposition that I might have passed through all the

The human organism is, and the self-conscious person is not, part of the material world of sense.

varieties of sentient experience of which I have been conscious since I was born, without being embodied? Why may I not have the mental experience called seeing, or that other sort called touching, without my present visual and tactual organs, or even without any organism of gross molecular matter at all? Our so-called five senses, too, might conceivably have been other than they are—more numerous, for example—and thus presenting outward things clothed in innumerable qualities which are now unimaginable by man; or they might be less numerous, in which case much that normally constituted men can now perceive and imagine would be unimaginable. Of this last we have examples in those human beings who are born entirely blind, and to whom, in consequence, all words expressive of visual ideas to us who see are meaningless and unrepresentative. For aught we know, there may be percipient beings in some other corner of the universe who are destitute of all our so-called five external senses, and endowed with five, or five hundred, other sorts of senses, each different in kind from any of ours. If so, what is matter, in *their* perceptions and conceptions of it? It can have none of the qualities or quantities which we refer to the things that we call outward; and it must have five, or five hundred, sorts of properties, all of which a human being would be as unable to imagine as the born-blind man was to imagine scarlet, which Locke's blind friend pictured mentally as like the sound of a trumpet.

Further, what in the nature of mental experience, as we find it when we examine our own introspectively, —what is there in this which forbids a continued percipient life—either like our own as it now is, or like that of any of those supposed percipients who may have been endowed with five hundred senses other than any of ours—after our present organisms are dissolved in physical death? I see no difficulty, Berkeley, at this point of view, would say,—I see no difficulty in conceiving a succession of mental states, following physical death, being maintained as well without as with organised body, in the future life. For it seems easy to suppose a self-conscious and percipient experience persisting, without those conditions of molecular movement on which it is found now to depend, and which in this life are its " physical basis,"—to suppose that the ego still continues to exercise itself as I am doing now, receiving ideas of colour but without the organ of seeing, and of sounds but without the organ of hearing. And yet, even if this should turn out to be more than a mere conjecture, reason can be suggested for the present existence of the elaborate organs that are contained in the bodily constitution of man.

The present correlation of bodily organism and mental experience.

But we must return from conjectures to facts. Let us look more carefully at the appearances which matter presents. We may see how, as things now are, the properties popularly referred to matter so hang upon percipient life as that with its extinction they must

Illustrative facts.

necessarily disappear too, and at last leave the molecules in all the nakedness of empty abstractions.

The properties of matter distinguished as primary or quantitative, and secondary or imputed.
It has been customary with philosophers to distinguish the properties of bodies as of two sorts—those, on the one hand, which are essential to what is called body, deprived of which it would not be so named; and those, on the other hand, which seem to be accidentally connected with it, or at least which might disappear without body ceasing for us to be called body. The first sort are said to be primary or essential properties of matter; the others are called secondary or imputed properties. In their primary or essential attributes, bodies—whether large or small aggregates of molecules, as well as the constituent molecules separately—are space-occupying: they are solid quantities of extension : they can be formulated mathematically and mechanically, in terms of quantity. The secondary properties, again, are those which invest bodies with their chief human interest; those in virtue of which they are of practical importance or useful to man, — their hardness or softness, for instance, their heat or cold, their colours, sounds, odours, and tastes,—all which, as distinguished from the former sort, are alone properly called qualities; for the former sort are quantitative. In fact, on the molecular final conception of existence, the atoms or molecules were supposed to be quantities only, without qualitative differences; and the innumerable differences which we observe in the secondary qualities that are imputed to

an external thing were referred to quantitative differences too minute to be seen by men at any rate,—
differences in the shape, size, position, and motions of
its constituent atoms or molecules. Democritus, the
representative of early materialism, argues that all the
qualitative differences in external things are caused
by—*i.e.*, are physically dependent on—their quantitative molecular differences. Water, for instance, presents qualities different from iron—in other words,
qualities different from those of iron are imputed to
it, because its constituent molecules are round and
smooth, and do not fit into one another; those of
iron, on the contrary, are jagged, uneven, and densely
aggregated. This hypothesis of Democritus reappears
in Descartes and in Locke, with the cautious qualification, introduced especially by Locke,—that if the
qualities thus imputed to outward things are *not*
differenced by their dependence on unperceived (but
conceivable) quantitative relations of their constituent
molecules, they must depend upon something in bodies
that is even more mysterious than an essence or substance that is molecular.

Now, looking in the first place only at the imputed
and interesting properties of the things we call outward, it appears that for all by which *those* qualities
are distinguished from the molecular modes and relations by which, on the atomic hypothesis, things are
supposed to be determined, in their several imputed
varieties, things depend entirely upon sentient and per-

Obvious depen-
dence of the im-
puted or secondary
qualities upon a per-
cipient.

cipient life. We cannot even imagine the secondary
properties existing externally in the absence of life,
except by reading them only in terms of the non-re-
sembling molecules and molecular motions by which,
on this hypothesis, they are supposed to be conditioned,
or of which they are thus the correlatives. For the
atoms of which fire, for instance, is composed have
surely themselves no *felt sensation* of heat, like that
which I have when I approach fire. Now, if the
sensation is abstracted, what remains that is at all
imaginable, in the objective meaning of the word
"fire," except—motion among the molecules of which
the burning object is composed? Heat is therefore
necessarily read in terms of motion whenever it is
imagined as external. When I cease to read fire in
terms of my own feeling of heat, I must read it, if
I read it at all, only in terms of molecular motion.
Then an orange becomes colourless in the dark; it
must lose all that we are percipient of in what we
call *its* odour and taste, when all *mental* experience
is withdrawn: the residuary issue is at the most
a mass of colourless, inodorous, tasteless molecules.
When one tries to imagine heat in an object that is
in combustion, or an orange in possession of its imputed qualities, but with no one percipient of them,
one is obliged to imagine, not the sensations now
named, but some correlative modification of molecules in motion. Analysis of what are called "properties of bodies" in this way obliges us to strip the

"outward" world at least of all its secondary and interesting qualities;—except so far as these can be formulated in terms of the atomic motions of which they are then the correlatives, but which have no resemblance to the qualities in question at all; for our sensations of heat in fire, or of sweetness in an orange, are not in the least like solid and extended molecules, nor like any relations that can exist among solid and extended molecules. Moreover, physical science itself finds a barrier to its perfection here; for it has not yet discovered and precisely formulated the innumerable varieties of molecular motion which, on the hypothesis of molecular correlation, correspond to the innumerable varieties of the so-called secondary or imputed qualities of the things around us. So that the latter cannot yet be read scientifically to any considerable extent in terms of the former.

But the disintegration of outward things that is consequent upon the withdrawal of all self-conscious and sentient life from the universe, it may be argued, at the point of view of Panegoism, does not stop here. It is not arrested as soon as it has stripped molecules and their aggregates of all that gives them human interest and utility. It may be argued that the aggregates of molecules, and the very molecules themselves of which things are believed to consist, become inconceivable abstractions after they have been stripped of all their imputed qualities, and left to exist in an absolutely unresistant, colourless, silent, inodorous,

Implied dependence likewise of solid quantity, or primary qualities, on a percipient.

and tasteless condition, neither cold nor hot. For one's imagination of the chief primary property of things—namely, their extension, or occupancy of space—is itself dependent upon the relative sensations of which we are conscious, with which it is blended so inextricably that we cannot even imagine a perfectly colourless mass of matter. An extended thing that has no secondary qualities cannot be imagined as an outward thing at all; for it must be a thing that is neither hard, nor soft, nor coloured. Try, in a word, to strip things of all the qualities imputed to them which obviously depend for their actuality upon the presence of a percipient, and then all that by which they are known to us, or can be imagined by us, disappears too. But this subtraction of *all their properties* is practically the subtraction of the things themselves: therefore things cannot be imagined actually existing independent of all percipient life. At the most, only an unqualified and unquantified *something* remains, of which nothing can be either affirmed or denied,—an empty abstraction or negation, not worth taking into account as a factor in the constitution of the universe.

Unperceived molecules thus become empty abstractions.

If all the properties of material things are in this way proved to be in their nature dependent upon the living percipient, the common but confused supposition that some of them exist externally, meaning by that independently of all percipient life, is argued to be contrary to reason. For they are kept in actual, if not also in potential, existence, by the sentient ego through whose sentient experience they become what they are, and in whom accordingly they are finally substantiated. The universe is not a universe of independent molecules: it is a universe of the independent ego; with molecules, aggregates of molecules, and qualities imputed to them, all sustained in the continued mental experience of the ego. In this conscious life the visible and tangible world is continually manifesting itself, and being delivered from abstraction. "For can there," we are asked, "can there be a nicer strain of abstraction than to distinguish the *existence* of sensible objects from their being *perceived;* so as to conceive them existing unperceived? One might as easily divide a thing from itself as do this. Some truths there are so near and obvious that a man need only open his eyes to see them. Such I take this important one to be, namely, that all the choir of heaven and furniture of the earth—in a word, all those bodies which compose the mighty frame of the world—have not any subsistence without a mind,—that their *being* is *to be perceived*" — either by me or by some other sentient ego, if another exists.

Accordingly, no man who reflects upon the universe of reality, at this point of view exclusively, can doubt that what we call "outward" things—stars, their planets, this planet with all its visible and tangible contents, including our own bodies—are really mental experiences, arising in an established order which somehow

Our conception of what is meant by the real existence of molecules is transformed accordingly.

enables us to expect mental experiences still future,
—all which orderly universe of personally perceived
phenomena would necessarily become extinct with the
extinction of the conscious and percipient life of the
ego, on which the whole is practically suspended. Our
final conception of what a material world is, and of
what reality means, is more deeply transformed in this
individual egoism than was the old-fashioned anthropocentric conception, by the modern discoveries of the
astronomer and the biologist. Instead of an external
flux of molecules, in imagined orderly motion in
space, the universe is now seen to be an eternal flux
of orderly perceptions or ideas in the history of the
self-conscious ego. In this transformation scene, self-
conscious life is the final supposition—not the starry
heaven, with its molecular occupants, in the immensity of an independent space, nor the unbeginning
and unending physical metamorphoses, in which this
earth and all its living inhabitants are supposed physically to participate, apart from living mind, and what
living mind involves. Nothing now seems great in
the universe of existence but self-conscious mind;—
and the only living mind of which I am conscious is
my own.

The con-
ception of
causality
or power
in outward
things also
trans-
formed.

At this individual immaterialist point of view, a transformation in our ideas of causality and power has been
likewise tacitly going on. The meaning to which the
words " cause " and " power " were confined when only

customary sequence or customary co-existence was recognised in them, is found to be inadequate when one
reflects upon the meaning of cause and power as found
applicable to one's personal acts. For the Ego is found
by reflection to be a centre of power more deeply and
truly than molecules, or aggregates of molecules, are
perceived by the senses to be powers. In particular,
in recognising one's self—and other persons, if there
are any—as moral agents, one finds that he is obliged
to acknowledge more in an agent, or in moral agency,
than sense reveals in the physical "agency" popularly
attributed to molecules and their masses. In merely
outward nature, *per se*, all that is perceived is phenomena followed by, or changed into, other phenomena,
in a continuous procession of caused causes—an endless, orderly procession of metamorphoses—each unit
in the procession, so far as appears, the passive subject
of a rule to which it seems to conform; but without
innate activity being found in any of the units of the
procession, in the way that innate activity, or self-
originated power, is found in the personal agent who
deserves praise or blame for what he does. For conscience obliges us to recognise *ourselves* as in a measure
originating agents—the ego as the real agent—in the
case, at least, of all states and changes which evoke
the feeling and conviction of remorse on the part of
the ego on account of their occurrence. The moral
and immoral acts of the ego thus differ in kind from
caused or dependent causes in the natural procession

which the physical sciences are so successfully interpreting. None of *them* are found by sense to be agents that absolutely originate their acts, as I am found by conscience to be when I am judged to be the creator of an act of my own for which I blame myself. When we seize this deeper meaning of power and agency, all outward things seem to be powers or agents only metaphorically. They are found empty of real efficacy, which one is obliged to refer to an intending personal agent. So power proper comes to be regarded as that in which a change of some sort is found to originate; not that which is found only as the customary antecedent of a change, under a rule or law which *a priori* one has no reason to suppose might not have been different from what experience shows that it actually is. The physically scientific conception of causality, as continuous sequence only, is seen, in the light of this moral experience in my own conscious life, to be thin and shallow.

Occasional causation, and Locke on power in outward things and in egos.

Those who take the philosophical position even of a modified Panegoism find power only in persons. The occasionalism of Descartes emptied sensible things of causality in any other sense than that of the regularity of sequence, which, it was assumed, was actively maintained by God, whose existence seemed to him as certain as his own. But by Malebranche, still more by Spinoza, finite persons as well as things were inferred to be powerless, in the exclusive unity of all in God. Locke, too, notwithstanding his tendency

to ultimate atomism, had an inkling of active causality being exemplified only in egos, in contrast with
the passive susceptibilities of molecules and their aggregates, according to Aristotle's idea of antithesis
between active and passive power. "We are abund-
antly furnished," Locke says, "with the idea of *passive*
power, or capacity for change, by almost all sorts of
sensible things. In most of them we cannot avoid
observing their sensible qualities, nay, their very substances, to be in a constant flux. Nor have we of
active power fewer instances ; since whatever change
is observed, the mind must collect a power somewhere to make that change, as well as a possibility
in the thing to receive the change. But yet, if we
will consider it attentively, bodies by our senses do
not afford us so clear and distinct an idea of power as
we have from reflection on the [moral and immoral ?]
operations of our minds." Again : "Whether matter
be not wholly destitute of active power, as its author
God is truly above all passive power [*i.e.*, above being
a mere unit in the procession of caused causes]; and
whether the intermediate state of created spirits be
not that alone which is capable, both of active and
passive power [*i.e.*, man participating at once both in
passive external nature and in active spirit], may be
worth consideration. Natural substances any way are
not so truly active powers as our hasty thoughts are
apt to represent them." So that instead of matter and
force, or molecules in motion, explaining everything

I

they really explain nothing: all their changes under gravitation, and their natural evolutions, as well as their gravitation law and their still wider law of evolution, themselves need to be explained; and the only light for explanation comes from reflection upon conscious life. Of conscious life there is one imperfect specimen somehow connected with the physical evolution of a human organism, on this locally insignificant planet. It would therefore seem that the only agents that are really agents are incorporeal, and, so far as morally responsible, "not properly of physical consideration," and beyond the sphere of astronomical, geological, or biological science. External things are agents only metaphorically: persons alone are really active.

The outward world only a world of sense signs, found by custom to be interpretable.

In this way, instead of being an aggregate of individual agents, to each of which certain issues may be absolutely referred, as those for which that agent exclusively is responsible, the world unfolded to our five senses presents only aggregates of passive sense appearances, called sensible things, which are related to one another, not as an agent properly so called is connected with the effects which originate absolutely in the agent, but only as sensible signs connected with events yet future, which they practically signify, so far as they are believed to be in constant sequence with them. What are called causes in the material world are really only premonitors, somehow supposed to warrant men in expecting the actual appearance of changes they are believed to signify. They are only the somehow established forerunners of events, for which they prepare those who are able to interpret them; and in each case the physical antecedent might *a priori* be supposed different from what in experience it is found actually to be. The world presented to our senses is conceived as a world, or a universe, only because it is conceived to be this system of interpretable sense signs: it is interpretable because certain sorts of its presented appearances are found in constant sequence with certain other sorts: faith in this constancy makes men infer that when an instance of the one sort appears, an instance of the other sort may be expected to follow. The world that is called outward or non-mental, becomes transformed under this conception into a system of mind-dependent sense signs; and we find that we are able to interpret some of the signs on which the pleasures and pains of sentient life depend — which, in short, signify pleasure or pain to an animated being. This world of sensible experience is found to involve happiness and misery for me. At the same time, one among many functions which the same world seems to discharge is, that of awakening and educating intelligence in me the percipient, by that exercise of intellect which is needed for the interpretation of changes in the sense-presented order of phenomena, and by the exercise of prudence and benevolence in the useful applications of which the interpretations admit, when they can be made to minister to the comfort and organic satisfaction of man.

What right has the individual egoist to assume the interpretability of sense phenomena?　But how comes it that the sense phenomena of experience *are* thus significant? and have I any reason for supposing their significance, which I always do? How, too, have I come into existence to be an interpreter of sense signs? If two of the three postulated existences of ordinary faith are neglected, and if the only reality presupposed is *myself*, it seems to follow that in perceiving and interpreting what is, without proof, treated as a universe of reliable sense signs, I am only entitled to say that I am perceiving and conceiving *unintelligible modifications of myself*. At the most it is an "outward" universe of impotent sense phenomena, dependent upon my conscious and percipient life and experience; for some of the changes I find myself obliged to acknowledge my own personal responsibility, and so conclude that I have power to regulate them: the great majority are either the issue of what is called (as an apology for ignorance) my "occult faculty" of perception; or else they originate in another ego foreign to my private consciousness, and therefore to my knowledge; unless, indeed, I choose to refer them to some absolutely incognisable power, —the term "power" then a cover for empty verbal abstraction. The procession of felt sense perceptions, which forms so much of my inward life—so far as conscience (itself unexplained by the Panegoist) does not oblige me to refer some of its changes exclusively to my own agency as their originating cause—must all be referred to something unknown and unknowable. Moreover, these hypothetical references are themselves only states of my own consciousness as intelligent. Individual egoism is eternally confined within the individual ego.

But sense perception still introduces an incalculable element into my experience of myself, even when outward things and God are overlooked or explained away. This is one impediment to Panegoism, when I pretend to reduce absolutely to the unity of my own individual consciousness the reality that is present in sense. At the point of view of individual egoism, the universe is born and dies with the person who experiences it, and the only person of whose existence I am conscious is myself. The postulated Matter and the postulated God of ordinary faith are absorbed and lost in me. The exclusive ego, in the last resort—as well as the exclusive molecules, in the last resort—reduces human experience of reality to an absurdity, if not to a contradiction; although Universal Immaterialism has more to say for itself than Universal Materialism. *The universe of individual egoistic immaterialism lives and dies with the individual ego.*

I turn now to the third and only remaining postulate, to ponder its adequacy to the need of reason and experience when it is conceived in the end to super- *Another alternative.*

sede the other two. May the desired intellectual and
moral satisfaction be found when the Infinite Being
is taken as the one reality, and when we think of
molecules and individual egos as alike only perish-
ing or illusory modes of God? This third alternative
will be considered in the next two lectures.

LECTURE V.

PANTHEISM.

LET me at this stage recall the train of thought to Retrospect.
which I have asked your consideration in the foregoing lectures of this course.   Let me also suggest
their logical connection with the remaining part of
the course, on which we are now entering, and in which
we shall find ourselves more immediately concerned
with Theism than we have been hitherto.

At the outset I put before you my own concep- The problem which underlies Theism.
tion of the philosophical problem which underlies the
intellectual treatment of religion, and with which one
is throughout concerned, when engaged with "Natural
Theology in the widest sense of that term." It is the
final problem of existence, or of human life in the
universe in which man awakes into consciousness.
That what is actually experienced really exists, is
what most of us take for granted : this primary faith
is illustrated whenever things and persons are pre-

sented to us in space and time. Some explanation there must surely be of the ultimate meaning and outcome of the all-embracing fact, that I find myself in an ever-changing universe, whether or not the explanation can be reached by man. What sort of universe is this in which I find myself when I awaken into percipient life? May I look at it with trust and hope? or must I resign myself to doubt and despair, as in an environment in which the presence of active moral reason, that is to say of Deity, is not to be found? What am I who have become self-conscious and percipient; and for what purpose am I conscious? In what, or in whom, am I at this moment living and moving and having my being? These are the questions in which the final problem of existence is raised; they are questions with which philosophy and religion are concerned in common. Philosophy culminates in them; religion presupposes an answer to them. The existence of religion does not, indeed, depend upon the possibility of an exhaustive solution of those problems by the intellect. For religion is a practical relation of thought, emotion, and will in man to a supposed divine environment; and this remains good even although the divine reality, being infinite, may turn out to be only incompletely comprehensible in a merely human understanding. A religious life of reverence and moral trust, vivified by love, is not only consistent with, but probably involves a recognition of the insolubility, by logical intelligence, of the divine problem ; and we may find that intellect alone, in abstraction from the emotional and ethical elements in human nature, is inadequate to its settlement. It may turn out that the highest human philosophy takes the form of a reasonable faith that man will not be put to confusion in the end, by indulgence either in scientific prevision or in ethical and religious hope. As Locke expresses it : " How short soever men's knowledge may come of an universal and perfect comprehension of whatsoever is, it may yet secure their great concernments, that they have at least light enough to lead them to a practical knowledge of their Maker, and the sight of their own duties." We may find in the end that our share of reason leaves us at last, alike in natural science and in religious thought, suspended on a faith that finds vent in the expectation that animates scientific discovery, and also in the expectation with which religious prophecy is charged.

So much regarding the final problem of human life, or of this Natural Theology. Our next step was to articulate it more definitely, according to the ordinary supposition about the constituents of the universe of reality. For reasons given, I took Locke's account of these. This presents three final existences—namely, myself, the outer world which immediately environs me, and God. These are for each man the three inevitable realities. Under various conceptions of what each means, they seem to be all, in some manner, con-

Articulation of this problem : three postulated existences.

sciously or unconsciously, assumed, in the interpretation of human experience that finds practical response
in common sense. For the history of man is really a
record of the gradual, often interrupted, evolution in
the human mind of the three central ideas of each
one's own personality—one's sense environment—the
absolute Being, or ground in reason of the whole.
The conception of each of these three existences is
modified by the manner in which it is held in relation to the other two. For the last question regarding
each cannot be fully raised without involving answers
to root questions about the other two. In the early
stages of man's development self, or the personal factor,
is only obscurely recognised. The idea of a real order
present in the sense environment is also dim in the
early ages of history, as well as at first in the life of
the individual. And the idea of God originally appears in the crude forms of fetichism and polytheism,
or of a capricious supernatural interference that is inconsistent with natural order. But without enlarging
on men's crude primitive conceptions of each of the
three postulated existences, or tracing their gradual
growth as presented in history, I took them as they
appear in ordinary thought in the modern world, with
Locke as their intellectual spokesman.

Their re-
duction to a
philosophi-
cal unity—
materialis-
tic, egois-
tic, or pan-
theistic.

Then we went on to inquire what three monist
philosophies say regarding the three commonly postulated existences. Speculative philosophy is the endeavour to see the intellectual unity that makes the

universe a universe. With his craving for unity, the theorist is dissatisfied when mysterious plurality instead of exhaustive unity is presented as the final thought about things. The primary instinct of the intrepid thinker accordingly makes him resolve two of the three postulated existences into the third. So it comes about that some who speculate are disposed to imagine that we are all living and moving and having our being in a materialistic unity—the things and persons that appear in space and time being at last only molecules in motion, in their various inorganic aggregates and their organisms—and then to take this as the last word about what exists, refusing to go further. More reflective thinkers, again, exaggerate their own conscious egos, as the materialists exaggerate the data of the five senses: they see in the outer world of our surroundings only conscious states, dependent on themselves who are conscious of them; and their last word about what we are living and moving and having our being in is,—that each is living and moving and having his being in himself, or in his own mental experience. To another mind, neither outward things—that is to say, molecules in their aggregates and organisms—nor yet the ego in its successive conscious states, provide the desired unity: a final reality, sought either in tangible things or in self-conscious persons, seems inconsistent with the omnipresence and omnipotence, the eternity and infinity, which must be supposed to belong to the final reality:

self, and also the outward things by which self is surrounded, lose their imagined separateness in a higher conception of what exists: they are conceived, or at least spoken of, as necessitated modifications of the One Infinite Reality, called God, in which the universe is consubstantiated.

Pantheistic unity and necessity alone, properly speaking, absolute.
Here are three attempts to form the ultimate conception of the reality in which we find ourselves participating—that under which All is resolved into an empirical materialistic unity; that under which All is resolved into the individual personal unity; and that under which All is resolved, still under a supposed necessity of reason, into the Divine or pantheistic unity. But while each of these three exaggerations of one of the three existences, to the exclusion of the other two, has its advocates, perhaps none of the three has ever been advocated with thoroughgoing consistency. In the last two lectures I asked you to consider final materialism and final individual egoism, both of them atheistic or non-theistic when logical and exhaustive. Now you have to look at pantheism, in which the idea of God is exclusive; and in pantheism alone among the three is the conception of an absolute unity consistently held. At least materialism, with its innumerable atoms and organisations of atoms, fails to afford a strictly monist conception at the last. Both materialism and panegoism give us "substances,"—extended and unconscious substance, or the conscious substance himself, at the last, —but not the Infinite Unity.

We found modern materialism, under the influence of the sensuous imagination, ready to accept the discoveries of the new physical and natural sciences as leading the way to the only possible solution of the problem of the universe. The natural history of the molecules of matter—the laws of their chronological evolution in the various degrees of living organism, some accompanied by consciousness—is offered as an account of the whole. The physical organism, through its natural functions, under which reason and will are consciously manifested in man, is supposed in some way to explain the contents of reason and will, as manifested in consciousness; and the natural history of the physical organism, which is the present condition of the rise of reason into consciousness, is substituted for reflective criticism of the rational and volitional consciousness itself, after it has thus arisen into life. The details of the organic evolution, in the natural sequence of biological causation, are without doubt full of interest; but they are surely irrelevant when we want to hear the voice of reason itself, which must be our final tribunal, if reason is supreme in reality. Indeed the materialistic dogma —for it is only a dogma, or unproved assumption— that the common substance of the universe of things and persons that appear in space and time is *matter*— meaning by this matter as endowed only with those properties which our senses find in what is presented to them — this unproved assertion has prob-

Materialism or atomism as the expression of the ultimate unity.

ably never been made in earnest by any one who
has thought out fully what it involves.   It is impossible to identify mind and motion *as phenomena.*
It is moreover irrelevant to theism that the physical
natural history of the visible organism should be as
the materialist alleges that it has been; for the procession of phenomena does not necessarily involve an
atheistic, or exclusively materialistic, inference.   I do
not see how it follows that rational consciousness
can be resolved into molecular motion merely because
its correlative phenomena in inorganic and organic
matter can be read in terms of physical causation, as
the natural outcome of antecedent natural conditions
of matter; nor does it seem to follow that the organisms themselves are adequately conceived, when they
are treated as only mechanical results of the accidental
experiments of an unpremeditated "selection" that was
originally incapable of any form of teleological interpretation.   But of this afterwards.

Individual
egoism as
the expres-
sion of the
ultimate
unity.

I proceeded next to test this materialism, that
claims finality, by showing what immaterialism had
to say for itself.   Accordingly, some of the consequences of thinking the universe of things and persons in an ultimately materialistic unity appeared in
a striking way when, in last lecture, we reversed our
point of view, and tried to look at things exclusively
in the light of our own self-conscious and percipient
life.   We found the universe of "outward" things
depending on that life in unexpected ways, while the

life contains the rational consciousness to which materialism necessarily appeals in all its own reasonings, as the final criterion of truth. It was chiefly in order to illustrate this inevitable dependence of the outward upon the inward, that I asked each person provisionally to suppose his own ego to be the final unity in the universal system, and so resolve into its subjective experience the postulated existence of outward things, and the postulated existence of God. It is true that panegoism has, even less than materialism, formed an accepted philosophical system, with a full recognition of its logical consequences. It has been attributed to Descartes, as the implicate of his method: Fichte, at a certain stage in his philosophical development, has sometimes been considered its representative. But, hypothetically accepted, it forms at least a *reductio ad absurdum* of exclusive materialism. It presents the only reality of the materialist as empty negation, when the light and life of percipient consciousness is entirely withdrawn. But this individual egoism is self-destructive: it shuts up each person in a suicidal isolation, because the postulates of reason, which connect individual persons with the outward and with the infinite, are on its narrow basis dissolved in the one postulate of an individual personality.

But, as I have said, there is another alternative to either universal materialism or the egoism that claims finality. There is the recognition of the third postu- *Pantheistic necessity as the expression of the ultimate unity.*

lated existence as finally the only possible, because
the infinite, Reality. Mind and matter, as we experience them — the finite things and finite persons
that appear in time and space—are in this supposed
to have only an illusory reality, and to be not more
or other than transitory phases or modifications of
Infinite Being—the Absolute Reality—of which the
finite universe, in all its known degrees, from minerals
up to men, is the absolutely necessitated manifestation. This vaguely is Pantheism. The universe conceived pantheistically is conceived as the eternal in-
voluntary evolution of the One Infinite Reality: we
live and have the conscious being which, speaking un-
pantheistically, we call exclusively "our own," only as
we are modifications of the only Being. Atoms in all
their visible organisations, and egos in all their invisible conscious states, emanate from, and in the end
return into, Divine or Infinite Being, the one, the
absolutely unique, Substance and Power: Absolute
Being, now revealed in things and persons, absolutely
ceases to reveal itself. This is pantheistic Monism,
or the necessitated unity of All. The innumerable
atoms of materialism present an empirical and generic,
rather than the unique, necessary, and infinite One.
Taken either separately or in combination, matter
and the individual ego present factitious unities. In
Infinite Being alone we seem to find a unity that is
logically inconsistent with real plurality; a necessity
that is inconsistent with contingency or imperfection.

For if anything exists of which God is not the substance and the innate power, the pantheist argues that
there would then be two gods, and neither of them
could be the Infinite, which the universe must finally
be conceived to be.

Infinite Being seems, therefore, to have a claim in
reason to exclusiveness which neither of the two orders
of finite reality can produce. For God is more truly
substance and power, even under ordinary conceptions of what substance and power mean, than finite
things and persons can be. Descartes accordingly defined "substance," taken absolutely, as that which so
exists that it needs nothing else to account for or
sustain its existence: what are called "created" substances — bodies and egos to wit — are beings that
need God for their beginning and continuance, and
are, therefore, substances only in a secondary sense,—
whatever that may mean; for substance is that which
exists in itself, and is conceived by itself, the one self-
existent reality. In consistency with this, Spinoza,
more logical than Descartes, concluded that substance, or what exists with a true reality, must necessarily be One—absolutely unique—so that whatever is
finite and plural can only be unsubstantial or unreal.

There is need, let me say, for guarding against
ambiguity in employing this word *substance,* so prominent in the pantheistic vocabulary. Also neither
Descartes nor Spinoza seem sufficiently to distinguish between substantiality and causality, and fail

(marginal note:) Are finite things and persons substances, in the way that infinite Being is Substance?

K

to see that qualities and powers *can* be referred to finite substances, although the substances themselves still depend for their existence upon God. It does not seem to follow from such dependence that the thing or person so dependent must be only a necessitated mode of Divine Being. There is wisdom in the words of Locke, when he " desires those who lay so much stress on the sound of these two syllables—*substance*—to consider whether, applying it, as they do, to the infinite incomprehensible God, to finite spirit, and to body, it can be used in each of these cases in the same sense ; and whether it stands for the same idea when each of these three so different beings are called substances." If it does, he asks, with Spinoza apparently in view, whether it will not thence follow that God, spirits, and bodies, agreeing in the same common nature of substance, differ not any otherwise than in a bare different *modification* of that One substance ; as a tree and a pebble, agreeing in the common nature of body, differ only in a bare modification of that common matter. This he considers " a very harsh doctrine." " If they say that they apply it to God, finite spirit, and matter, in three different significations, and that it stands for one idea when God is said to be a substance, for another when the soul is called substance, and for a third (still different) idea when body is called so ;—if the one name substance stands for three several distinct ideas, they would do well," he thinks, " to make known these distinct ideas, or at least to give three distinct names to them, to prevent, in so important a notion, the confusion and errors that will naturally follow from the promiscuous use of so doubtful a term ; which is so far from being suspected to have three distinct significations, that in ordinary use it has scarce one clear distinct signification ;—and if they can thus make three distinct ideas of substance, what hinders why another may not make a fourth ?" These words of Locke may be pondered when one is investigating the scheme of a pantheistically united or necessitated universe, especially as in Spinoza.

Yet Pantheism, in one or other of its many protean forms, is a way of thinking about the universe that has proved its influence over millions of human minds. Looked at in one light, it seems to be Atheism ; in another, it is a sentimental or mystical Theism ; in a third, it is analogous to Calvinism. It has governed the religious and philosophical thought of India for ages. Except in Palestine, with the intense consciousness of personal deity there found, it has been characteristic of Asiatic thought,—under one phase in Brahminism, under another in Buddhism. It is the religious philosophy of a moiety of the human race. In the West we find the idea at work in different degrees of distinctness—in the pre-Socratic schools of Greece, as in Parmenides ; after Socrates, among the Stoics ; then among the Neo-Platonists of Alexandria, with Plotinus in ecstatic elevation as a signal representative ; again, in a striking form in Scotus Erigena, who startles us

Pantheism in its protean forms pervades the intellectual and emotional history of mankind.

with active and intrepid speculation in the darkness of
the ninth century, the least philosophical period in
European history; yet again, with Bruno as its herald,
after the renascence: and in the seventeenth century
the speculative thought of Europe culminated in Spinoza's logically articulated conception of pantheistic
unity and necessity. Pantheism was uncongenial to
the spirit and methods of the eighteenth century: it
is a favourite idea at the root of much present
religious and scientific speculation in Europe and in
America: it was formulated philosophically in the
superconscious intuition of Schelling: it has affinities
with the absolute self-consciousness of the Hegelian:
it appears in the Absolute Will and the Unconscious
Absolute of Schopenhauer and Hartmann, in Germany,
and in England in the Unknowable Power behind
phenomena of Herbert Spencer. Its history is in a
manner the history of philosophy, which might all be
unfolded in its relation to the pantheistic solution of
its supreme and final problem.

The word
Pantheism.
This philosophical form of religious thought is older
and more widely spread than the name now appropriated to it, for the term "pantheism" is of modern
date. The 'Pantheisticon' of John Toland, early in
last century, brought the word in some degree into
vogue in this country, although the pantheistic idea
was an exotic among us in the earlier part of this
century. And those now called pantheists were called
atheists, because they identified the One Absolute Sub-

stance with the infinite material universe, or spoke of it as an incognisable *tertium quid*—superconscious and impersonal—neither matter nor mind. On the other hand, when the finite universe of things and persons was seen strongly in its dependence on Spirit, the resulting form of sentiment, if not of reasoned speculation, seemed to admit of monotheistic interpretation. " Whether God be abstracted from the sensible world," Berkeley remarks in 'Siris,' "and considered as distinct from and presiding over the created system; or whether the whole universe, including mind together with the mundane body, is conceived to be God, and the creatures to be partial manifestations of the divine essence,—there is no atheism in either case, whatever misconception there may be;—so long as Mind or Intellect is understood to preside over, govern, and conduct the whole frame of things." I suppose Berkeley here to imply that this is so, only provided that there is a practical recognition of morally responsible persons as well as physical things in the universe, with acknowledgment of the subordination of the visible world to the active ideals of moral government. With this proviso the speculation referred to is not pantheism, either in its cosmic or its acosmic phase.

" Pantheist," all this implies, is an ambiguous term. Deism. It is apt to be applied to theists who emphasise what distinguishes them from deists. Deism, theism, and pantheism may be distinguished. Under a gross deistical conception, God is imaged—as living in a place apart —determined at a certain date to create the aggregate of things and persons that have since appeared in space —these all after creation being left in a vague way by this external deity to the implanted forces in nature,— God at a distance, either doing nothing, or occasionally interfering with the natural order, by miracle or extraordinary providence,—a wholly transcendent and, in this sense, alien God, in short—an individual being among other individuals, instead of Being absolutely unique.

Pantheism as opposed to Deism.   The pantheistic conception is at the opposite extreme to the deistical: God is, so to speak, coextensive with the now evolving infinite universe of individuals, which being coextensive with God, or Deity modified by rational necessity, could present no other appearances than those in nature: finite things and persons are therein related to God as its waves are related to the ocean whose surface they occasionally disturb— though to satisfy this analogy they must be the waves not of a finite but of infinite ocean. Even as the waves are always water, so the ever changing things and persons of the finite universe are always modifications of the one only reality called God :—

> " In Nature see nor shell nor kernel,
> But the All in All and the Eternal."

These, after all, are only crude pantheistic metaphors, which imperfectly represent the unique conception of

all that exists as of necessity one in power and substance.

Intermediate between the deistical conception of an
idle God, outside nature, and the pantheistic conception of God as the Universe in its substantial and
potential infinity, is the theistic conception of the
universe of experience as a revelation—an incomplete
revelation—of God: God expressed in the contents of
space and time, but not exhausted in the expression;
—and, above all, not so expressed in the contents of
space and time as that whatever enters into temporal
existence is finally necessitated to appear; so that
there is no room or freedom for ideals of duty, or
for the rise into existence of anything that ought
not to appear, and that therefore could not be finally
necessitated to appear. *Theism as inter- mediate.*

The idea of God as the ever-present life of the world,
operating in and through natural laws, is common to
philosophic theism with pantheism, and is part of what
modern theism owes to pantheistic exaggeration. It
distinguishes both from the deism in which God is conceived as a person living at a distance, and leaving the
ordinary evolution of nature and society to the regula-
tion of its own natural sequences, whatever that may
mean. The thought and feeling of divine immanence in all natural appearances; of the finite being
pervaded by and sustained in what is infinite,—comes
out, in ancient and modern poetry and religion, as the
intense expression of a theism so conscious of the *The im- manence of God or Active Reason in external nature.*

uniqueness and pervadingness of the Divine as to refuse to place God apart,—one among many. Hebrew
literature, with its abundant representations of God,
still leads up to the idea of divine presence latent in
the heart of reality.   Instead of an individual and
distant God, apart from the cosmos, but occasionally
operating as a disturbing God, its voice is,—" Whither
shall I go from Thy spirit ? or whither shall I flee
from Thy presence ? If I ascend up into heaven, Thou
art there: if I make my bed in hell, behold, Thou art
there.   If I take the wings of the morning, and dwell
in the uttermost parts of the sea ; even there shall
Thy hand lead me, and Thy right hand shall hold me."
Then there is the expressed sense of finite despair,
apart from the enveloping and pervading infinite : " The
way of man is not in himself: it is not in man that
walketh to direct his steps."   Again of faith : " God is
not far from every one of us: for in Him we live, and
move, and have our being."   So it is too with the poets
and prophets of Christianity, in the early Greek Church,
as in Clement and Origen, and in the medieval—all followed by the more deistical conception of early Protestantism, in the seventeenth and eighteenth centuries,
which tends to divorce the natural or secular procession from God.   Reaction against this finds expression in the familiar words of our own religious
poet, who had learned—

> " To look at Nature, not as in the hour
>   Of thoughtless youth ; "

and was wont to feel—

> " A presence that disturbs me with the joy
> Of elevated thoughts ; a sense sublime
> Of something far more deeply interfused,
> Whose dwelling is the light of setting suns,
> And the round ocean, and the living air,
> And the blue sky—and in the mind of man."

This is still the theistic conception of God in nature ; not the pantheistic conception of man and moral government reduced to natural law, or to abstract dialectical necessity, or made to disappear in the end in abstract undifferentiated Substance.

The dreamy abstract character of pantheism is found in its protean forms of representing the relation of what appears in space and time to the absolute Substance and Power, of which those appearances are assumed to be modifications. Is God eternally under modification and change ; or had the modifications, in the form of finite things and persons and their changes, an apparent beginning, and will they all come to a final end ; so that all things and persons at last disappear in God, with an eternal cessation of change, time and therefore change being truly an illusion of sensuous imagination ? The great medieval pantheist, Scotus Erigena, here speculates boldly, but without verification of the speculation, in his philosophic dream about " Nature,"—the idea of which with him expresses not only, as now commonly, the external world under mechanical law, but the totality of real and even pos-

Pantheistic dreams of Scotus Erigena.

sible existence. Nature, he supposes, must consist of God,—the one Substance and Power out of which all things that appear in space and time must emanate, and into which they must all return, beginning and ending their transitory or unreal history in the un-created and unchanging God, apparently manifested in time. The finite universe in its total evolution is thus, as it were, as a flash of light in the darkness and silence of eternal undifferentiated Being. God is the term in which all things and persons seem to begin, and in which they must at last eternally and unconsciously repose. I find no proof offered of these tremendous assertions. They illustrate the freedom and elasticity of pantheistic imagination, and its indifference to the demands of experience. Imagination first determines what reality must be, and then disdains to be regulated by a human experience which is disparaged as inevi-tably only human imagination. The actual universe of experience is disparaged, as an illusory descent from the universal to the particular, from the abstract to the concrete. In the end, as in the beginning, all resolves into undifferentiated Being, abstract and universal.

Spinoza presents pantheism in abstract demonstra- tiveness.

This much in illustration of some of the phases of Pantheism, as it occupies in its history various points in the interval between Atheistic Nescience and Philo-sophical Theism, or between this last and Supercon-scious Impersonalism. But it is by Spinoza that the idea of pantheistic unity and necessity, as the final conception of existence, is put before us in the most systematic form, and with claims to unbroken demonstrativeness. In Spinoza a purely intellectual philosophy is identified with religion. He is the prince of the systematic divines who bid defiance to the wisdom of Bacon, when he warns us that "perfection or completeness in divinity is not to be sought" by man; that "he that will reduce a knowledge into an art or science must make it round and uniform," whereas in divinity or philosophy "many things must be left abrupt," if we are to remain faithful to the reality. That is to say, philosophical or theological thought must, in a human understanding, become at last aphoristic thought, and can never be an exhaustive system of the universe, as seen at its divine centre in the heart of eternity.

It is for us here an interesting fact that when thought about the universe represents it in the form of a pantheistically necessitated Whole, with finite things and persons, finite spaces and times, as its necessitated modes, it is adopting the conception under which Lord Gifford seems to desire that the problems of Natural Theology should be investigated, as the point of departure at least. And in a way we *are* making it the starting-point in this course. For in the negative course of thought through which I led you in the four preliminary lectures, we found ourselves repelled, first from exclusive and thoroughgoing materialism or atomism, and then from exclusive and thoroughgoing individual egoism, on account of the crudeness and inadequacy of each of these attempts to reach a satis-

The three alternatives of modern religious thought.

factory unity in existence. Each leaves us isolated, without absolute support; for in neither is there the divine synthesis. This support Pantheism offers, emphatically, in its fashion, for it deifies everything. If we fail to find an intellectual home here, we must abandon the hope of satisfying the desire for unity in one exclusively of the three postulated existences, repelled from each in turn, as a philosophy adequate to human experience. Pantheistic Reason, Universal Nescience, and Theistic Faith are the three philosophies now before Europe and America, with some educated and more half-educated thought oscillating between the first and the second. Of these three, which is the most reasonable, because the fittest to provide for man, in the fulness of his physical and spiritual being, a true home in needed moral as well as intellectual satisfaction? The remainder of the present course should prepare the way for an answer to this question.

Spinozism and Lord Gifford.

It is, as I have said, an interesting fact, at least for us, that the pantheistic idea of *consubstantiation* of the outward world and man in the One Infinite Substance or Reality called God should be the central idea of Lord Gifford's Deed of Foundation, and the idea which he seems to desire to get worked out and tested under his bequest, in some of the innumerable fruitful ways which it seemed to him to open up to mankind. This is implied even in his words quoted in my opening lecture. "Natural theology" was described as "knowledge of God, . . . the One and the Sole Substance, the Sole Being, the Sole Reality, and the Sole Existence;" and the true and full knowledge of the relations of man and the outward universe to the Sole or Infinite Reality is presumed to be "the means of man's highest wellbeing, and the security of his upward progress." But this idea is more fully expressed in a lecture by Lord Gifford on "SUBSTANCE," delivered some years before his death, after which it was printed and circulated among his friends. I make no apology for quoting some sentences from this curious tract, to show how near the idea of the consubstantiation of finite things and persons in God lay to his heart; so that Pantheism might well be made the centre of interest in a course of lectures associated with his name.

That God is the one and only Substance, the one hidden reality which exists under the qualities or appearances of all finite things and persons, and to which all their phenomena are to be ascribed—this is the leading idea; and so he tells us that the word SUBSTANCE is "the grandest word in any language." Substance, he explains, is "that which is below and above and around and within" all material things, and all individual minds or egos ; coextensive with them all, and in which they all exist; so that whatever is predicable of them must be predicable of the one divine substance of which they are the parts. Let me take from the tract now before me some sentences

All things and persons consubstantiated in God, the one only Substance, in Lord Gifford's idea.

in which this thought is applied, and in which the reader is invited to contemplate the universe, so to speak, Spinozistically.

His idea of the impotence of finite things.

"To come to the root and bottom of the matter at once, I ask you," Lord Gifford says, "to look at the forces and energies and laws of nature, and the laws of life which have so much to do with the phenomena [of external nature and of man] which we have been examining. . . . What are these *forces* and *energies*, innate in matter forsooth, innate in protoplasm, innate in organisation, and on which so much reliance is placed? Do these forces and energies explain anything? Do they not just put the question further back, or further on? For *the* question is, What is the *substance* of all the forces and energies themselves? *They* are not final and ultimate; they themselves need explanation; there must be something behind and beyond them. They are not self-originated: they are not self-maintained: they are but words, telling us to go deeper and to go higher; they all seem to say to the anxious inquirer, '*Not* in us, *not* in us.' . . . The force behind and in all forces, the energy of all energies, the explanation of all explanations, the cause of all causes and of all effects, *the* soul that is within and below and behind *each* soul, *the* mind that inspires and animates and thinks in *each* mind—in one word, the substance of all substances, the substance of all phenomena, is—God. 'Nature! 'tis but the name of an effect.' The cause is God. *Now* we have reached

a substance that does not in its turn become merely
a phenomenon, a substance which has nothing behind
it, but of which all things [and persons], past, present, or future, are but the *forms.* . . . *Substance* is
the true name of *God.* Every line of thought meets
here. Every eager question is answered here. Every
difficulty and perplexity is resolved here. Here the
philosopher must rest. Here the ignorant must repose.
This universe and all its phenomena—other universes,
unthinkable by human minds—all are but forms of
the Infinite, shadows of the Substance that is One
for ever. . . . There cannot be a finite energy that is
due only to itself alone, and which is independent
of everything else; for there can be but One Infinite.
. . . It is mere repetition to say, That if God be the
very substance and essence of every force, and of every
being, He must be the very Substance and Essence
of the human soul. The human soul is neither self-
derived nor self-subsisting. It is but a manifestation,
a phenomenon. It would vanish if it had not a substance; and its substance is God. . . . Then if God be
the substance of our souls, He must also be the substance of all our thoughts and of all our actions.
Thoughts and actions are not self-sustaining, self-
producing, any more than worlds. They are mere
manifestations, first of our souls, but next, and far
more truly, of God, who is our ultimate Substance. In
Him we live, and move, and have our being. We are
parts of the Infinite—literally, strictly, scientifically so.

A human soul, or a human thought and action, *outside of God*, would be a rival deity.

"In all this," he continues, "I have not gone a single step out of my way as a student of mental *science;* and if I have had to speak to you of God—frankly and freely—that is only because God is necessarily found by all who fairly follow up the *purely scientific* idea of substance to its deepest roots and its highest sources. The highest science always becomes religious —nay, religion itself. . . . Science knows no authority but the intuition of truth." (We see here why Lord Gifford insists, as I showed in my opening lecture, on Natural Theology being a "science," seeing that it is involved in the self-consistent intellectual unity which all science postulates.) Then he thus proceeds: "If God be the substance of all forces and powers, and of all beings, He must be the *only* substance,—the only substance in this universe, or in all possible universes. This," he insists, "is the grand truth on which the system of Spinoza is founded; Spinoza's whole works are simply drawing deductions therefrom. 'I am, and there is none besides Me'—no being, no thing, no existence besides. I am, and nothing else is. If there could be two Substances; if anything else but God existed [any other thing or person], anything outside God, anything of which God was not the substance,—then there would be two gods, and neither of them would be infinite. But I must forbear," he says at last, " I must forbear to trace further the *consequences* of God being *seen* as the one eternal and only Substance. The subject may be expanded into many volumes."

It is this "expansion" into its innumerable consequences of the idea of *God as the one only substance,* with criticism of the same, in the innumerable ways in which it may be handled by different minds, that Lord Gifford seems to have had before him, as an ideal for successive generations of Gifford lecturers, who might work it out according to their respective individualities. The idea itself, in the first place, is a very elastic one, apt to evade the intellectual grasp, and, in the next place, while attributed by him to Spinoza, is, as held in fervid sentiment by Lord Gifford himself, probably more and other than intellectual Spinozism — itself ground on which it is difficult to stand steadily when tested by the facts of moral experience.

Is this abstract idea of the Absolute Substance called God, scientifically or otherwise prolific ?

I will ask you, in next lecture, to look more closely into the grounds and consequences of Spinoza's conception of the universe of things and persons in a necessitated pantheistic unity. This will open the way from Panmaterialism, Panegoism, and Pantheism to the modern point of view of Experience, and what physical and moral human experience presupposes. After we have reached this point, we shall proceed, in the four concluding lectures, to inquire whether theistic faith is not as much at the bottom of our

Prospective.

L

moral experience of the infinite reality as physical faith in the order of nature is at the bottom of our physically scientific experience—all human science of what is experienced being at last faith in what is reasonable. You may call this pantheism if you please, but it is pantheism accommodated to man's moral and religious revelation of the reality in which he lives and moves and has his being.

LECTURE VI.

PANTHEISTIC NECESSITY AND UNITY: SPINOZA.

DAVID HUME has been called the "prince of agnostics." Spinoza, in like manner, is the prince of pantheists. As I said in my opening lecture, the intellectual dimensions of "natural theology, in the widest meaning of the term," are recognised more fully by none than by these two—Spinoza and Hume—at opposite extremes, —extremes which curiously approach one another in the end. Spinoza starts from the divine centre, in abstract thought; Hume from the circumference, in sensuous experience. *Deus,* or the abstract *unica substantia,* is the criterion with the one; *homo mensura* the regulative principle of the other—the *homo* being only the individual *homo* of sensuous impressions and associated ideas. In these two, Spinoza and Hume, the chief matters of discussion in the present course are in a manner personified: Spinoza in those especially treated in this and in the last lecture; Hume, directly

Spinoza and David Hume severally personify Pantheism and Philosophical Nescience.

or indirectly, in the four that are to follow. But while each personifies this subject-matter, I do not intend an exhaustive criticism of either, but ask leave to follow my own course, while not forgetting these two names.

The elasticity and ambiguity of Spinoza's pantheism.   Spinoza is a puzzle to his interpreters. Those who have lived for years mentally in his company, seeking to think the genuine thought of this speculative genius, are obliged to confess doubt about their interpretations, and the adequacy of their insight into the purpose of the singular recluse, who made his appearance in Holland early in the seventeenth century, three months after Locke entered the world. In the age that followed his birth Spinoza was regarded as an atheist and a blasphemer. In the nineteenth century he has received homage as a saint. The amiable Malebranche, Samuel Clarke, the representative English philosophical divine of his generation, the sceptical Bayle, and the cynical Voltaire, all see in Spinoza the enemy of religion. By Lessing and Novalis, Goethe and Schleiermacher, he is canonised for his virtues and piety. Once anathematised by Jews and Christians, this proclaimed atheist is now described as a god-intoxicated mystic. Between these extremes men oscillate in their reading of the life of the poor spectacle-grinder in Holland, as they see in him the logical reasoner who treats Deity as an empty abstraction, formed by definition, or recognise a devotee, ready in the spirit of self-abnegation to lose his individual will and individuality in a divine environment. The elasticity of pantheism of which I have spoken may explain the contradiction; for the pantheistic conception is susceptible of either a materialistic or an idealist explanation: under one light it reads intellectual atheism, under another sentimental theism, yet again superconscious or transcendental impersonalism. An alien in the prevailing spirit of the eighteenth century, probably no other personage living in the preceding century has so powerfully affected theological philosophy in the nineteenth as this solitary reasoner, who devoted the thinking part of his short life of forty-four years to meditation and speculation about God. The purely intellectual love of God, realised in the realisation of his own participation in Infinite Being, was the ideal of Spinoza's life, and the religion in which he sincerely aspired to live. It was a life of more than common simplicity, frugality, and indifference to sensuous pleasure, that this swarthy, slender, consumptive-looking youth passed through in his lonely lodging at the Hague. As Coleridge, I think, suggests, his very innocence and virtue, matured into an invincible habit, in which the man was lost in the abstract reasoner, may have blinded him to the defects of a doctrine which seems to overturn morality in a theory of necessitated existence, which he nevertheless describes as ethical theology.

The resigned consciousness that I and all other persons are living and having our being as mathe- In Spinozism the absolute reality is regarded as at once infinite and finite; substance and modes; undifferentiated and determined in necessary forms.

matically differentiated modifications—transitory, yet which somehow make their appearance—of the infinite attributes of one undifferentiated Substance,—this resigned state of feeling seems to be the essence of Spinoza's religion and morality. He finds himself under an intellectual obligation to acknowledge one and only one substance or reality, indifferently named God, Nature, or the *Unica Substantia*. Its attributes are infinite : the modifications which these attributes may assume are each of them finite. The attributes of the Divine Substance that are known to man are only two—infinite extension and infinite thought: God or Nature is known, in short, only in modes of infinite incorporeal extension, and in modes of infinite thought. To enter within the range of human sense and sensuous imagination, the infinite extension and the infinite thought must be distinguished in finite modes of each attribute. The extension is differentiated, for instance, in the circles, triangles, and other mathematical figures which can be formed with it ; thought in the correlative conscious states in which it becomes concrete.

In Spinozism all individual things are illusions of imagination.

Individual things and individual persons are formed by human imagination out of these several modes: the things and persons have no real or independent existence: their appearance of reality is explained by Spinoza as an illusion of imagination, which arises when they are erroneously conceived in abstraction from the Divine Reality of which they are modes.

Taking the metaphor of the ocean and its waves to represent the *Unica Substantia* and its finite appearances, individual persons and things, composed of modes, have been likened, in this system, to those waves changed into lumps of ice. Imagination deludes us in the supposition that they are more than finite modifications of infinite space or of infinite thought, these two sorts being absolutely correlative. All this making of individuals out of the undifferentiated Unity is truly illusion according to Spinoza, whose supreme principle was—*omnis determinatio est negatio :* the finite can be only a negation of the Infinite, never a positive reality. Nevertheless, he proceeds as if the One Infinite were decomposable by abstraction, capable of being regarded alternately as Infinite and finite, Substance and modes, the Undetermined and the differentiated in mathematically necessary forms.

So it is that the only two attributes of God known to man are represented by imagination in the aggregated modes commonly called individual things and persons, and endowed by imagination with an illusory reality. Both sorts are reasoned about as geometrically necessitated ; for extension and thought, being substantially identical, are necessary correlatives, so that theology may be philosophically unfolded in mathematical terms. They form between them the *natura naturata*, which, by a logical but not real distinction, Spinoza contrasts with the *natura naturans*. These names, substituted for finite universe and God, express the identity of the

The modes of the *unica substantia*, read as geometrical quantities.

One Substance, which, as I have said, may all be
modally interpreted in terms of geometrical quantity,
seeing that extension and thought are in necessary
correlation. The One Substance, in which I find myself
a mode, may be speculated either in its abstract unity
or in its concrete modes,—at once infinite and finite, undifferentiated and yet under mathematically necessary
forms. God without the universe is not self-existent,
with a life of His own: God as the *Unica Substantia*
is an empty substance, without attributes and therefore without meaning: the *natura naturata* is as necessary as the *natura naturans:* it *is* God substantially,
not merely one of the manifestations of God. We are
living and moving and having our being as a necessitated part of the One Immensity, which comprehends
as part of itself all that can possibly exist. The universe of so-called things and persons *must* be modally
what it is. There is no room for the introduction into
existence by finite persons of acts which conform to
ideals of duty and goodness; nor yet for the entrance
into existence of wicked action, or what is evil or
ought not to exist, and therefore is not necessitated to
exist. Reality and perfection are one, under Spinoza's
demonstration of what existence must be : the spiritual
homo mensura is no test of thought about existence.
It is an obvious conclusion of this mathematical pantheism that there can be no real contingency, even at
the human point of view : apparent freedom from the
mathematical necessity is a delusion of imagination,

the issue of inadequate knowledge of the divine immensity: it is derogatory to the perfection of infinite Space. So too is every conjecture about the final reality which supposes *natura naturata* ruled by man's ideas of good and evil, order and disorder, or by those ends which seem desirable under a human imagination of things. Human desires must be regulated by the mathematical necessities of Nature, which is another expression for the necessary nature of God —not by the otherwise irrational interests of men. It is here that this form of pantheism looks like atheism, so that Dugald Stewart applies to Spinoza what Cicero has said of Epicurus: Spinoza has in words left us nothing but God, yet he gives us in fact no God; for a God who is stripped of rule, providence, and purpose must be taken as only another name for blind fate.

Is not this way of looking at the universe, in which all is finally regarded as pantheistically necessary Immensity, profoundly unlike the reality found in our spiritual experience? When we enter into the speculative thought which is unrolled in the abstract demonstrations of Spinoza, we seem to be carried away from the world of facts, which with him is only another name for the world of illusion-breeding imagination. Yet we are emphatically summoned into the presence of the sublime idea of Infinity, which connects itself in some minds with pantheistic unity and necessity,

The ideas of space, time, substance, and causality, as avenues to infinite reality.

while in others it is that which sustains monotheism and religious devotion. The Infinite is not very far from any one of us, for all our mental experience suggests the idea in the forms of Immensity, Eternity, and Causality. Dwell on this for a little. The various phases of the idea of infinity, contrasted with the limits within which we find ourselves involved, are not artificial constructions that have nothing to do with actual everyday life. When we reflect we find intellectual tendencies, of which we cannot rid ourselves, which connect all that is present in sense and in our inner consciousness with infinite reality. Places and dates, persons and things, the changes of which persons and things are the subjects—each and all are found at last to have their roots among ideas which we are obliged to recognise as in our thoughts incomplete, but which necessarily tend towards a mysterious *incompletability*, of which, notwithstanding, we cannot rid ourselves. The place where I am now standing, for instance, is actually contained within the space that has no boundary—the Immensity, whose centre is everywhere, while its circumference is nowhere. Instead of space, contemplate duration: the hour within which I am addressing you is somehow connected with timeless Eternity: change or succession is connected with what seems inconsistent with the possibility of change and succession. Then, again, when we try to get at the Substance of the things or the persons whose phenomena are presented in experience, we find that we are pursuing something that continually evades us, in an endless yet unavoidable regress. What actually appears in sense is always connected with something beyond ; and this something more, when made to appear in sense, again leads on to more still beyond it ; and so on in an always unsatisfied pursuit after finality in the form of the absolute substance. " If any one," says Locke, "if any one should be asked what is the subject or substance in which a colour that he sees inheres, or in which a weight he feels inheres, he would have nothing to say but that they inhere in the solid extended parts or molecules of which the coloured and heavy body consists ; and if he were next asked in what this solidity and extension themselves consisted, he would find himself obliged to go again in quest of something else—like the Indian who, saying that the world was supported by a huge elephant, was asked what the elephant rested on ; to which his answer was, a great tortoise: and being further pressed to tell what supported the tortoise, replied—*something*, he knew not what." And as with substance, so too when we are in pursuit of the Power that originates changes. If it is intellectually impossible to suppose a quality existing without a substance in which it inheres,—an adjective without a substantive,—so too it is intellectually impossible to suppose a change without a cause into which the change may be refunded: but every finite cause in turn demands another cause to explain its own existence, and that other, if finite, equally a cause out of

which it has emerged; and so the causal regress imposed by intelligence is lost in the mystery of endlessness—a chain with an infinite number of links, whatever that means. In this, as in the foregoing instances,
we find ourselves inevitably dissatisfied with what is
finite—with finite figures in space, with finite times
in duration, with finite substances, and with finite
causes. However far we go we are under an intellectual obligation to go further. The universe presented in experience seems to extend itself to infinity;
and when we try to limit it, we have to regard the
limited portion as inconceivably related to what is
beyond.

Is the in-
finite a
quantity?

Do we think truly of the *infinite* reality when we
think of it as a "Whole"? It cannot be supposed
to be a completable quantity, or indeed a quantity at
all, if quantity means absolutely rounded Immensity,
or absolutely rounded Eternity. An indefinitely great
finite object *is* a quantity; for it has its boundary,
although the boundary may be too remote for a merely
human imagination to represent the quantity with distinctness. But is the Infinite Reality, towards which
we are carried by spaces, durations, and changes, capable
of quantitative presentation?

Finite
spaces and
infinite
Space.

Take space to begin with. Imagine any finite quantity
of space you please, however vast—say the area included
within the orbit of the planet on which we are living.
You *can* subtract from this the total space contained
within the orbit of Mercury; you have to that extent
reduced in imagination the finite area which was con-

tained within the Earth's orbit. Or, instead of sub-
tracting, you *can* add to the spacial quantity of the
Earth's orbit, by including all that is within the vaster
expanse contained within the orbit, say, of Mars, or of
Jupiter, or of the whole solar system. In short, you
can either diminish or enlarge the quantity of space
with which you are dealing in this instance, because
you are dealing with a finite quantity. By subtraction,
too, the remaining space is diminished in exact proportion to the quantity withdrawn ; and by the addition
it is increased in exact proportion to the quantity
added. In all this imagination is dealing with finite
spaces, which may be indefinitely great or small, but
which are imaginable in their nature, even if human
imagination can represent only an obscure image of
quantities indefinitely vast or small. In each instance
we are holding up in imagination a finite quantity of
space; or we are trying to picture a finite expanse which,
because it is finite, is capable of being diminished and
capable of being increased in quantity. Not so with
space, when regarded by intellect in its mysterious infinity, independently of sensuous imagination and sense-
perception. For we are intellectually obliged to add to
every imaginable or finite space, however vast : we find
something in our mind which forbids us to suppose
that we can ever arrive at the absolute boundary of
space, with no space at all beyond : something in our
minds obliges us, too, to think of *every* finite or imaginable space, however small, as still divisible into
parts smaller than itself. We are obliged to believe

that the largest conceivable finite space is still incomplete; for there *must* be a larger: we cannot but suppose that the smallest is incompletely divided; for there must be a smaller. The noteworthy fact in this mental experience is, that each addition is believed to bring us *no nearer* to the Infinite Reality than we were before we began to add, and each subtraction to carry us *no farther away* from it. The addition of the quantity of space contained within the orbit of Mars to that contained within the orbit of the Earth *is* a definite addition to the second-named quantity, because both are finite, and consist of finite parts. But no addition of parts to parts brings one nearer to the absolute reality of Immensity; and no subtraction carries us farther away from it. Finite spaces, large or small,—large enough to include the whole known stellar system, or small enough to defy the most powerful microscope,—finite spaces are all at last confusedly spoken of as " parts " of the Infinite that nevertheless cannot consist of parts, and which is therefore not truly a quantity, having transcended that category. There is, as it were, as much more space beyond the largest as there is beyond the smallest quantity. Stretch imagination to the utmost,—suppose, if you please, an imagination inconceivably more powerful than the human,—infinite space is as much out of its reach, and as far short of exhaustion by its processes, as it was at first—the additions being all, as it were, irrelevant to *it*. In the light of reason, the spaces of sense and imagination, large or small, disappear in the Infinite Reality.

Space thus becomes one of our human avenues towards the Infinite. Turn next to time and duration. This is another avenue which, perhaps even more than space, brings infinity home to us all. However far back in time we make imagination travel, we are obliged to suppose a time still more remote; however far forward we look, we are obliged to suppose a yet remoter future. We can set no boundary, either in the past or in the future, to the succession of changes by which the idea of duration is evoked in human consciousness: when we imagine any finite period, long or short, our minds oblige us still to imagine a duration, longer or shorter, by the addition or subtraction of which the first is increased or diminished. But just as space at last passes into Immensity, so time at last passes into Eternity. Unbeginning time does not admit of addition, nor does unending time admit of subtraction. The Eternity in which each is lost does not admit of parts, although sensuous imagination has to picture it as divisible. We are as far from exhausting eternity *ante* when we have travelled back millions of years as we were when we commenced our journey into past time; and no passage of time now elapsed diminishes the eternity that seems to be in front of us. "How anything can have existed eternally," as says Samuel Clarke, "that is, how an eternal duration can be now actually past, is

[margin note: Finite times and Eternity.]

a thing as impossible for our narrow understandings to comprehend as anything that is not an express contradiction can be imagined to be. And yet to deny the truth of the proposition that an eternal duration *is* now actually past, would be to assert something far more unintelligible, even an express and real contradiction." Endless movement, which is our concrete idea of time, thus always loses itself in the mysterious rest of the eternal. The unbeginning past seems to misleading imagination as if it were a definite quantity, subtracted from the unending future, it too being supposed a definite quantity; but thought is lost in an Eternity greater than either the unbeginning past or the unending future, and yet somehow continuing each of the two as its parts. Unbeginning and unending existence implies not merely that there may, but that there must, be continuous addition to every finite duration, however lengthened, and yet that each successive addition brings us no nearer to the infinite in the form of Eternity than an hour or a moment does. Add to a finite time and we are brought nearer to a longer finite, however long that finite; but we are brought no nearer to Eternity than we were, and are left always at the end to express the unavoidable dissatisfaction of intelligence with every duration that is limited or determined. Positive or imaginable time, necessarily supposed to be incapable of being completed, makes imagination commit suicide when it tries to imagine its infinity, by obliging it to enter a region in which picturable quantity can no longer survive; but in which

"immutably survive,
For our support, the measures and the forms
Which an abstract intelligence supplies,
Whose kingdom is *where time and space are not.*"

The space by which we are now surrounded in this room, and the time that is included within the hour during which we are here together, both seem to stretch, the one into unexpanded Immensity and the other into timeless Eternity—each in this way an avenue to the infinite Reality. The finite in each of these forms irresistibly transcends itself, and seems to become undifferentiated Reality in doing so.

Space and time carry us into the Infinite.

How to connect finite places with the Immensity in which place seems lost, or finite times with the Eternity in which duration seems to disappear,—the placed with the placeless, the timed or dated with the timeless,—is the mystery of an experience of the infinite reality which, like ours, is conditioned by place and time, in a way that must always keep it under a sense of incompleteness and dissatisfaction. The pantheistic conception of Spinoza looks like a vain attempt to think the final reality, called Nature or God, at a point of view where past and future disappear—all undetermined by time and place,—*sub specie æternitatis,* —seen intellectually at the eternal unquantified centre —not in real succession, but somehow under geometrical relations of necessity. It treats the one only

Temporal succession or change an illusion, and reality intelligible only *sub specie æternita tis,* according to Spinoza.

M

Reality as a boundless geometrical unity, to express which in finite modes mathematical figures, with their changeless, because intellectually necessary, relations, are substituted for an actual succession which he relegates to the finite imagination. The *Unica Substantia* in its two infinite attributes is unchangeable, undifferentiated by the misleading accident of succession. Pure Intellect knows nothing either of temporal change or of antecedent purpose. Effects and ends are as alien to this philosophical conception of what really exists as they are to the abstract conceptions of pure geometry. They belong to the illusory sphere of sensuous imagination, which is, with Spinoza, another name for ordinary experience. The universe being the absolute necessity of reason, could not be other than what it is; and it is misleading finite fancy that makes it either a theatre of change, or an aggregate of contrivances in which means are chosen to reach ends that might be attained by other means, or ends other than those with which the so-called means are truly in necessary mathematical relation. Spinoza's universe, seen *sub specie æternitatis*, or in the light of his philosophy, is as empty of cause and purpose as the multiplication-table, or the demonstrations of Euclid. The illusion of temporal and dynamical succession is exchanged for the timeless statical certainty of geometrical relations.

With Spinoza nothing really hap- He who thinks the reality in which he lives and moves and has his being in sympathy with Spinoza, must therefore think it, not as an imaginable succession, but in the unimaginable eternity. For our imagination of succession is to the reality like trees and houses seen from the windows of a carriage in motion. *They* seem to be moving, but the motion is in ourselves; for they are really at rest, under their necessary relations of place, not under changing relations of time. The supposition that change is real is, under this pantheistic conception, the great delusion of the unreasoning. Nothing happens: all exists simultaneously. The past is not really past: the future is not still unactual. Even our thought is not successive: the succession is only what seems, when imagination invades the province of knowledge. The All is the eternal Now. Under the geometrically necessitated conception, history and experience are dissolved in illusion: what has not yet happened is as real as what has already happened; what is future and what is past is identified in the form of what must be. Nothing really happens: all must eternally be. *[pens: all exists simultaneously, under mathematically necessary relations.]*

It is instructive to follow Spinoza as he sublimates finite things and persons, individualised by the deceptive imagination, out of which the illusory world of common consciousness or experience is supposed to emerge, but which reason refunds into the true being of the One Divine Substance in which all things exist in absolute perfection. Substance, so far as matter is substantial or infinite, cannot, he argues, be added to or divided. If asked why we are apt to suppose *[Two ways of conceiving quantity.]*

the contrary, he would say that quantity may be conceived in two ways—either in imagination or in pure intellect. If therefore—so the argument would proceed — we regard quantity, as we often and easily do, as it appears to imagination, we find it divisible, that is to say, made up of parts; but if we regard it intellectually, and think of it as in the One Substance, " *which is difficult for us to do,*" then it can be demonstrated that it must be infinite and indivisible, or not composed of parts. Thus we can imagine water divisible, so far as it is a finite individual thing, separated from the infinite reality by our distorting imagination, and then it is found to be composed of separable parts: but when it is refunded into the divine substance, it cannot be thought of; for as such it is not divisible or determinate, but indeterminate or indifferentiate.

The supposed logical impossibility of contingency in Nature: whatever is must be.

Again, the All must be eternally necessary; for otherwise we are involved in the contradiction that Nature (*natura naturans*) might be different from what really is. What we call contingency and change is the issue of our imperfectly rational apprehension of the infinite reality, in the many delusive forms of sense and imagination. What exists cannot be contingent in reality: it seems contingent only because it is viewed in the imperfect light of deficient knowledge. Things are absolutely perfect in the reality, for whatever is is divine. But even the opinion which refers all to capricious will is nearer the truth, according to this pantheistic conception, than the supposition that things are what they are, for the sake of some supposed good thereby secured to man, and of which man is the final cause. For this is to suppose an end in existence that is independent of God, an end outside the infinite Reality, and to which the *Unica Substantia* is subordinate.

The alleged prejudice that purpose or final cause, and a humanly related purpose too, is the connecting principle of existence, is what Spinoza throughout his demonstrations labours to remove. Man, with his disposition to think things in a temporal succession—not *sub specie æternitatis*—takes his own finite and imaginable experience as the measure of reality, and looks at things as events, or historically; not *sub ratione*, or intellectually. Magnifying the importance of his own desires and appetites, he supposes that the final cause of what is must be human happiness, as seen in the ends and motives by which he himself, as a part of nature, is usually determined to act. As pleasure is the motive of his own actions, he comes to interpret Nature or God as a system of means constructed for securing this for man; which involves the further supposition of an anthropomorphic Ruler of Nature, endowed with a capricious freedom, able to act in this way or in that; who, moreover, does nothing in vain, which only means nothing that is inconsistent with man's happiness. And whenever experience of the reality contradicts this human fancy, in the actual experience of pain to which man is often

Pantheistic explanation of the supposed prejudice, that the universe is charged with final causes, which centre in human interests.

subject, then, rather than surrender the vain imagination of a reality that can be measured by human pleasures, its anthropomorphic advocates suggest man's ignorance, and conclude that the rule of the gods somehow surpasses our narrow comprehension. This favourite refuge of narrow minds, Spinoza thinks, would have kept the human race in darkness to all eternity, if mathematics, which excludes regard to causes final or efficient, had not placed before us a higher criterion of truth, and made men acknowledge the necessary nature of things. For the mathematical conception of the universe shows—so he argues—that God or Nature can have no human end in view, and that to suppose the universe to be charged with purpose is a fiction of imagination, not a scientific conception. It is because in the eye of imagination the worth of things is determined by their human relations or utilities, that the irrational prejudices arise which are expressed by the words good and evil, merit and sin, praise and blame, order and disorder. For "good" is the term popularly applied to whatever promotes the interests of man, or ritual of worship as the imagined interest of God. Ignorant of things in their substance, men imagine an order of their own to be in the things: when objects are so placed that they can be *easily* imagined by themselves, they call them well arranged, and when placed otherwise, they call them confused; as if this order were something in the things themselves, and not in their own imagination. They say that God must have created the universe in an order which they find easy to apprehend, weakly attributing their own imagination to God; perhaps, Spinoza sarcastically adds, on their own principle of final causes, meaning that God, out of consideration for human imagination, has disposed all things in the way in which they are most easily imaginable by man.

Spinoza sees human life crowded with examples of this substitution of finite imagination for the infinite reality of pure reason, with endless controversies and hopeless scepticism as the consequence. Men imagine things without truly understanding them. If they truly understood things, they could not but be all alike convinced scientifically, though not all necessarily pleased. The vulgar methods of interpreting the Infinite Reality are only different exercises of sensuous experience and play of imagination, which reveal nothing that is eternally or absolutely true. The perfection of things is to be judged by what they must be, not by the ways in which they delight or offend men.

A dilemma confronts this logical elaboration of pantheistic necessity. Either we reduce the universe of individual things and persons to shadows of reality, and then the undetermined substance or Deity of Spinoza comes in as an abstract featureless unity; or we must assume that the presented data of our temporal experience are real, so far as they go, and that

Marginal notes:

Consequences of what exists being imagined instead of being reasoned.

A dilemma.

God is signified, not modified, in the finite universe. For determining between these alternative theories we must have recourse to facts: if facts oblige us to admit that that with which experience brings us into contact and collision is not shadows and dreams, but individual realities, and a real succession of events, we must accept the alternative which it imposes on us. It is by means of *monads*, says Leibniz, that Spinoza is refuted: Spinoza would be right if there were no *monads:* in that case all that is not God would be evanescent accident of fancy.

Our moral experience and the pantheistic necessity.

But it is in the moral experience of remorse and responsibility that an insurmountable obstruction to pantheistic necessity seems to present itself. A logical pantheism is inconsistent with ideals of unattained good, and with the entrance of real evil into existence. Deified reality must be perfect: reality and perfection must be taken as synonymous. Nero and Borgia, Socrates and Jesus, are all alike and equally divine. But if we find that actually existing which *ought not* to exist, and which has come into existence by no absolute necessity, we find what involves a disruption of Spinoza's divine unity and necessity. Now this disruption is the implicate of remorse, which is as much a necessity of moral reason as physical causality is of scientific reason ; and neither can be proved to be inconsistent with the other. In the universe there exists that of which God cannot be the substance, unless either God is evil, or evil only one of the illusions of human imagination. Individual persons cannot be real substantially, we are told, because this is inconsistent with the pantheistic definitions of substance and reality. They must be only modifications of One Substance. Be it so ; for this may be made only a dispute about words. Life implies that in point of fact they are as if they were distinct substances, for we so treat them in our moral judgments and in our actions : men govern men by rewards and punishments, and whatever the speculative idea presented in our definitions may be, duty determines the good man's conduct in a way that makes *him* responsible for it. Viewed in the dry light of a pure reason that consists in our arbitrary definitions of words, it may be concluded, as has been said, that " Regulus and his tormentors, the spikes which tore him, the body which they lacerated, the mind which felt the agony and would not yield, nay, Rome and Carthage themselves, with all their angry feuds and contrary interests, are all essentially One and the Same Substance." But if this is consistent with moral experience, it must also be true that " modifications " of one and the same Substance *can* bear to each other the *moral* relations commonly expressed by *governors* and *governed*, and that the modifications can differ from one another in various degrees of wisdom, power, and goodness.

While Spinoza insists upon the identity of theological with mathematical certainty, he seems to identify it in much of his reasoning with the merely verbal certainty

Spinozistic theology only verbal consistency with definitions.

that is founded on arbitrary definitions of words. He
banishes efficient and final causes, change, and temporal
succession, as artifices of fancy. He puts only names
and their definitions in their place, and the names so
defined are used in verbal demonstrations in which
the conclusion only makes explicit what was already
arbitrarily introduced by him into the definitions. So
far as it is worked out in consistency with the definitions, the pantheistic system is a logical evolution of
what is contained in the connotation of certain words
of extreme abstraction. But the result only asserts
necessary connection between the dogmatically assumed definitions and the conclusions. "It is possible," as Dugald Stewart remarks, " by devising a
set of arbitrary definitions, to form a science which,
although professedly conversant about moral, political,
physical, or any other ideas, should yet be as certain
as geometry. It is of no moment whether the ideas
correspond with facts or not, provided they do not express absolute impossibilities, and be not inconsistent
with each other. From the definitions a series of consequences may be deduced by the most unexceptionable
reasoning, and the results will be perfectly analogous
to mathematical propositions : but the terms true and
false cannot be properly applied to them." The upshot
is, that they are logically connected with the nominal
definitions which are the only principles of this verbal
science. The terms true and false can refer merely
to formal connection with the verbal premisses, not to

correspondence with things existing, or with events which we expect to be realised. Spinoza's theological philosophy is, I think, an apt illustration of this.

That the pantheistic conception ultimately refunds all that exists into an undifferentiated unity emptied of events, is an unsurmountable difficulty in thorough-going impersonalism or pantheism. It vainly asks us to conquer the region towards which we are carried —as we found in the former part of this lecture— when we try to surrender place for Immensity, time for Eternity, manifested substances for the absolute Substance, causal succession for the final mystery of Causality. It demands an impersonal faculty in which the individual person must be identified with and lost in the impersonal unity; and to meet this, pantheistic thinkers have been reduced to hard straits. The impossibility of thinking what is undifferentiate is met by some in a supposed intellectual intuition, which can hardly be distinguished from blind mystical sentiment; by others in that avowedly sentimental phase of pantheism, poetical more than theoretical, which is suited to the less robust intelligence, or to the dreamy fancies of the less active races of mankind.

Plotinus, in the ancient world, and Schelling in this century, may be taken, each in his own way, as advocates of a sort of intuition, which seems at last to resolve into mere feeling, sublimated into supercon-scious entrance into the spaceless and timeless — the

[margin note:] Undifferentiated impersonal unity unattainable, under the conditions of a self-conscious experience.

Nirvana of the Buddhist, who is weary of a conscious experience of the temporal succession.

Theecstasy of Ploti- nus.

We find Plotinus asserting a claim to this sort of ecstatic vision of the Eternal, into which, however, he is reported to have said that he had risen only four times in his life—a vision or feeling in which he would have realised Spinoza's indifferentiate Substance; and it is told of him that in his pantheistic enthusiasm he disclaimed his own birth or introduction into time, looking with contempt on the contents of space, and ashamed of the appearance of connection with temporal succession. The "ecstasy" is surely an empty name for an illusory superconscious state from which all that human intelligence can recognise is withdrawn.

The ec- static in- tuition of Schelling.

Schelling's vaunted intuition of the Absolute is beset by a like difficulty. "To reach the point of indifference," it has been said, "Schelling by abstraction annihilates first the object and then the subject of consciousness. But what, then, remains? *Nothing.* We then hypostatise the zero; we baptise it with the name of Absolute; and conceit ourselves that we contemplate absolute existence, when we only speculate absolute privation." Without contradictory assumptions it seems impossible, under the conditions of human thought, to connect infinite with finite intelligence; temporal succession with the eternal Now. It is impossible to ascend intelligibly from finite experience into the Infinite, which refuses to enter as a completed object into experience, and to be presented under any form of experience; or to return, if we could start from the Infinite, into the relations which constitute the finite. It is impossible, in short, for man to see All from the divine centre.

It seems as if Locke had in view this supreme pan- *Locke re-* theistic difficulty, and Spinoza in particular as its *calls men to the facts* representative, when he insists that the chief cause of *of mind.* error in philosophy and theology is that men begin at the wrong end in their inquiries, and in vain seek for satisfaction in the possession of the truths that most concern them, whilst they let loose their thoughts into the vast ocean of Being, as if all that boundless extent were the undoubted possession of human understanding. We must employ instead the less pretentious but surer method, and inquire what the real universe that is in a small measure revealed in our experience of the temporal succession therein shows itself to be, physically and morally. In next lecture, accordingly, we shall exchange the abstract necessity and undifferentiated unity of pantheism for the tentative experience that seems more suited to man, in his place in the hierarchy of existence, intermediate between the merely sensuous animal and Divine Omniscience. For the alternative seems to be — *Homo mensura*, in some interpretation of this formula, or *Nulla mensura*.

LECTURE VII.

UNIVERSAL NESCIENCE: DAVID HUME.

Summary. IN preceding lectures we have passed through various phases of thought regarding the ultimate problem of existence. The first phase was an inquisitive one. What sort of universe is this in which I find myself living and moving and having my being? In what sort of reality do I find myself sharing; and what is likely to be the issue of the venture, which, without leave asked or given, I find myself obliged to make in being obliged to live? The next phase was dogmatic. I found myself taking for granted, in accordance with prevalent belief or opinion, that consciousness means myself; and myself, too, percipient of innumerable things outside of my inward life; and absolutely certain, moreover, that this inward self-conscious and percipient life is dependent upon Something Eternal, more definitely the Eternal Mind called God. Our third phase was scientific, in the narrow physical

meaning of the word science : science, so understood,
seemed to lead to the conclusion that you and I are
ephemeral material organisms, composed of molecules
in motion, and that we are living and moving and
having our being among other molecular organisms,
each somehow endowed with conscious life while it
lasts, but its short self-conscious life only a passing
event in the universal molecular history which makes
up all that exists. The fourth phase of thought through
which we passed was more reflective. In it we saw that
the universe, resolved at last into molecular motions,
was after all not so satisfying to reason as it seemed
at first; and that instead of the percipient ego and its
perception of outward things absolutely depending
upon outward things in their atomic constitution, the
molecularly constituted things were themselves unintelligible without active and percipient consciousness
in me. Accordingly, instead of supposing with the
materialist that I am living and moving and having
my being as only an insignificant organism among
other organisms, in a purely outward universe, it seems
true, in a deeper sense, that all visible things, including my own organism, exist in my mental experience ;
or at any rate that they depend for their existence
and activity on some percipient mind that is having
actual sensuous experience. I found that Panegoism
had at least as much to say for its proposition, that
the outward world is all really living in me, as Panmaterialism had for *its* assumption—that my percipient

life is only an accident which has occurred in the endless history of a dark unconscious universe of molecules
and aggregates of molecules in motion or in growth.
Still deeper reflection, however, showed the insufficiency both of this empirical materialism and this empirical egoism, by reducing each, when taken apart, to
an absurdity. This deeper reflection seemed to lead us
nearer to a true philosophy, which should contain the
answer to our original inquiry about the final meaning and destiny of existence. Neither the molecules
moving in space and time, nor the perceptions of
them and of myself of which I was conscious, could, I
now thought, be the last word about the absolute
reality. They, and I, and all other percipient beings
like me, were ephemeral, as far as I had experience of
them ; and as nothing ephemeral could, it was assumed,
be the absolute reality, one was led to think of molecular things, and self-conscious persons, with Spinoza, as
interdependent modifications, co-existing consubstanti-
ally, *either* under mathematically necessary relations of
infinitely extended thought, or else as the unique
absolute reality—the *unica substantia* or perfect Divine
Being, in which they really exist, as seen at the eternal
centre, in an indeterminate or undifferentiated unity.
Or else escaping from the rigid geometrical conceptions
of Spinoza, one might think of them as transitory phenomena, under relations of time rather than of space,
evolved by an utterly inscrutable Power, eternally
manifesting itself in phenomena ; yet a Power which,

notwithstanding, is eternally hid from us behind those appearances, and in which the appearances—often consisting of suffering conscious and percipient lives—are all finally absorbed.

But the pantheistic unity and necessity seemed to be broken up by inevitable pre-suppositions of human action, necessary implicates of all moral experience, which make us refuse to call evil good, or to see deity in disorder, virtue in crime, and truth in error. I even say to see truth in error; for if human experiences, under the disparaging name of "imaginations," are themselves modes of the perfect being, how can *they* be condemned as illusions, or how can there be any error if all is divine? *The pantheistic necessity and unity contradicted by moral experience.*

Universal Nescience seems to be the *reductio ad absurdum* of each of the three philosophical attempts to reduce to unity that triplicity of existence which is dimly presupposed in the common faith. Pan-materialism, Panegoism, Pantheism, each so far true in what it affirms, are all challenged as inadequate and inconsistent expressions of human experience, or on the ground that they reach verbal consistency through inadequacy. In the ages materialistic and egoistic atheism and empiricism, and pantheistic rational necessity, in some form of each, hold their ground, for each expresses in part what is real; and each I daresay has in its own way contributed to a deeper and truer intelligence of the universal problem. It is probable that for some minds each may continue to be found satisfying in *Absolute Nescience, or the reductio ad absurdum alike of pure Materialism, pure Egoism, and pure Pantheism; each of which, nevertheless, serves a purpose.*

N

the future as in the past.   But each leads logically
into universal scepticism.

Universal Nescience—doubt about everything, the
mental paralysis involved in a universal scepticism—
is accordingly the next condition of mind I would ask
you to enter into provisionally.   Is it our only remaining alternative?   Must we in the end subside
into the impotence of a speechless suicidal scepticism,
or is there another position which man is able to
occupy?

Is the
problem
of the uni-
verse and of
human life
in the end
in every
way in-
soluble?
A sixth and negative phase of thought meantime
succeeds to the five already passed through: it is one
in which faith is professedly eliminated.   The inquisitive mood in which we placed ourselves at the outset,
it would now seem, was vain.   A point of interrogation
becomes the symbol of human life, in relation to itself
and to the outside universe and to God.   I cannot
really tell what sort of universe this may be into which
I have been ushered.   My existence may or may not
be dependent on the eternal existence of the Being
who was believed to bring me and all else, except
this Being, into appearance.   The sum of passing
appearances may or may not be explicable, as the
issue of innumerable molecules in motion: the same
may or may not be at last sufficiently described in
terms of my inward life; or each of them metaphorically as outward and inward sides of the same Something.   The reality is Something hid behind both the
molecular and the conscious appearances—concealed,

not revealed by them — for this is indeed what the pantheistic phase of thought and faith in the end amounts to : the geometrically necessary ultimate unity of Spinozism, and the evolutionary physical unity of less rigid forms of pantheism, disappear alike in undifferentiated unity. I find no ultimate issue other than nescience of abstract pantheistic reasoning, or of the pantheistic feeling of mystery ;—neither speculative nor emotional pantheism is an adequate or self-consistent interpretation of life and moral experience, so it leaves me finally in doubt. Whether there is or is not at the centre of existence supreme living mind of God now appears as a speculation less capable of being brought to an issue than the question about a plurality of inhabited worlds. Like this famous question, it must remain an abstract question about a concrete matter of fact that lies wholly out of the range of sensuons experience ; and as all inquiries about matters of fact must be determined by experience and not by abstract thought, both questions are for ever indeterminable. Whether a living Person is the supreme Power seems even *more* indeterminable than the question about the existence of persons analogous to human beings in the other planets : for an improved experimental apparatus may some day conceivably bring one or more of the planets so within human experience that men can determine whether or not it is the scene of an intelligent population ; but wider experience can never relieve the incomprehensibility of the infinite existence within which men awaken into consciousness, if it is an incomprehensibility that is imposed by the very constitution of a human knowledge of the concrete universe. The supposition that man can so get outside of the universe and of his own private consciousness as to have the infinite reality within his intellectual grasp; and then find, by this ecstatic experience, what its universal principle is, and whether it is a trustworthy principle, and ours, by participation in it, a trustworthy intelligence, — *this* can never come within the range of human, or indeed of finite, power. Paralysed thought withdraws the final problem, as one which must have made its appearance only through an obstinate unreflecting delusion. At the best this discovery can only warn us emphatically to address ourselves to practical and provisional interpretations of the small fragment of world-appearances and their uncertain relations which human experience in the five senses presents, leaving the substance of the infinite reality in a darkness which these transitory appearances do nothing to remove.

Agnosticism: demands logical proof instead of ultimate moral faith.

To think of life and the universe thus is, according to the favourite conventional expression, to look at existence agnostically, or to be an agnostic. This, we all know, is the name suggested by Professor Huxley to express his own mental attitude to the problem of " natural theology, in the widest meaning of the term "; and it has passed current because it expresses a vision or conception of the universe that has returned into fashion in this latter half of the nineteenth century. "When I reached intellectual maturity," Mr Huxley tells us, "I began to ask myself whether I was an atheist, a theist, or a pantheist." This, I suppose, was to ask whether his own last word about life and experience was that of the atheistic materialist and atheistic individual egoist; or that of the theist, by whom the three existences are finally postulated; or that of the pantheist, who sees in the finite universe an illusory succession of changes in a really unchangeable metaphysical unity. "I found," he goes on to say, "when I put this question to myself, that the more I reflected, the less ready was the answer. At last I came to the conclusion that I had neither lot nor part with any of these denominations, *except the last*. The one thing in which most of these good people were agreed was the one thing in which I differed from them. They were quite sure that they *had* attained a certain Gnosis—had, more or less successfully, *solved* the problem of existence: while I was quite sure I had not; and had a pretty strong conviction that the problem was insoluble. And with Hume and Kant on my side, I could not think myself presumptuous in holding fast by that opinion. So I took thought, and invented what I conceived to be the appropriate title of *agnostic*. It came into my head as suggestively antithetic to the *gnostic* of Church history, who professed to know so much about the very things of which I was ignorant." "Agnosticism" is otherwise described by the inventor of the name as a method of intellectual procedure, rather than as a state of doubt about the final meaning and purpose of life and the infinite reality. It is a method, we are told, "the essence of which lies in the application of a single principle, which is the fundamental axiom of modern science. Positively this principle may be thus expressed: — In matters of the intellect, follow your reason as far as it will take you, without regard to any other consideration. And negatively :—In matters of the intellect, do not pretend that conclusions are certain which are not demonstrated or demonstrable." Agnosticism, according to this account of it, is a term invented to express dutiful submission of human belief to the limits imposed by logical understanding and experience,—rejection of all assertions and denials that are inconsistent with this purely intellectual integrity.

Agnosticism made a question-begging term.

It is difficult to see how this intellectual integrity can be the distinctive mark of agnostic scepticism without question-begging. In the present case the very point in dispute is, whether any positive assertion about the final meaning and purpose of life and experience *is* reasonable. That many unreasonable assumptions and conclusions, positive and negative, about the sort of universe we are born into, its principle or want of principle, its purpose or want of purpose, have more or less prevailed, is a superfluous truth. But it still remains for criticism and proof that all positive assertions of this sort must be unreasonable assertions. To assume this at the outset, in a question-begging definition, is almost to illustrate agnosticism in the act of defining it: it is to determine a matter of fact not by proof, but by an arbitrary definition of the word agnostic.

It is of course true that the theological conception of existence has given birth to abundance of fallacious reasoning. The theistic interpretation of things has been often the issue either of abstract metaphysical arguments, in which a disputed matter of fact is settled by manipulation of abstract propositions; or it has been the outcome of irrelevant facts, in the form of insufficiently tested human authority — the authority of mankind in general, or of men reputedly good and wise; or it has been credited to the account of those facts in history, which suggest that religious faith has been a means of increasing individual happiness and the prosperity of communities. Nay, without even the semblance of an appeal to reason, it has been sustained by superstitious reverence for the words of a book accepted as infallible, or for the dogmas of a society which claims infallibility. In all this the final appeal to reason and experience is either evaded, or rested on a narrow foundation. Abstract propositions can never show us what exists in fact; at the most they can show only what must be fact, in case conditions of which only experience can inform us are actually fulfilled. So it is argued that

Theological fallacies.

as to authority, it is worthless when it relates to what
can never come within the range of human experience.   No man can ever actually see the Eternal
Spirit, or hear him speak; or see those who saw him,
or who heard his voice.   Tradition reports the occasional occurrence of physical miracles; and animal
organisms which seem to involve adaptation of means
to ends are familiar to us all.   But man cannot know
enough about the ultimate constitution of the universe
to justify him in concluding that the reported signs
and wonders, even if they really did come within the
experience of a human being, must be understood to
mean the active interference for a purpose of the
supposed Eternal Mind; and as for Paley and the
curiously constructed organisms, we now know enough
about the natural history of cosmical changes to justify
the conclusion that their curious construction may be
the gradual issue of ordinary natural growth; so that
divine creative irregularity would be superfluous.   It
is unnecessary, the sceptic says, to *prove* the absence
of supernatural interference; the proof of a negative
is always difficult: it is enough that there is no proof
of more than natural sequence, and that the admission
of more without reason is contrary to reason.   Assumption is not argument.   Least of all can the burden
of human life be rested on the dogma that what
seems to be useful for man must therefore be true;
or that a belief ought to be accepted merely because
it relieves desires and aspirations of the believer; or

because its reception seems to make its recipients happier. To make the wishes of men a test of the reality of the thing wished for, is to reverse the method of science, and to substitute indulgence in agreeable anticipation for intellectual insight. An Infinite Being that, by the very nature of human experience, can never present itself in that experience, even if it exists, must be to man as though it were not; and when men suppose that they are having experience of Infinite Being, they are really mistaking unhealthy states of consciousness for something above them which they choose to call divine. Knowledge of unexplained human feelings is not properly named when it is called knowledge of God.

This Agnosticism, thus confident that man must for ever find in the ultimate problem of life and experience his one insoluble mystery, is in curious contrast with the absolute certainty that was claimed for theistic faith by the illustrious spokesmen of philosophy in the first period of the modern philosophical revival. I hope that to refer to them is not an unreasonable recognition of authority. "Depth in philosophy," Bacon says, "bringeth men's minds alone to religion; for while the mind of man looketh upon second causes scattered, it may sometimes rest in them, and go no further; but when it beholdeth the chain of them confederate, and linked together, it must needs fly to Providence and Deity: nay, even that school which is most accused of atheism doth most demonstrate religion; that is the

The assumption that man must for ever remain ignorant of all beyond phenomena of sense reverses the teaching of Bacon, Descartes, and Locke.

school of Leucippus, and Democritus, and Epicurus—for it is a thousand times more credible that four mutable elements and one immutable fifth essence, duly and eternally placed, need no God, than that an army of infinite small portions, or seeds unplaced, should have produced this order and beauty, without a divine marshal." Then hear Descartes : "With respect to God, if I were not preoccupied by prejudices, and my thought beset on all sides by the continual presence of the images of sensible objects, I should know nothing sooner nor more easily than the fact of God's existence. For is there any truth more clear than the existence of a Supreme Being, or of a God, seeing it is to His Essence alone that existence necessarily and eternally pertains ? But although the right conception of this truth has cost me much close thinking, nevertheless now I feel not only as assured of it as of what I deem most certain, but I find further that the certitude of all other truths is so absolutely dependent on this one, that without the knowledge of God it would be impossible ever to know anything else. . . . For if I do not first know that there is a God, I may suppose that I have been so constituted by mere nature as to be deceived, even in matters which I apprehend with the greatest seeming evidence and certitude ; especially when I recollect that I have frequently judged things to be true and certain which other reasons afterwards constrained me to reckon as wholly false. . . . I now clearly see that the certitude and truth of all science depends on knowledge of God and on that alone; so that as before I knew God I could have no perfect knowledge of any other thing. But now that I know God, I possess the means of acquiring knowledge of innumerable matters, as well relative to God as to corporeal nature." Next take Locke: "We cannot want a clear proof of God as long as we carry *ourselves* about us; since He has plentifully provided us with the means to discover and know Him, so far as is necessary to the end of our being, and the great concernment of our happiness. . . . It is plain to me we have a more certain knowledge of the existence of a God than of anything our senses have not immediately discovered to us. Nay, I presume I may say that we more certainly know there is a God than that there is anything else without us. But though this be the most obvious truth that reason discovers, and though its evidence be (if I mistake not) equal to mathematical certainty, yet it requires thought and attention; or else we shall be as uncertain and ignorant of this as of other propositions which are in themselves capable of clear demonstration." So far Bacon, Descartes, and Locke, three early leaders of modern thought. How comes it that what they, in the seventeenth century, regarded as self-evident reality, or at least demonstrated certainty not less cogent than mathematical, should in the nineteenth century be judged by speculative physicists to be wholly and for ever incognisable by men?

It boldly claims for its parents, Hume and Kant; and the theory of knowledge which was proposed by Locke.

The history of European thought in the interval goes far to explain the revolution through which what was accepted as the supreme certainty by the intellectual leaders of the seventeenth century has become the supreme uncertainty of the physical theorists who aspire to lead philosophic thought in the nineteenth. Professor Huxley thinks that with " Hume and Kant," the great authorities of the eighteenth century, presenting themselves as advocates of the insolubility of the final problem of the universe, it cannot be " presumptuous " to hold fast by this opinion. Agnosticism is for him new only in name. He thinks it is a new name for the philosophy of Hume and Kant: their philosophy has now determined the limits within which a positive human knowledge of the universe must be confined. And their message is reported to be, that men can know reality only so far as they have sensuous experience of it: without this experience knowledge is only a sham—an empty abstraction. Except so far as the three commonly postulated existences—outward things, myself, and God — are actually presented in experience, no positive conclusions regarding any of them can be drawn: our assertions about them must all be negative.

The Kantian Philosophy as a whole not agnostic, seeing that Kant offers moral rea-

Kant is associated by Professor Huxley with Hume as one of the two leaders of agnosticism. This is on account of Kant's theory of causality, and his application of it to natural theology. But Kant's intellectual negation of theological knowledge does not necessarily mean that his philosophy as a whole is theo- son for supermundane realities. logically negative. To assert the contrary is scarcely to do justice to it as a whole; for it implies that his total thought is not consistent with itself—that his second great work was intentionally a vain attempt to restore what he had destroyed in his first. But the arguments in the first Critique against the possibility of a theological solution of existence through a causal construction of sensuous experience by the logical faculty, which neither demonstrate nor disallow the existence of God, do not foreclose the more practical argument from man's moral experience, in the later Critique, and in this is to be seen the complementary issue of the Kantian inquiry as a whole. Hume, not Kant, is the modern representative of what is called agnosticism. It is thus formulated by Hume:—" When you go one step beyond the mundane system, you only excite an inquisitive humour, which it is impossible ever to satisfy." And Hume sees that this agnosticism involves total nescience, and not merely theological nescience.

For in truth the revolution in our conception of the The Pyrrhonism of Hume is theological agnosticism thought out. universe of reality which was proposed by Hume, in his 'Treatise of Human Nature,' is a great deal more bold and thorough than the later agnosticism which claims him as its parent : it involves the complete disintegration of knowledge of every sort, not of theology only. It issues in dissolution of reasonable reality in a scepticism which leaves men impotent and speech-

less ; or, if expressed in speech, it must be speech in
the form of a question, never in the form of a proposition, either affirmative or negative, on any matter
whatever.   The " Que sais-je ? " with the even balance
as its symbol, which Montaigne adopted to express the
hopeless universality of his spontaneous doubt or ignorance, represents all that Hume finds at last in sensuous
" experience," at the close of a reflective analysis of its
contents.   The only philosophically lawful sort of intellectual life for man, according to Hume, is a life
of question-putting, with no answers about anything.
Experience consists—if it can be spoken of as a " con-
sistence "—not of what is substantial, but of isolated
appearances, empty of substance or reality.   We can
have no experience of a substantial material world ; we
can have no experience of substantial personality in
the form of a self ; we can have no experience of the
unica substantia in the heart of the whole.   The whole
at the most is a succession of empty shows, too insignificant to be worth fighting about, so that martyrs
of all sorts are madmen.   The essence of wisdom, as
with Montaigne, is to oscillate, to doubt, to inquire, to
feel sure of nothing, to make one's self responsible for
nothing.   It was the lesson of Pyrrho of old.   If actual
sense is for us the measure of the universe, experience
is only the feeling of each moment.   What is not felt
at the moment cannot be a part of it : this experience
is transcended whenever assertions are made regarding
the past, the distant, or the future ; even in memory,

and in the supposition of the existence of permanent things behind the present phenomena which are attributed to the permanent things; in the supposition, too, of a permanent self behind the momentary sensations which are supposed to be in some way connected with this spiritual substance of which there is no experience; or when assertions are made about Divine Substance, also unexperienced, on which the other two illusions are supposed to depend, while this last is itself the chief illusion of all.

If belief must in all cases be confined within the transitory actual feeling of the moment, and if feeling, under this stringent limitation of reality, cannot be interpreted as the sign of aught beyond itself, it seems to follow that our only possible intellectual expression must be a transitory interrogation. All assertion about what is outside the limit of present feeling must be unproved assertion. Intellect can at the most only have strength enough to extinguish itself. Intelligence can only be a momentary experience of the impossibility of intelligible experience, if even so much as this. *Interrogation, not proposition, the only legitimate expression of universal nescience.*

Hume seems to find outside of argument a practical counteractive to this intellectual suicide. An intense view of the disintegration of a knowledge that is limited to the isolated impression of the moment at first disposed him " to reject all belief and reasoning," so that he " could look upon no opinion as more probable or likely than another," especially any *Hume himself finds in his felt needs what practically arrests his scepticism.*

opinion concerning the ultimate meaning of the universe. " Where am I, or what am I ? " he asks. " From what cause do I derive my existence, and to what condition shall I return ?　Whose favour shall I court, and whose anger must I dread ?　What beings surround me ? and on whom have I any influence, or who has any influence on me ?　I am confounded with all these questions, and begin to fancy myself in the most deplorable condition imaginable, utterly deprived of the use of every member and faculty."　But if " experience," in the narrowest meaning of the word, when made the criterion of reality, brought him to this pass, " experience " in a wider meaning, and including the mental experience of an irresistible faith, carried him out of what he calls his " philosophical melancholy and delirium."

A universal disintegration of reasoning by reasoning is self-contradictory, and practically impossible.　　For it is impossible for a human being to subside practically into Pyrrhonism, or total inability to assert anything about anything.　There is the " secret force in nature " of which Pascal speaks, which sustains the weakness of our finite understanding, and arrests " philosophical delirium."　The sceptic who declines the attempt to interpret for action any of the appearances presented in experience, because reality in its infinity is incomprehensible by man, must cease to live.　This total scepticism, it has been well said, can never be more than an amusement of the understanding : its only serious effect must consist in exercising acuteness, and in humbling the pride of dogmatism :

no human mind can permanently acquiesce in it: by professing to render *all* the principles of reasoning and conduct equally uncertain, it leaves all opinions in the same degree of certainty or probability, relatively to each other, which they occupied before. David Hume himself discovered in faith or trust the only extrication from the sceptical dilemma that seems available for finite intelligence with finite experience; and even his attenuated faith carries in it the rudiments of the three commonly postulated existences—self, the outer world, and God.

It is instructive to trace the steps which led Hume to what he calls a "sceptical solution of sceptical doubts" about the possibility of finding meaning in experience. It is Pascal's case: those who pretend to doubt everything are confounded by natural faith, while dogmatists who claim infallibility are confounded by sceptical criticism. The finite intelligence of man, incapable of comprehending the infinity of existence, is instead, Hume finds, "carried by custom" to believe in objects and events that "lie beyond the present testimony of our senses and the records of our memory." In all human reasonings from experience, he finds that a step is taken in a faith "which is not supported by any argument or process of the understanding;" and yet it is sanctioned as a step that is reasonable: though not obliged by argument to take the step, one is induced to do so by "another principle of equal weight and authority" with argument. All "inferences

In all reasoning about the absent from present experience, a step must be taken which is "not supported by any argument."

o

from experience" are really examples of trust in uniformities that are customary in the experience which we seek to interpret. Hume, accordingly, reconstitutes the experience which his sceptical criticisms had disintegrated. We are inevitably disposed, he virtually says, to put trust in the universe, when it addresses us in its tried uniformities, confident that if we do so our intelligence will not be put to confusion by the issue. Now this faith in the past customs of nature is virtually, and so far, faith in God immanent in nature. It is in the exercise of this reliance on the surroundings amidst which we live and move and have our being that men are able to transcend immediate and momentary experience, and to bring into a larger or scientific experience what was never actually present in their senses, and was, therefore, not recorded in their memories. We are carried blindly by custom to expect, and expectation is in all cases a faith. This may mean that we put *so much* trust in the reality that envelops us, and in which we participate, as to recognise that this credit is reasonably given; although we cannot demonstrate its reasonableness, or demonstrate that what is continually manifesting itself in our lesser or immediate, and also in our larger experience, in which the lesser is inductively interpreted, is a revelation, so far as it goes, of the Infinite Reality. We put trust in the customary behaviour of the universe, because without this trust we could not live even the life of sense, while we find nothing that is self-contradictory implied in our doing so. The faith works in harmony with our circumstances. It is "an operation of the soul" which seems to meet the order in which the universe is wont to be experienced. It is as unavoidable in its occurrence as it is to feel the passion of love when we receive benefits, or hatred when we meet with injuries. In all these operations alike, Hume sees what he calls "a species of natural instinct," which no reasoning is able either to produce or to prevent.

Hume even suggests a theory of the natural law under which this faith in natural law arises in the minds of men. The faith itself he describes as a feeling of trust in reality, which can be understood only by our being actually conscious of it. "Were we to attempt a definition of this belief or faith, we should perhaps find it an impossible task; in the same manner as if we should endeavour to define the feeling of cold, or the passion of anger, to a creature who never had any experience of these sentiments. Every man is every moment conscious of the sentiment represented by it. It is that act of the mind which renders realities, or what is taken for reality, more present to us than fictions, causes them to weigh more in the thought, and gives them a superior influence on the passions and imagination. Belief consists not in the peculiar nature or order of ideas, but in the *manner* of their conception, and in their peculiar *feeling* to the mind. It is impossible perfectly to explain this feeling. We can go no further than assert that belief [in reality] is some-

All inferences about matters of fact are ultimately expressions of faith in the trustworthiness of the ever-changing Universe.

thing so felt by the mind as to distinguish ideas of the judgment from mere fictions of the imagination. It gives them weight and influence; enforces them in the mind, and renders them the governing principles of our actions." A recognition of the practical trustworthiness of the universe—for so the mental state now under consideration might be described—is, according to Hume's theory, a natural issue of the fact that real events outside our minds follow one another in steady order. The past natural history of our surroundings occasions faith in the continuance of their natural order—that is to say, in their interpretability. But whatever the occasion of the rise in us of this faith may be, the matter of relevant concern is,—that the faith *does* naturally come into exercise, and that the expectation which it involves finds a response in our experience of surrounding reality. The universe, in short, is so far comprehended, when it is found in fact to correspond to the expectant judgments of man: man and his universe are united in an experienced harmony. Man's power to interpret, verified by this experience, suggests that the outward succession is determined by laws which correspond to laws that regulate his own interpreting mind; for otherwise he could not become its interpreter. Is not this interpretability of nature another expression for its immanent divinity, its final supernaturalness in germ? For it meets and so far satisfies the human feeling of absolute dependence on the otherwise unknown Supreme Power, herein no longer unknown, but *so far and thus* revealed, in a real revelation of what in its infinity passes knowledge. One can almost read this within the lines even in Hume.

In the "correspondence" that appears between our trust in natural order and the facts of that order, he sees "a kind of pre-established harmony." It is a "harmony" between "nature and the succession of our ideas: though the powers and forces by which the universe is governed be wholly unknown to us, yet our thoughts and conceptions have still, we find, gone on in the same train with the other works of nature. *Custom* is that principle by which this correspondence has been effected. . . . Had not the presence of an object excited in us the idea of the objects commonly conjoined with it [in nature], all human knowledge must have been limited to the narrow sphere of our memory and senses; and we should never have been able to adjust means to ends, or employ our natural powers, either to the producing of good or avoiding of evil." And that a universal purpose, as well as a universal order, is latent in this trust in the universe, even Hume suggests. "Those who delight in the discovery and contemplation of *final causes*," he continues, "have ample subject to employ their wonder and admiration," in contemplating the harmony between our expectations and the course of things. For the "wisdom of nature" has implanted in us an instinctive faith, "which carries forward the thought in a correspondent course to that which she has established

(margin note): They presuppose an established harmony between our thoughts and the course of nature; so that all natural evidence is fundamentally cosmic faith.

among external objects, though we are ignorant of those powers and forces on which this regular course or succession of objects totally depends."

The three primary postulated existences are virtually implied, each in a thin attenuated form, in these notable words—" self " and " outward things " distinguished, yet in an established harmony with each other ; and withal a rudimentary faith in order and purpose embodied in the whole, but with ignorance otherwise of the Power to which the order and purpose are due. The Supreme Power is credited with " wisdom," because wisdom is manifested in this established harmony ; yet, as with Herbert Spencer, so with Hume, " the power which the universe manifests to us is utterly inscrutable." But one may ask, How and why " utterly " inscrutable, when the " wisdom " latent in its " powers and forces " is acknowledged ? Its very manifestations must not be spoken of as if they concealed it, when they are its revelation and embodiment. Is not the opposite conception the issue of a defect in the comprehension of the *homo mensura* principle ? The revolution in the method of interpreting existence for which Hume claims credit, in his ' Treatise of Human Nature,' may be said to be,—substitution of the concrete *homo mensura* for the abstract *Divina Mensura* principle of Spinoza. But by Hume only a shadowy film of the *homo* is taken into account, with the result, as Thomas Carlyle puts it, that to him life and the universe " was little more than a foolish Bartholomew

Fair show-booth, with the foolish crowding and elbow-ings of which it was not worth while to quarrel, the whole would break up and be at liberty so *soon* ";— himself " with factitious half-false gaiety taking leave at death of what was itself wholly but a lie."

In David Hume, the gentle benevolence which charmed his friends, which Henry Mackenzie has pa-thetically illustrated in the story of 'La Roche,' was united to a temperament to which religious life was by his own account foreign. Warm in friendship, he was indifferent in religion, with a natural repug-nance to every sort of enthusiasm, founded on the narrow rationalism of an understanding measured by external sense. We see this in his objections to de-votion and prayer, and as he himself tells us, to " everything we commonly call religion, except the practice of morality, and the assent of the under-standing to the proposition that *God exists*. It must be acknowledged," he adds, " that nature has given us a strong passion of admiration for whatever is excel-lent, and that the Deity possesses these attributes in the highest perfection ; and yet I assert that God is not the natural object of any passion or affection. He is no object either of the senses or imagination, and very little of the understanding ; without which it is impos-sible to excite any affection. And, indeed, I am afraid that all enthusiasts mightily deceive themselves. Hope and fear perhaps agitate their breasts when they think of the Deity ; or they degrade him into a resemblance

Hume's reason for regarding religious worship as irrational.

with themselves, and by that means render him more comprehensible. Such an affection cannot be required of any man as his duty. Neither the turbulent passions nor the calm affections can operate without the assistance of the senses and [sensuous] imagination; or at least a more complete knowledge of the object than we have of the Deity. In most men this is the case; and a natural infirmity can never be a crime."

Hume's
difficulty
about the
theistic
conclusion
of Clean-
thes.

This recognition of "natural infirmity" as non-moral may be taken as tacit acknowledgment that the ground of morality lies in supernatural freedom. But apart from this, of which more afterwards, this argument for the impossibility of religious devotion "in most men" is interesting when taken in connection with the sympathy which Hume nevertheless avows for the intellectual position of Cleanthes, one of the three interlocutors in his 'Dialogues on Natural Religion.' It is Cleanthes who takes the part of reasoning himself into faith in omnipotent and all-wise Deity, as the supreme principle in existence, by an induction from our experience of the order and mechanism that reign in the world. To his mind, "the most agreeable reflection which it is possible for human imagination to suggest is that of genuine theism; which represents men as the workmanship of a Being perfectly good, wise, and powerful, who, having implanted in us immeasurable desires of good, will prolong our existence to all eternity in order to satisfy these desires." Some of this suggests analogous reasoning of Kant's, but I introduce it here on account of Hume's expressed sympathy with the conclusion, combined with his hesitation to receive it as truth, on account of the absence of adequate human experience in verification. " I could wish," he remarks in one of his letters,—" I could wish that Cleanthes's argument could be so analysed as to be rendered quite formal and regular. The propensity of the mind towards it," *i.e.*, the support it has in human experience — "*unless that propensity were as strong and universal as that to believe in our senses*— will still, I am afraid, be esteemed as suspicious foundation. 'Tis here I wish for your assistance : we must endeavour to prove that this propensity is somewhat different from our inclination to find our own figures in the clouds, our faces in the moon, our passions and sentiments even in inanimate matter. For such an inclination [as this last] may and ought to be controlled, and can never be a legitimate ground of assent."

The legitimacy of an extension of "experience" which takes in and accepts as part of it the moral and religious sentiment of mankind, is in the question at issue with modern agnosticism, and it is interesting to find Hume struggling with it. It is difficult to determine what his final opinion was, or how far below the thin surface of external sense experience he meant to go. That a principle of intelligence is supreme in the universe, however little an object of human understanding this principle may

The limit of experience according to David Hume.

be, was sometimes strongly maintained by him. "The whole frame of nature," he asserts in his 'Natural History of Religion,' "bespeaks an intelligent author; and no rational inquirer can, after serious reflection, suspend his belief for a moment with regard to the primary principles of genuine theism." Perhaps the key to Hume's negations may be found in a remark which his friend Boyle (recorded by Hill Burton) reports that he made, when it was alleged that he had "thrown off the principles of religion." To which the good David replied: "Though I throw out my speculations to entertain the learned and metaphysical world, yet I do not think so differently from the rest of the world as you imagine." But this about Hume personally is by the way. I return to agnosticism.

Is the religious "leap in the dark" more irrational than the inductive ?

The scientific agnostic, we now see, is ready to take the inductive leap in the dark through faith in a natural order believed to be immanent in his sense surroundings; this leap is essentially an act of faith, and not the result of a purely logical process of reasoning, emptied of all trust. Is he not also required, under pressure of moral or spiritual necessities which remain latent in some men, to regard as also reasonable that still deeper interpretation of the universe which makes it at last the supernatural manifestation of supreme moral purpose ? That to do so is fallacious only "because it substitutes faith for reasoning" cannot *per se* be pleaded in arrest of this further

leap in the dark. For every step in the physical interpretation of the external world equally involves the
substitution of *trust* for a perfect rational insight of
the infinite contingencies of nature. Boasted inductive verification in natural science is finally an act of
faith, not of reasoning ; for we cannot prove by abstract argument that what has happened even a million
times *must* therefore happen again. The agnosticism
that retains physical science is not really a protest
against faith; it is only an arrest of faith at the
point at which faith advances from a purely physical
to the moral and religious interpretation of life and
the universe. Is an arrest of faith *at this point* justified by reason, or by the experience of mankind? I
must try to answer this question in the three following
lectures.

LECTURE VIII.

GOD IN NATURE.

David Hume's faith in a pre-estab-lished har-mony. IN last lecture we found David Hume emerging out of universal nescience, not by means of reasoning, but through faith in the supposition of an intelligible harmony between our ideas and the succession of events in sense. The long experienced custom of events, in presenting themselves in an interpretable way in human experience, seemed to him to occasion, and also to justify, this faith in a correspondence between them, as at least a working hypothesis. Without faith in this "correspondence," human beings could not adjust means to any ends they might have in view, or use their natural powers in procuring good and avoiding evil. The harmony, too, he seems to allow, wears the aspect of what, according to the analogies of human experience, we should call a designed arrangement. It looks as if the course of nature—that is to say, the temporal succession of events, in the midst of which we find ourselves, and in which we must take our respective parts—were thus far like a constant manifestation of contrivance on our behalf, and that it may even be so conceived when man tries to form his final conception.

May we then interpret the harmonious correlation, between the succession of changes in the universe as it appears in sense, and our faith in their orderliness, —as the manifestation of persisting purpose in the Supreme Power? And if so, must we also suppose that this temporal succession, with its supposed order and semblance of purpose on the whole and in special details, had an absolute beginning in time? Have we reason to believe that there was a time in which there was no cosmos—no orderly course of nature—no universe proceeding as the physical universe seems now to proceed, in a course of natural evolution, including cycles of integration and dissolution? And must we believe that, when there was no cosmos, the ordering or designing Power existed unmanifested in any form of natural manifestation; so that at a particular date nature, or the finite universe, was ushered into existence by a sudden creative act? And if there actually has been a time in which there was neither cosmical evolution nor dissolution going on as now, did there then exist stuff or material out of which the ordering and designing Power fashioned the cosmos, and set its evolutions agoing, charged with " powers " which enable the natural successions and their cycles to persist without further " interference" by the designer? Or was

How to interpret this harmony.

this cosmos, of which men have some experience, originated without pre-existing material—there being in that
case no primordial chaos out of which the earliest cosmos could have issued in any imaginable sort of way; so
that, according to the theological formula, *it* must have
come " out of nothing," not out of chaotic material.
Yet again, is it a more reasonable supposition than
either of these two, that cosmical evolution and disintegration has been going on always — that it is an
unbeginning succession, and may be expected to be
an endless process? This third supposition may seem
to imply that the idea of cause and effect is capable
of being exemplified only by the changes that occur
within the supposed natural or orderly system, but
not *ab extra*, as explanation of the existence of the system, or of a succession of cosmical systems. For it
may be argued that the fact of the cosmos being a
cosmos cannot in any manner be an effect of something beyond itself — that this would even involve
the contradiction that its supposed cause must be at
once a part of the cosmos yet wholly external to the
cosmos. May not the universe in which I now find
myself, in the deepest interpretation which I can put
upon my present experience of it, be just this unbeginning and unending succession of orderly or significant,
and therefore interpretable, changes, in the midst of
which I am living and moving and having my being,
and of which I and other human beings are parts,
even if their significance in it is only trivial. May

not this now experienced universe, in its eternal
natural or orderly evolution, be the final reality ?

It is questions of this sort, charged with infinity, that
the agnostic naturalist puts aside as unanswerable.
He does so on the ground that answers to them must
be answers that come from a faith which is irrational,
because it does not admit of being verified by experience ; whereas, on the contrary, answers to questions
about the finite causes of events within the temporal
succession of the natural evolution *may* be accepted in
a faith that is assumed to be sufficiently enlightened by
verification. Now, if the faith is reasonable which sup-
ports the presupposition of natural order, on which all
scientific verification depends without previous proof
from experience,—why must the teleological interpretation of nature be rejected, on the ground that *its*
only support is faith ? The scientific trust in cosmical
order, on which all inductive verification depends, cannot itself be proved by experience, because no interpretation of experience is possible unless this faith is
accepted without proof. The religious trust in the
immanence of design, in the universe as a whole,
as well as in the narrow portion of it which passes
through human experience, seems to stand on the
same footing. If it is not unreasonable to *assume*
natural law as a constructive principle in the interpretation of sensuous experience, why is it unreasonable to *assume* design, if the facts may be read in harmony with this other and deeper assumption ? Order

The faith that is accepted, and the faith that is rejected by the scientific agnostic.

means reason, and this for us means conscious reason or living mind. Purpose brings the mind thus immanent in the scientific order into analogy with human intending will; and the circumstance that we bring the idea of purpose to the facts to enable us to interpret. them, instead of receiving it from them as a necessary conclusion, seems in itself to be no more a reason for arresting religious faith in God as immanent purpose, than for arresting scientific faith in God as immanent physical order.

Imma-
nence of
order and
purpose
in nature
does not
determine
what the
term
"God"
morally
means.

When I speak of order in nature as the expression of objective intelligence, and of purpose in nature as the expression of objective intending will, I do not mean to foreclose questions which meet us later on, regarding the Orderer or the Designer, named God in the religious interpretation of the universe. Recognition of order and design that is sufficient for the mechanical and even the teleological interpretation of nature, does not settle what is meant by the Divine Orderer or Designer. It does not tell us fully what God is.

Nor does it
determine
that the
natural
universe
ever began
to be.

Further, the fact that I take for granted that I am living in a cosmos, and in a cosmos charged with purpose, in the sense that it presents innumerable examples of means naturally adapted to secure human and other ends—this fact does not necessarily settle what I may call the historical question of the origin and final outcome of the system of natural changes now in course of evolution.

I do not find that the presence of order and design within the cosmos necessarily means that the cosmos must have had a beginning. The *eternity* of the universe in its natural succession, the alternative to the contrary hypothesis, must be *proved* to be inconsistent with the interpretable order and perfect adaptations with which it is now apparently charged: those who assume that it had a beginning must prove, and not assume. They are bound to find evidence of what, if true, would be a historical fact. Now, historical proof that the presently manifested cosmical order and purpose long ago began for the first time to be manifested is not only difficult to find, but seems to involve contradiction.

Is there proof that the cosmos had a beginning, or that it was "specially created."

Is there evidence that the existing natural universe of matter and mind had a beginning? Can facts be brought to show that the subject of the natural succession of metamorphoses, in their periodical cycles of integration and disintegration, was absolutely brought into existence, at a particular date, by a Mind that had no beginning, and which existed before this date without any cosmical manifestation? What proof is there that the universe made its first appearance as a sudden supernatural effect, and that it has not existed without beginning, as a succession of essentially supernatural changes, similar in the "naturalness" of their appearances to those changes in which we all find ourselves and all things participating to-day? May not the actual matter of fact have been, that the unbe-

Unbeginning natural metamorphoses may be really and constantly supernatural, instead of superseding God.

ginning past has been the scene of an endless succession of orderly evolutions and dissolutions—ordered cycles or natural economies—in which the existing material has been undergoing constant metamorphoses; that human beings are living in one of these cycles, which had *its* natural beginning in a remote past, and is naturally destined to end, and pass into another economy in some remote future, followed by other universes (if we choose to call each cycle a new "universe") in an unending future? Is not this an eternal natural succession that may be essentially supernatural, and that may be conceived of as unbeginning expression of eternal intending Will? Is it not a more reasonable supposition than the idea of special creation, which seems to mean that the material now in natural course of metamorphosis was once non-existent, and did absolutely enter into existence, as an effect of the Will of solitary Mind existing antecedently? Moreover, if the actual state of the universe, at any given moment after its original creation in time, must be accounted for, or naturally refunded into, its state in the preceding moment; and if the "special creation" is a refunding of the whole, at a particular period, into "creative" Mind, does not this logic of causation demand a still remoter antecedent cause of the solitary creative Mind itself, which in this reasoning is inferred only under the ordinary postulate of natural science, by which changes are physically identified with antecedent conditions on which they depend? What is meant by the "supernatural" act, in which nature is supposed absolutely to begin, at some remote era in the past, unless it means an antecedent mental process, which itself needs a cause as much as any other process in the succession?

This last question was suggested by David Hume. Self-conscious mind, so far as civil or natural history informs us, first made its appearance at a comparatively late date,—in the form of human conscious life on this planet. This, we are told, was preceded by ages of merely sentient matter: before that there was only insentient matter. It is therefore with a *material* cosmos *only* that we are supposed to have to do, in the earlier stages of the history of the universe, if we confine our regard to the only cosmical economy of which man has any authentic record—either documentary or in the form of geological phenomena. Hume suggests that, for aught we can know *a priori*, matter may contain the source or spring of order originally within itself as well as mind does; and that there is no more difficulty in conceiving that the several elements or molecules of matter, from an internal unknown cause, may fall into the most exquisite arrangement, than to conceive that their ideas in the supposed Universal Mind, also from an internal unknown cause, have fallen into that arrangement which forms the succession of ideas in the mind of God. If the material world is caused by an ideal world in a universal Mind, this ideal world must in its turn rest upon some other; and so on

A question put by David Hume.

without end. "It were better, therefore," the sceptic conjectures, "never to look beyond the present material world, and to suppose a natural succession of unbeginning and unending changes in it. By supposing Matter to contain the principle of order within itself, we really assert *it* to be God; and the sooner we arrive at that Divine Being so much the better. A mental world, or universe of Divine Ideas, requires a cause as much as does a material world, or universe of visible and tangible objects." So that, if the principle of merely natural or caused causality is taken as the one ultimate category, and if this requires us to presuppose Mind to account *naturally* for the beginning of nature, the same principle of natural causality seems to require us to presuppose some natural antecedent to account for the existence of the ideas of this Mind.

The common "proof" that the cosmos is not eternal.

An argument of natural theologians has been, that there *is* evidence, supplied by civil and natural history, that the presented universe *was* created "out of nothing" at a particular time, but that there is no similar evidence that Mind had a beginning, or that Mind needed to be created by an antecedently existing Power. This argument is pressed by Dr Chalmers, in his interesting and eloquent book on Natural Theology. "The precise difference between the two," he says, "is, that we *have* proof of a commencement to our present *material* economy, but we have no such proof of a commencement to the *mental* economy—*i.e.*, the Divine Mind—which may have preceded it. There is room for the question, How came the *material* system of things into its present order? because we have reason to believe that *it* has not subsisted in that order from eternity. There is no such room for the question, Why might not the material have fallen into its present order of itself, as well as the mental which is conceived to have gone before it, in the form of a Divine Mind? We have no reason to believe that this mental economy ever was otherwise than it now is. The latter question presumes that the mental did begin to enter into order of itself, or, which is the same thing, that God *had* a commencement. In the material economy, we have the vestiges before our eyes of *its* having had an origin—or in other words, of its being a consequent; and we have furthermore the experience that in every instance which comes under full observation of a similar consequent—that is, of a consequent which involved, as the mundane order of things does so amply, the adaptation of parts to an end — the antecedent was a purposing mind, which descried the end, and devised the means for its accomplishment. We might not have been called upon to make even a single ascent in the path of causation, had the world stood forth to view in the character or aspect of *immutability*. But, instead of this, both history and observation tell of a definite commencement to the present order; and we therefore just follow the lights of experience when we move upward from the world to an intelligent mind that ordained it. It is this which carries us backward one step from the world to God; and the reason why we do not continue the retrogression *beyond God* is, that we have not met with an *indication* that He has had a commencement. In the one case there is a beginning of the present material system forced upon our convictions [by the evidence of natural vestiges in geology, and also by the testimony of historic records]. In the other case, the case of the antecedent Mind, there is no such beginning forced upon our convictions by experience. We have therefore ample *reason* for regarding the world as a posterior term, and seeking after *its* antecedent. But we have no such reason for treating this antecedent as also a posterior term, and seeking for *its* prior term in a higher antecedent. The one we *see* to be a changeable and a recent world. The other, for aught we know, may be an unchangeable and everlasting God. The one order, the material, we *know* not to have been from everlasting. The other, the mental, which by all experience and analogy must have preceded the material, bears no symptoms which we can discover of its ever having required any remoter economy to call it into being."

A "catastrophe" may itself have been a natural sequence, not an absolute cosmic beginning.

What is here alleged to be proved by the records of history, contained in Hebrew and other literatures, and by the physical vestiges discovered by geology, seems to be only this—that the metamorphoses which this planet of ours has passed through include a succession of *catastrophes;* and that these can be explained only by what is called supernatural "interference," particularly those economies which contain living matter, and, above all, the organisms with which, as in human organisms, self-conscious life is somehow associated. An economy into which life, and emphatically self-conscious life, has *for the first time* entered, is one, it is argued, which needs interference with a natural economy that is supposed, on account of its naturalness, to be itself empty of the supernatural. But the antecedent creative Mind is presumed to be a Mind that itself had no beginning; inasmuch as neither the records of history, nor geological phenomena, afford any evidence that the living Mind which suddenly created matter, and introduced life on this globe, was itself a caused cause.

This argument scarcely touches some important previous questions regarding theological inference from facts of experience recorded in history, and the nature of the causal judgment which we are obliged to presuppose in our interpretation of change. In the first place, it leaves the perpetual presence in nature of an absolutely independent and therefore eternal Mind so far an open question, that it has to be determined, and can be determined, by documentary records of what has happened; instead of accepting theistic faith, as well as faith in physical law, as a postulate—unless it can be disproved—on the ground that it enables man more adequately or deeply to interpret his surroundings than faith in natural uniformity taken alone does. The postulated eternal presence of providential Mind, im-

Empirical evidence of the non-eternity of the cosmos inadequate in two respects.

manent in nature, is reduced to a contingency dependent on the records of history, like the existence of any particular dependent cause among the physical sequences in nature. In the next place, it seems to foreclose discoveries in natural science, which are continually revealing natural causes of changes that were formerly presumed to be independent of the natural order, and as such called supernatural, as if the natural succession was undivine.

Significant metamorphosis of phenomena is not causality in its full Aristotelian meaning.

How can natural causation with its dependent causes be thus final? It is always sending us in quest of a cause that is not itself *caused*. One thus finds at last in natural causation the demand for a self-determined or supernatural, not merely for a caused cause,—this last being the sign of the approach of its invariable or natural successor, rather than the really originating cause. A God that might conceivably have had a beginning, and is thus essentially dependent; or who is inferred to be unbeginning, only because we have no historical proof that God ever began, is really thought of only as a part of physical nature,—an antecedent that happens to be eternal because it does not seem to have any natural predecessor. But are we not obliged to bring to the consideration of change the conviction that natural change *as such* is, now and always, dependent upon a Power that is independent of change, or an uncaused cause? Is not this conviction independent, too, of any evidence which history or external nature might present, in regard to the question about the beginningness or the unbeginningness of the now manifested natural order ? That order may, it seems to me, be unbeginning, and yet throughout for ever dependent—an eternally dependent cosmos—an eternally supernatural evolution. The fact that men have risen into individual self-consciousness in an eternal course ,of nature does not necessarily mean that the eternal natural succession is the whole; or indeed that succession, if unbeginning, can be thought of as a "whole" for what is infinite, as argued in a former lecture, is not in subjection to the category of quantity.

Again, the progress of scientific interpretation of external nature is continually extending our information about what is natural, and, as natural, imaginable, in the form of the temporal process of phenomena. Scientific inquiry discovers natural processes, which can be presented to the senses or represented in the sensuous imagination, to fill gaps in the physical succession that were before conceived to be bridged over by a supernatural agency that was somehow opposed to the "causes" presentable in sense, which alone interest natural science. The continuity of natural change becomes less and less interrupted, as science advances in its unravelling of the intricate web of natural causation : with each advance the need is lessened for interpolating divine acts merely to bridge over the interval. But under the conception of nature as causally supernatural, what forbids an unbeginning history of this planet, through all its changes, in-

The possibility of reading an unbeginning and unending succession of cosmic changes in terms of natural causation, does not exhaust the demand for Infinite Reality.

organic and organic, and especially the evolution of its human organisms, being read throughout in terms of divinely dependent natural causes, most of which, indeed, have still to be discovered? And as these changes in our planet are only a very few of the changes in the material universe, of which this planet is an insignificant part, what forbids that—if not in the progress of human discovery, yet to the mind's eye of higher intelligence — the eternal natural, yet supernatural, succession may arrange itself in an intellectual view of the infinite system of caused causes, in which every change, whether in the history of extended things or in the history of conscious lives, has its correlative natural cause? This would be the infinite universe read in terms of natural science. Yet, while true to the facts, as far as it goes, would not this reading of it, exclusively in terms of mechanical causality, be after all inadequate to the demands of the higher *homo mensura* criterion, and therefore, even for man, an insufficient answer to the final question—In what, or in whom, am I, now and always, living and moving and having my being? Do I not still find myself obliged to deepen this mechanical interpretation of the universe by a teleological interpretation, and to see that in and through the natural world itself, even if it is an unbeginning and unending world, I am really living in what is finally a supernatural universe?

The "course of nature"   The natural history of the material world, so read, is a history of instrumental, subordinate, or secondary causes, which are only metaphorically called *agents.* They are virtually *signs* of their so-called effects,— signs in which the Divine Reality is continually revealing order, meaning, and purpose to the percipient beings that have risen into conscious perception, on this planet, in the course of the natural evolution. At this point of view, sensible signs, not ultimate causes, make up the whole visible course in nature. Natural causation is really sense symbolism. Without natural causes, one may say, " there could be no calculable course of nature. And without a calculable course, nature could never be understood ; mankind must always be at a loss, not knowing what to expect, or how to govern themselves. Therefore, in the government of the world, physical agents, improperly called *agents*—that is to say, mechanical second causes—are necessary to assist, not indeed the governor, but the governed. Yet if the explaining of a phenomenon be to assign its proper, efficient, and final cause, it should seem that natural science never *explains* anything, its province being only to discover the laws of nature."

may be only a system of significant appearances, which, as significant, are more or less interpretable by man.

Natural causation does not supersede the divine power that is always latent in the natural universe, if God is the ultimate cause of all natural causation. The discovery of a previously unknown physical cause is then only the discovery of one additional significant expression of the universal fact that we are living and moving and having our being in an interpretable world; which, although by us interpretable

Natural causation is a term expressive of the interpretability of the world in which we find ourselves ; and the interpretation of

nature im-
plies inter-
preting
mind de-
pendent
on corre-
lation of
that mind
with Mind
immanent
in Nature.

only in part, yet can so far appeal to a human intelligence that is practically in analogy with itself.
There is presupposed a microcosmic and a macrocosmic
intelligence—the one in each of us, the other immanent
in the world. The elaborate order of nature is God
continually speaking to us; and its elaborate web of
natural connection is a means to the end of its being
a revelation of God. Living in and through this order,
we are living in and through what is virtually a perpetual creation; which may have been going on without
beginning, and without end in prospect—at once natural
and supernatural—a nature significant of the supernature with which it is constantly charged. So far
pantheism seems in harmony with theism. A constant divine determination of nature is the share of
truth which theism may be said to have received
from pantheism. "Men," says Spinoza, "have been
wont to call only that whereof the natural cause
is unknown the work of God. For people in general
think that the power or providence of God is then most
plainly manifested, when they perceive something to
happen in the course of nature which is uncommon, or
contrary to the opinion which they have formed from
custom concerning what the course of nature actually
is. And in no way do they think that the existence
of God may be more clearly proved than from this—
that nature doth *not* keep her order. Wherefore they
deem that all those set aside God who explain events
by natural causes, or try to understand the conditions

on which they depend. For they suppose that God is doing nothing, as long as nature is moving on in her accustomed order; and on the other hand, that the powers of nature and natural causes are idle so long as God is acting. They imagine therefore two powers, distinct from each other, to wit, the power of God, and the powers of natural things; which last they suppose to have been at first determined by God, or, as most nowadays express themselves, to have been created by Him. But what they mean by *nature*, and what by *God*, they know not; except that they suppose the power of God to be a sort of regal government, and that they attribute a mechanical force all its own to nature. The common herd, therefore, call unusual works of nature miracles, or works of God; and partly out of devotion, partly out of desire to oppose those devoted to natural science, even wish to be ignorant of the natural causes of things, and delight only to hear of those things which they are least able to interpret, and are therefore most apt to admire."

The question at the heart of all this is, Whether what are commonly called natural causes can otherwise than metaphorically be called *causes*, if cause means that the final human conception is of Reason ever active in the universe. The point to be kept in view seems to be, that natural causation, with the alleged equivalence between effects and *its* causes, presents only a system of interpretable signs, which, because a system, is found

Does "natural causation" explain anything finally?

charged throughout with order and purpose. Natural science unfolds the uniformities, and can give a provisional interpretation of nature; each genuine scientific discovery is an illustration. The theologian may suggest particular examples of purpose, or what is analogous to purpose, gathered with more or less skill from appearances presented in the inorganic world, particularly in living organisms. But the perpetual existence of the cosmos, charged throughout with natural order, and with means that lead to ends, is the constant miracle of God in nature. Order and end may be each presumed in faith to be latent in all the phenomena and events of inorganic and organised nature. Indeed the special instances of each, in the form of discovered law and discovered purpose, embrace only an insignificant proportion of the illimitable number of special laws and special ends. The complexity of the phenomena obscures their actual order in regions still closed against confident scientific inference; the astronomer, for example, has been more successful than the meteorologist. And examples of adaptation of means to ends are more abundant and impressive to a human mind in the appearances presented by living organisms than in those of inorganic nature. But withal are we not intellectually obliged, or at least at liberty intellectually, to read experience in the faith that it is experience of a cosmos in which providential law and purpose are always immanent, throughout, and even in events which seem to us insignificant?

To determine between the alternative mysteries of a sudden creation of cosmos at some period in the past, and the mystery of an eternal natural and yet divine cosmical evolution, is a task that perhaps transcends understanding, for without doubt it transcends sensuous experience. We have no reason to suppose that the ever - changing cosmical growth may not have proceeded always, in absolute or constant dependence on the principle that makes us now try to construe any of its phenomena in terms of order and of purpose. We are born into what may be unbeginning and unending natural evolution; but the world into which we are born is, we find as a fact, an interpretable world, which even for the limited intelligence and experience of man is more or less successfully the subject of tentative interpretations. Men are inevitably dependent on the contingencies of a narrow and broken experience, for their scientific understanding of the qualities and behaviour of the unconscious things, and the conscious persons, of which the universe is found to consist. Each finite thing and person is so connected with every other, in the past and in the distant, that a complete knowledge of each is possible only to omniscient intelligence. Accordingly, unconditional certainty, or an absolute knowledge of the natural causes and ends of the things that are presented in our experience, is unattainable. Yet human life rests on the faith, that a working intelligence on our part of the Intelligence that is expressed in the orderly sequences and adaptations of nature *is* within our reach; so that in intellectual intercourse with the Intellect that is latent in Nature our human intellect will not in the end be put to confusion. When we try to interpret nature as sense symbolism, we often find our hypothetical interpretations verified by the event; and although there is for us no demonstrable certainty that, with innumerable unknown causes in existence, what has been now verified will be undisturbed, this faith sufficiently sustains us. This is that faith in the harmony between the course of nature and the thought of man which, as we found, was the last word even with Hume. The mathematical, mechanical, chemical, and vital causal relations of things presented to our senses may be treated as an intelligible language. And that this natural language can in some measure be interpreted by man, the gradual growth of his sciences of nature is a practical proof. May we not therefore assert that, in our surrounding universe, we are continually in the presence of a Power that reveals itself in articulate language of law and purpose? Are we not, when in the presence of external nature, in a condition which is in analogy to that in which we are when beside a human being who is speaking to us, or otherwise making signs that enable us to enter in some degree into his thought? The natural order and natural ends of the economy into which we enter at birth may be the visible expression of a

Power which uses, and perhaps has always used, the visible universe for self-revelation; even as men use their bodily organs in communicating to one another the invisible contents of their respective minds—with this signal difference, that nature, like the Power at work in and through it, may be an unbeginning and unending process, while the words of men are transitory conventional signs.

This difference need not hinder, as far as I can see, recognition of special design any more than of special law, in particular examples of natural causation; and that whether the end recognised is found in a natural catastrophe, or in the slowly reached products of long series of natural metamorphoses. The spiritual interpretation of all natural causation is equally valid, or equally incapable of disproof, however complex the natural links may be, and whatever obstacles are thus offered to the scientific knowledge of the observer. If natural causation is all ultimately supernatural, no increase in our physical science of the special causes in the visible succession can dissolve the spiritual significance that is immanent in each caused cause and in the whole. *Natural causation admits of a spiritual interpretation.*

Perhaps, too, the very complexity of the web of natural causation, which man finds that he is able in some degree to unravel scientifically, so as to live within it, may itself be regarded rightly as an example of adaptation of ends to means, when this complexity is considered in relation to man. The complex constitution *The complexity of the cosmos an education of intelligence and character.*

Q

of the cosmos seems to be fitted by its elaborateness for educating our latent intelligence, and for the moral discipline involved in a laborious mastery of the causal secrets of nature. It may even suggest with more emphasis than a simpler constitution, the constant presence of Active Reason in nature; expressed more impressively, and in a way more apt to induce reverence, when the natural language costs us time and labour to interpret, or when it is interpretable only tentatively and to a small extent, for the operative purposes of men.

The cardinal fact is, that the universe into which we awake in becoming conscious *is* interpretable and not chaotic, not when or whether it began to be.

The basis of human life is surely found in the faith that the ever-evolving universe *is* charged with meaning and purpose. It does not depend on the transcendent alternative of whether the natural signs, with their divine meanings and adaptations, had an absolute beginning, or are, on the contrary, an unbeginning and unending revelation of eternal Spirit We still presume that we are living and moving and having our being in the midst of intelligible relations, out of which human sciences of nature gradually construct themselves. As relations of natural causality express thought, while they are independent of individual human thinkers, true science of nature, so far from contradicting the supposition that one entered at birth into an essentially intelligible universe, proceeds unconsciously throughout all its inquiries, experiments, and verifications, upon this very assumption, as its ultimate and indispensable working hypothesis. Natural science is a product which depends for its existence upon the fact of intellectual affinity between man and his surroundings.

This fact, which is suggested by every circumstance and event in life, seems to bring light to us in dealing with the final inquiry regarding the *sort* of existence or universe in which *we* are having our being. The phenomena, of which we have experience, are either extended and unconscious, or unextended and conscious — matter or spirit, — with unconscious life, as in vegetable organisms, intermediate between the two. The history of the universe, as far as it discovers itself to man, is a history of action and reaction among these beings. If *we* are to form any conception of the substance or supreme principle of the whole, it must be the conception either of substance that is unconscious and extended, or of substance that is intelligent and foreign to extension. The alternatives for us are a materialist or a spiritual conception of the Power finally at work in nature. *Two ultimate alternatives.*

Some one may ask indeed whether there is need for having recourse to either of those alternatives. Can man proceed further than to recognise that he is living in an interpretable universe, so far as scientific interpretation of its sense signs implies this? I do not find that I can arrest inquiry at this point. For I have found that what are called natural " causes," so far as my knowledge of them can go, are not causes and effects *in their own right*. They are causes and effects that are brought into, and kept in, this relation, *The need which impels us to one or other of these alternatives, instead of resting in the fact that we find ourselves in a physical cosmos, not in a physical chaos.*

by some principle that is superior to themselves, and to which they are in subordinate dependence. I find no evidence that unconscious things originate change in one another; nor is the term "agent" intelligible till one has experience of a self-conscious being, or more definitely of the self-conscious being that each one calls "myself," and of self in the exercise of morally responsible activity. I touched on this in the lectures on materialism and egoism, when it appeared that the hypothesis of an evolution of inorganic and organic things throws no light upon the reason that awakens in consciousness, to be appealed to as finally in the heart of things. To find with the biologist what the external conditions are under which a human being enters on his life of intelligence, is not to resolve the final problems of which intelligence becomes aware : these must be determined, if at all, by spiritual data contained within invisible intelligence itself; not by external data in the material world. Matter, as we perceive it, *explains nothing* in the way of ultimate explanation; nor does it, as I think can be shown, afford even the deepest and truest explanation that is within man's reach. Motion of molecules can only explain motion in other molecules, and not even this finally; for there is no necessary connection perceptible in sense between contact of moving masses in space, and the motion of other masses which follows the impact. What one can say is, that we are accustomed to expect the latter when we see the former. The former is thus to us the intelligible sign, and so the foundation of a natural prophecy, upon which we proceed in faith.

Self-consistent materialism is an impossible, because self-contradictory, position, and the tacit assumptions of the materialist alone conceal its absurdity. "The materialistic assumption," as Lotze says, "takes upon itself to show how, from bare properties of space filling divisibility, inertia, and mobility, the whole universe, and therefore its spiritual constituents, could be naturally developed, without admixture of any other principle or cause whatever. Now, psychology compels us to see that states of motion in matter, or in material organisms, are only the occasions upon which there arise in us spiritual processes, such as sensations or other feelings and thoughts. But *why* these occasions are followed by those spiritual states is not only not a subject of possible empirical knowledge, but it is even possible to see that man can never reach the point where it could be seen that a mode of motion in a mass of molecules, however curiously elaborated, would have to cease to remain a mode of motion, and would be under an absolute necessity to transform *itself* into a process of thought, or even of sensation. According to all ascertainable principles, from *motions alone* nothing but a new distribution, propagation, or arrest of *motions* can follow. A spiritual sequence can

Lotze on the materialistic alternative.

be attached to them only indirectly—that is to say, through their natural relation to another substance which in its own nature possesses a capacity for the manifestation of spiritual processes; in which capacity the mere motions themselves, as such, as perceived by us are wanting. So that in each particular instance, as well as in the totality of the universe, with a barely material ultimate principle, in which matter is endowed only with those characteristics which are in science assumed to be essential to it, it is incapable of originating the world of spiritual processes." In short, the acknowledged interpretability or divinity which appears in the significant relations of natural things, to which I have been asking your consideration in this lecture, can make no appeal to, or receive no response from, a universe that consists ultimately *only* of atoms in continuous motion. The conception of existence as absolutely or ultimately spiritual is therefore deeper than the conception of it as ultimately an evolution of atoms in infinite space and time—scientifically true, so far as it goes, as this last conception of it may possibly be. For there is no inconsistency between theism and the hypothesis that fire - mist was the physical beginning of our world.

The revelation of God in and through what is

It is the revelation that is involved in the self-consciousness of man that supplies the key to this deeper or spiritual interpretation of nature. Apart from this,

the outer world, with all its laws and ends, is dark- highest in
ness; for external nature in itself, or apart from the ᵐᵃⁿ·
contents of moral life in man, conceals the God whom
it nevertheless reveals when it is looked at in the
light of spiritual consciousness.

In next lecture we shall look for some light, through
this opening, into the mystery of existence.

LECTURE IX.

MAN SUPERNATURAL.

Retro-
spect.

THE purpose of last lecture was partly to show that
obligation to presuppose order and purpose in nature,
as the condition of interpreting it, is independent of
the question whether the cosmos had a beginning; for
even if at birth we are ushered into a cosmos that had
no beginning, we find ourselves *now* living and moving
and having our being amidst surroundings that must
be presupposed to be ultimately and essentially supernatural, or an expression of intelligent purpose, as the
condition of their being adequately interpreted.

Nature
and super-
natural-
ness.

But of whose intelligence and purpose is this the
expression? Of what sort is the ordering and designing principle? What is meant by its supernaturalness? Have we any example within our experience
of a reality superior to the natural causation that is
alone recognised in physical sciences? Does not the
applicability to man of the idea of moral obligation

involve supernaturalness in him, and thus supply an analogy to supernaturalness in nature? These questions lead to the subject of this lecture, which is concerned with the supernatural as presented in man, a moral and religious being, who shares as a responsible agent in the universal reason, and who, as a free spirit, is connected with the centre of a moral world, to which nature is in harmonious subordination. Under this final conception, advance of the natural sciences only deepens and enriches man's conception of God. When an event can be referred in science to a natural cause, it is not by this divorced from God, if all natural causation is the immediate manifestation of Divine Power. May I add that the idea of natural causation being essentially divine is not new to me. It pervades the thought which I have given to the world in the last five - and - twenty years, for it is implied in six volumes of which Berkeley was the text, and in three in which I have essayed a critical reconstruction of Locke.

I find the signal example of the divine in the Man. spiritual being of man. For do we not see in man a being at once natural and supernatural, intermediate between brute and Deity, with an intelligence and experience that is neither nescience nor Omniscience,— equally unable, as Pascal suggests, to know all, and to be ignorant of all, who is great even in knowing himself to be miserable, and who constantly seeks to support the present by the future interpreted through the past ? Let us examine the supernatural experience into which man may rise when he realises his true ideal.

External
organic
conditions
not to be
identified
with the
self-con
scious life
of which
they may
be the oc-
casion.
The visible organic conditions under which conscious-ness makes its appearance in man, and in terms of which its gradual development may be expressed in biology, must not be identified with the moral and spiritual life, itself invisible, of which the organic motions are the natural occasion. Intelligence may be manifested in and through visible processes, in inorganic and in organic nature; but those visible processes are not the invisible conscious intelligence, nor are they the emotional and volitional life, which is blended with the intellectual, in a complete per-sonal consciousness. The presumed interpretability of nature, and the fact that I find myself in an in-terpretable world, is something more or something other than the sense-presented phenomena them-selves in their illimitable varieties. That these sense appearances are capable of being understood, I am mentally obliged to pre-judge; for this pre-judgment is the fundamental condition of the formation of natural sciences by man, as well as of every calcu-lated movement in daily life. A chaos of letters of the alphabet, presented in a heap on a table, is not confounded with the same letters organised into a book, and therein so charged with meaning, that the reader finds the book in objective intellectual affinity with his own intelligence. Man in like manner treats

nature on the hypothesis that, in trying to understand its phenomena scientifically, he is exercising himself in an intelligible, if not in an intelligent or personal cosmos—not in a meaningless chaos.

But living consciousness is more than potential intelligibility; more, too, than the sensuous signs in which the reason latent in nature receives expression. Meaning, abstracted from a living conscious thinker, is an unactual abstraction. Let us once more suppose all conscious life in the universe suddenly annihilated. What then becomes of the latent interpretability of natural phenomena ; or of the phenomena themselves, which we are obliged to presuppose interpretable, and therefore in correspondence with our own intellectual constitution — the macrocosm in analogy with the microcosm ? *Conscious intelli-gence.*

Is it not within the rational consciousness of man, not in the natural phenomena presented to our senses in the organism of the human body, that we are to look for the true key, or at least the best within man's reach, for his final interpretation of the universe ? Those very sciences which express some part of what the physical universe in which we live is saying to us, are themselves products of rational consciousness; not of unconscious, nor even of merely sentient, life. And rational consciousness in man is not yet proved experimentally to have its natural equivalents in phenomena of matter ; but even if this could be physiologically proved, so that the scientific *Conscious life the light of the world.*

equivalent for every conscious state could be found in the organism, this spurious monism leaves unaffected the constructive principles of reason as criteria for the determination of truth. Whether conscious perception by man is a transitory or a permanent fact in the universe, matter, apart from all perception of it, is an empty, unactual abstraction. Conscious life is the light of the world. The sciences themselves—physical, chemical, biological—have their concrete existence only in the conscious life of a person; so that it is only through invisible personal life and agency that the mysterious reality of existence is actualised into sense and science. Living science is a function of invisible conscious life. The biologist, in *his* living science, reads the symbols of that life in the form of visible organic processes. Each discovery of an instance of physical causality in the constitution of the world is a mental act. Success in science depends upon the amount of intellectual development in the individual discoverer. The validity of his discoveries depends at last upon mental presuppositions, which something in his mind obliges him to make, and not merely upon the transitory visible phenomena. He is obliged to presume, without proof, an orderly constancy in nature, for apart from this, expectation and scientific verification have no ground to rest on. Sensuous experience is only of the past: it cannot be identified with the future, in the way that inductive science virtually identifies it, without this disposition to take its orderly constancy, or rationality, for granted. The very power the biologist claims of concluding that he is himself a natural issue of the evolution of the material world is refunded into rational consciousness. This makes man the most significant, and indeed his only known organ, for a revelation of what God is, that the universe contains. Man, the microcosm, is the unique example of the supernatural, in which, if anywhere within experience, religion finds the type of the infinite supernatural Macrocosm. The ideal man, including his body, is for us the symbol of God in nature. The spirit of man, incarnate in his body, is the symbol of Infinite Spirit, incarnate in the universe presented in time. As containing what is highest in human experience, the spiritual life of man, in its full development, may be said to signify to man what is final or supreme in existence — in short, what we call God—in the only form in which God can by us be apprehended.

Hence the philosophical inadequacy of all merely natural or biological interpretations either of nature or of man,—their inadequacy, I mean, even to our modest intellectual resources, as well as our needs, moral and religious. A physiological account of the so - called " action " and " reaction " between man's animal organism and its material environment, under a law, let us say, of natural selection, omits man's supernatural intelligence and moral agency as revealed to reflection. It overlooks that in man which distinctively reveals God,—so far as the infinite principle of

The necessary inadequacy of all merely biological or other natural interpretation of existence.

the universe *can* be revealed to an intelligence intermediate between nescience and the perfect intuition of
the Omniscient.   Is it not in and through that which is
found by reflection in man's invisible life of consciousness, not through that which is presented to any or all
of his five senses, that the world is finally interpretable
by him ?

The lan-
guage of
Nature and
Comte's
maxim.   The progress of the physical sciences themselves is
an evidence that natural evolution is a continual
address to man, expressed in the significant language
of caused causes ; for those sciences, so far as they go,
are an interpretation of this language. \Scientific intercourse with the natural universe is virtually intelligence
in intercourse with intelligence — the mind of man
learning to think the thought or reason that is latent
in things.   Yet curiously it was a maxim of Comte,
that the heavens declare no other glory than that of
Hipparchus, Kepler, Newton, and the other illustrious
astronomers, who have interpreted the causal language
that is uttered by the masses of matter that occupy
space.   On this principle the glory of Newton's 'Principia' was not the glory of Newton, but only of those
readers of the 'Principia' who are able to appreciate its
physical theory and demonstrations.   If the Book of
Nature receives the meaning which it is supposed to
express only from the astronomical discoverer, must
not the book which was supposed to make Newton
illustrious receive *its* meaning, not from Newton, but
only from its intelligent interpreters ? (

But it is in man's life as a moral being, in the responsible exercise of deliberate will, not in man as purely intellectual, that the facts of his experience seem to resist the limitations of physical evolution, and refuse to be read exclusively in terms of a natural action and reaction between the *individual* organism and its surroundings. The inadequacy remains even when we take account also of the *inherited* results of organic and extra-organic interaction, as contained in the history of the animal ancestors of the individual organism, or even in the previous history of the whole material world, of which a living body is of course a part. It is in the exercise of morally responsible will that man so rises, *as a person, above* all that is merely physical and impersonal, that the divine principle at the heart of existence seems to be illustrated in him. And if so, it is then illustrated in a way that does not admit of sufficient expression in the terms, or under the conditions, of sciences which only formulate the customary processes of visible nature. Is not the responsible will in man supernatural: self-determined, not determined from without: so that man may be said to hold the unique position of being at once an outcome of the physical evolution, and a creative agent in respect of all in his history and surroundings that he is morally responsible for? For rational consciousness blended with volitional consciousness cannot be identified with any processes of natural causation: in spiritual action man seems to erect himself, as a personal agent, above himself, as merely an event in the succession of natural occurrences. Unless above himself, as merely a part of visible nature, he *can* erect himself into an active, and therefore rational or supernatural spirit, how mean a thing is man. If he is under an absolute obligation to obey moral law, he cannot be in every respect part of the dependent causal mechanism. The way of looking at the universe that makes visible nature and natural causation the sole measure of reality must, if man is a moral agent, be inadequate as a philosophical theory.

Science and morality in man imply more than natural sequence. Thus science and morality in man both seem to involve more than physical sequence. The dogma of the speculative naturalist, that an outer world of interpretable things acts upon a human intelligence mechanically, as bodies in motion "act" upon bodies at rest, so that the scientific interpretation of this experience by a discoverer is itself only a physical effect of the causality of the body,—is a dogmatic postulate, which seems to leave out of account man's participation in intuitive reason, and power of distinguishing between fancy and reality, in which the essence of our knowledge and its certainty consists. Defect in the dogma is still more obvious, when the speculative naturalist argues that the relation of motives to acts for which a human agent is responsible must be the same in kind as the causal relation which one body bears to another body, when motion in one physically follows impact by another in motion ; for this leaves out of account the difference between that superiority to physical nature which responsibility attributes to all agency that is either moral or immoral, and the dependence that is only natural and non-moral: for a natural cause is not held morally responsible for any of its physical effects, whether it is a sentient or insentient cause. The intellectual power of distinguishing between transitory appearances and the deeper realities which they signify—between immediate sense and even natural science—is a power in which the intellectual man erects himself, as supernatural, above himself, as merely sensuous and a part of nature. But the power of morally responsible choice between good and evil in action is emphatically that in which man is free either to erect himself above physical law and dependent causation, or to let his proper personality be wholly merged in nature.

Thus in man two ultimate mysteries seem to meet— the mystery of natural causation, and the mystery of moral or immoral will. In natural causation we find intelligible signs of an order with which nature is charged. Here we are involved in the mystery of eternal succession: since no natural cause can be self-determined, each physical antecedent presupposes one anterior, of which it has been in its turn the physical effect or equivalent. Self-determining intelligence, and responsibility for what is personally determined, seems to contradict the presupposed universality of natural causation, and puts us face to face with an origi-

The ultimate mysteries of infinite temporal regress and a moral causality.

R

native cause, as that to which alone power is rightly attributed.

Natural or dependent, and moral or independent, causality. Man, intermediate between the nescient and the omniscient, can neither imagine nor comprehend the final reality in either of these two ways. He cannot comprehend an unbeginning and unending series of causal metamorphoses of dependent phenomena, all connected under physical laws, and as means to ends; nor can he comprehend a universe of self-determining spiritual agents. Natural causation in its ultimate implicates, and morally responsible agency in its ultimate implicates, are both alike *incompletely* intelligible, at the scientific point of view. Each conception, necessarily incomplete, is therefore necessarily mysterious for an intelligence that can comprehend and judge only in part, and not at the eternal or infinite centre. But this human incompleteness deprives man of the right in reason to conclude, that natural causation, on the one hand, and, on the other hand, morally responsible *acts* of which the human agent, not the Active Reason immanent in all natural causation, is the originating source—are two contradictory conceptions. Man's conception of natural causation is not complete enough to justify the conclusion that a sinful action *must* be determined by the Power revealed in the sequences of nature;—not by the person who is regarded by the moral reason as morally responsible for it. The presence in the universe of agents who are responsible for what ought not to enter into existence, and therefore had not any material necessity for existing, is accordingly *intellectually possible*: man's experience of remorse is a practical proof that man's supernatural independence is true in fact. Conscience points to supernatural agency, in the form of intending self-conscious acts of persons, whose *self*-originating causality can be brought home to them by their moral experience. This experience introduces a deeper meaning into causality than that which this word connotes when it is affirmed of a merely natural or caused cause. An immoral act *must originate* in the immoral agent; a physical effect is not *known to originate* in its physical cause.

Thus cosmic faith and moral faith are both alike concerned with what is incompletely intelligible under the conditions of physical reasoning; therefore neither can be scientifically proved to be so related to the other as to be incapable of mutual reconciliation under a higher principle. Scientific faith in physical necessity need not subvert moral or religious faith in what is higher than physical necessity, yet not necessarily inconsistent with it. Cosmic faith and moral faith.

The profound question of the relation between persons morally responsible for acts and the order of nature is suggested by some sentences in Professor Huxley's interesting essay on the hypothesis that animals may be automata,—including, of course, the human animal. " It seems to me," he says, " that in The relation between natural changes and personal agency.

men as in brutes there is no proof that any state of
consciousness is the cause of change in the motion of
the matter of the organism. . . . It follows that our
mental conditions are simply the symbols in consciousness of the changes which take place automatically in
the organism ; and that, to take an extreme illustration,
the feeling we call volition is not the cause of a voluntary [overt] act, but the symbol of that state of the
brain which is the immediate cause of that act." As
viewed in this statement, men are only organisms,
not persons, — visible and tangible *things*, with each
of which conscious life is inexplicably found connected, — consciousness in men being more fully developed, under *its* natural causes, than the sentient
intelligence which is associated with the organisms of
other animals on this planet. But in all animals conscious life is impotent: it is discounted as wholly
irrelevant in this scientific explanation of man. The
metamorphoses which the inorganic and organised
material world undergoes, in the persistent processes
of natural causation which science tries to register and
formulate, are all independent of conscious "agency"
as a factor. Man is not entitled, on account of his
felt responsibility for his acts or otherwise, to be
included as a factor of actions, or even among those
conditions of events which constitute collectively, in
each case of change, what natural science means by
a "cause." For conscious self-determination is not
found to be an ingredient in the constitution of physi-

cally conceived causes, the external process of trans-
forming these into the new relations that are called
their effects being alone of scientific interest. Absolute
origination is not an *imaginable condition* which is
connected, in the way a physical cause is, with the
occurrence of events in the historical evolution of the
universe. We are deluded, it seems, when we suppose
personal or self-contained agency; for no volition of
which one is conscious can either increase or diminish
molecular motion in the brain, as its physical cause:
all cerebral changes must be naturally caused by
motions, organic or extra-organic, external to themselves, which it is the office of biological science to
observe and formulate.

But although biology may reasonably confine itself
in this way to the natural causation of physical phenomena, and may thus banish from biological thought
the hyper-physical ground of the moral relations of
persons, either to one another or to the physical
phenomena they are commonly supposed to modify,
I am unable to see with Mr Huxley that this justifies
"the gradual banishment from *all* regions of human
thought of what we call spirit and spontaneity;" for
by "spontaneity" I suppose he means acts which,
when regarded as morally referable to an agent, are
inferred to be free or independent of natural causation, on account of the agent's exclusive responsibility
for them. Instead of this banishment of "spontaneity,"
biology, as well as every science of visible nature, seems

(marginal note:) The relation of
"spirit and
spontan-
eity" to
the physi-
cal order.

to place us face to face with an ulterior reality, suggested by the intellectual and ethical correlation between the material world and the intelligent and intending person to whom moral responsibility is referred. It makes us ask, what the presumed agreement between human intelligence and natural causation means. It also makes us ask, how the numerous seeming "interferences" of moral and immoral agents with the otherwise customary course of nature can be reconciled with the exclusive sufficiency of visible causation, illustrated in inorganic and in organised processes, which biological naturalism confines itself to. The certainty of human knowledge surely implies some deeper connection between what are commonly called "conscious" agents and the molecular motions in the brain of the supposed agent, then, through the brain, with molecular motions throughout the universe. Moral responsibility for a human act depends upon the agent who is morally praised or blamed for it being an independent or self-contained power, *so far as* that act is moral or immoral,—so far, therefore, independent of the natural causation to which "states of the brain" are subject. A community between the intelligence that is manifested consciously in man, and the intelligence that is latent in nature, signified to man in interpretable sensuous signs, is the explanation of human sciences of nature. The postulate of a self-contained power that is above the conditions of physical causation, seems to be indispensable for any act of which the agent can be

morally praised or blamed ; although the relation of
man's moral or immoral acts to the supreme natural
order and purpose must be only imperfectly intelligible,
if both the idea of physical causality and the idea of
free agency are ultimately incomplete or mysterious.

The exclusion of questions of this order, not only
from biology as a special science, but also from "all
human thought," seems to land the persistent thinker
in some curious paradoxes. If blended rational and
volitional life, and all that is involved in this, are
irrelevant accidents in the inorganic and organic
causal history or evolution of the universe, it seems
to follow that all changes in the material world would
have occurred exactly as they have occurred, even if
rational and volitional consciousness had never arisen.
The contrivances in nature with which *men* are credited or discredited must all be placed, in that case,
to the credit or discredit of the Power manifested in
nature. Commonly supposed products of the human
spirit must be conceived of as only part of the natural
history of human organisms. The books contained in
the world, for example, might have become what they
are by a law of natural selection, under which their
visible contents might have been evolved as we have
them, yet without consciousness on the part of the supposed authors and printers. The brilliant additions to
scientific literature for which we are grateful to Professor Huxley, when we refer them to his self-conscious
agency, are only the natural issue of an organism,

Some curi‑
ous para‑
doxes.

itself one of the issues of the gradual evolution of the material universe: his published works might have existed exactly as they exist now, if neither his conscious life nor any other had ever made its appearance in the universe. If consciousness and postulated personal activity are really irrelevant accidents in the procession of molecular motions, what proof can I have that at this moment mine is not the solitary conscious life in an unconscious world? On what reasonable ground can I assert that I am now speaking in the presence of conscious persons; or how can each hearer know that the words which he hears are not undulations of the air, that have been naturally caused by molecular motions in a visible organism, themselves the natural issues of molecular changes in organic or extra-organic nature, conveyed under the natural laws of sound to the organ of hearing in human organisms? Perhaps I am now in the presence of unconscious automatic organisms.

Sense phenomena significant of other self-conscious persons.

In Berkeley's 'Minute Philosopher,' Euphranor, one of the interlocutors, in a dialogue concerning the religious conception of the universe, argues that we have at least as clear, full, and immediate certainty of the supernatural existence of an infinitely wise and powerful Spirit as each of us has of the existence of any other self-conscious life besides his own. "What!" rejoins Alciphron, the other interlocutor, "What! do you pretend you can have the same assurance of the being of a *God* that you can have of *mine*, whom you

actually see standing before you and talking to you ? "
"The very same, if not greater," is the reply. "How
do you make this appear?" asks Alciphron. "By the
person Alciphron," Euphranor replies, "is meant an individual *thinking* person, and not the hair, skin, or
visible surface, or any part of the outward form,
colour, or shape of Alciphron." "This I grant," replies the sceptic. "And in granting this," Euphranor
argues, "you grant that in a strict sense I do not *see*
Alciphron, but only such visible signs and tokens as
suggest and infer the being of that *invisible* thinking
principle or soul. Even so, in the self-same manner,
it seems to me that, though I cannot with the eyes
of flesh behold the invisible God, yet I do in the
strictest sense behold and perceive, by all my senses,
such operations as suggest, indicate, and demonstrate
an invisible God, as certainly and with the same evidence as other signs, perceived by sense, do suggest
to me the existence of *your* soul, spirit, or thinking
principle,—which I am convinced of only by a few
signs or effects, and the motions of one small organised
body; whereas I do at all times and in all places
perceive sensible signs which evince the being of a
God."

The argument here is, that the universe must be the The agency
of Mind in
expression of Universal Mind, because of the order, the uni-
and relations of means to ends, which mark the course verse.
of its events: we have the same sort of evidence for
the Universal Mind, although that Mind is invisible,

as we have for the existence of other self-conscious human persons in the phenomena of their visible organisms, which are reasonably taken to signify their invisible self-conscious existence. Just as I am assured that the intending activity of another human being is the explanation of the audible words and visible actions which I refer to him, so I am bound in reason to recognise, with at least equal assurance, the existence of supreme intending Will, as the explanation of the order and purpose presupposed in a scientifically interpretable world. Divine spirit is embodied in the great sense-symbolism of the world, just as human spirits are embodied in the little sense-symbolisms presented to us in the history of the small organised bodies which resemble what we each call " our own body." But if, even in the case of human organisms, there is no possibility that self-determined conscious agency is the origin of any of their motions, it follows that the ordering and designing purpose of a man is as illogically concluded from the words and actions of a human organism as Divine Purpose from the laws and ends with which the infinite organism of the universe seems to present. There is as little room for originative human agency as for originative divine agency. All that is commonly attributed to a calculating consciousness in men is explicable, it seems, as the natural issue of the unconscious processes of natural causation in organisms. The human race, and the whole animal world, with all their so-called works, may be part of an unconscious evolution of which I am the solitary conscious spectator. Morally responsible personality, with free intending will as its implicate, is a practically superfluous adjunct of the organism I call mine, and a like superfluity if it is annexed to other organisms as well as to mine. But I have no proof that the other organisms are also connected with conscious life, if all their words and overt actions might be what they are, only through organic and inorganic natural causality. The unconscious natural succession of molecular changes in each human organism, without the "interference" of any conscious intelligence and will, would be a sufficient explanation of this printed essay on animal automatism. Neither world - making nor watchmaking would presuppose spiritual activity ; for worlds and watches are equally the issue solely of the natural orderly evolution of the visible and tangible phenomena that form into watches and into worlds. Each is an ultimately meaningless natural growth; and the "adaptations" in each are at last merged in unexplained and inexplicable original variations in atoms, which therein appear to exemplify a law of unconscious natural selection.

But what, I would again ask, are natural automatic changes in an organism, and through organisms in extra-organic things, when the changes and their subjects are totally abstracted from perception and consciousness ? What is the 'Principia,' or what the 'Essay Concerning Human Understanding,' without

Matter, inorganic and organic, presupposes mind ; but mind does not equally presuppose matter.

conscious intelligence and intending purpose in Newton and Locke, who are responsible for them, and
without conscious activity in their supposed readers?
The words printed on the pages of a book *become
significant* only when consciousness makes its appearance. The continuous drama of natural creation, in
the course of which the visible 'Principia' is supposed
duly to take its place, has proceeded in harmony with
an immanent reason; so that although I have no
physical proof, on account of its appearance, that
another mind is responsible for it, I yet find the
sensible signs so in harmony with my own conscious
intelligence that I cannot resist the conviction that a
great intelligence was the author. Whether the relation between another person and the visible evolution
is called a relation of cause and effect or not, it is
a relation such as that the visible appearances are
accepted as a reasonable guarantee for the invisible
and foreign intending mind. I cannot banish the
latter, and then fully think out my experience on the
hypothesis of the exclusive reality of the former. A
human intending will is responsible for the sensuous
signs of meaning and purpose which a human organism
presents. The immoral act for which the individual
murderer is held morally responsible cannot be shifted
off to the non-moral organism, and thus finally to the
Power that is supreme in nature.

Natural
causation
is descrip-
When the meaning of the words "matter" and
"force" is considered, in the light of sensuous and

spiritual experience, it would appear that the discovery of the natural sign of a change is no real explanation of it; and also that our idea of originating power on which change finally depends is got from reflection upon our own irresistible conviction of moral responsibility for all deliberately intended acts, which must therefore be self-originated. "I *ought*, therefore I *can*," is the moral index which points to the *agency of persons* as man's highest conception of causality or power in himself and in the universe. Consciousness of the moral ideal is consciousness of duty or moral obligation; but there can be no obligation of duty unless there is, so far as duty, absolute power within the agent either to obey or to disobey. The human subject of a moral obligation must, as capable of the obligation, be free from a divine mechanism of natural causation. The act must be his own, not merely a term in that chain of physical causes and effects, which is otherwise conceived as the continuous metamorphoses which the Supreme Power makes visible nature gradually pass through. The only ultimate or originative power that enters into human experience seems to be moral or spiritual, so that this is the only sort of ultimate explanation of the universe causation that man can apprehend.

tive of processes; conscience is the index which points to their originating cause.

Intelligent self-originated volition — under obligation of duty, — necessarily involved in personal responsibility,—is that in man which I call supernatural. As a merely sentient being, he is wholly, or almost

The supernatural in man.

wholly, an event in the orderly natural system, as empty of supernatural causality as any other phenomenon in the passive natural sequences. In his moral acts man appears to exemplify that final principle on which natural order ultimately depends; and in the elements of his moral personality we seem to have what man may take as (for him) the type of the supreme supernatural principle of the universe—a principle deeper than, yet consistent with and presupposed in, cosmic faith in natural uniformity, and called God when conceived as the ever active moral Reason. See the contrast between the mechanism of nature and supernatural agency in the familiar words of our great religious poet :—

> " Look up to heaven ! the industrious sun
>   Already half his race hath run ;
>   He *cannot* halt, nor go astray,
>   But our immortal spirits *may*."

Causality and conscience.

The final meaning of cause is thus reached through conscience, and in the ethical conception of the universe we seem to have a deeper and truer hold of reality than when it is treated only as a scientifically interpretable system of sense signs. *Man at his highest*, acting freely under moral obligation, with its implied intellectual and moral postulates, is suggested as a more fitting key to the ultimate interpretation of things than man only as an animal organism, abstracted from the moral experience that is often un-

conscious in the human individual, but is realised fully
in the Ideal Man, and can be disclaimed by imperfect
men only by disclaiming human responsibility.

The Macrocosm in analogy with the microcosm—the
supreme Power in nature in analogy with what is
highest in man, the *homo mensura,* when the *homo*
means the moral and spiritual, as well as the merely
sensuous man,—in this analogy, for which the contents
of consciousness supply the materials, we seem to have
the best light within man's reach for the true philosophy of the universe. The Macro-
cosm in
analogy
with the
human mi-
crocosm.

I do not know whether the leading suggestion of
this lecture, indeed of this whole course, is or is not in
contradiction to the thesis of Professor Drummond,
when he announces "natural law in the spiritual world,"
and especially in his 'Ascent of Man,' because I do not
fully understand its philosophical meaning. If this implies that the natural world of things, as distinguished
from the moral world of persons, is a continual and
immediate manifestation of God, it is a fundamental
conception which I am trying to recommend. But if
it were meant to subordinate spiritual life to natural
causation conceived only physically, and so to make
physical causation the final mode of looking at the
universe, with a sufficient explanation of the spiritual
world in organised matter, the 'Ascent' would be a
fanciful historical exposition of Universal Materialism.
Perhaps the intention is to suggest that no hypothesis The
'Ascent of
Man.'

regarding changes merely in the material organism can be inconsistent with the supremacy of spiritual law throughout the perennial evolutionary struggle in the natural world.

The religious instinct in man.

The religious consciousness in man is nearly connected with the consciousness of moral obligation, and implied power to make personal action conform or not conform to the ideal of duty. I suppose that religion postulates the faith that nature is an ally dependent on active moral reason, and this for us at least means dependence on a *personal agent*, along with the state of feeling and will which is the accompaniment of this faith, in its different degrees of intensity and intelligence. As a feeling religion includes reverential trust in the principle that is supreme in the universe; and for those with whom a merely cosmic faith in uniformities of natural order is the deepest principle which they recognise, this faith is, in a manner, their religion. But when faith goes no deeper than the cosmic postulate; when it is emptied of the ingredients contributed by man's experience of himself as a moral or supernatural being—this non-moral faith contains no *absolute* guarantee that intelligence may not be in the end put to confusion, even in the scientific application of an ultimate trust in physical uniformity. Seeming cosmic order may in the end be physical and moral anarchy, and life intrusted to a faith so thin and shallow is, after all, not worth living. Pessimist despair, instead of religious hope and reverence, is not uncongenial to the worship of a wholly physical causality, that god of agnostic science. So that although this cosmic faith in an impersonal or non-moral universe, when it is the final trust of any, may be called *their* religion, it is not religion in the full meaning of the word. It falls short of it, in so far as religion involves reconciliation through what is spiritual or supernatural being at the heart of things. Now man's rational and volitional consciousness contains the only example, in his experience, of what the words moral and supernatural mean. This makes it true that on earth "there is nothing great but man;" and that "in man there is nothing great but mind" or personal consciousness, with its implicates of reason and will and love. Does not the scientific agnosticism which explains away or overlooks this destroy the only foundation for a final faith that is absolute?

The religious instinct which interprets the final Power practically as perfect moral personality, not merely non-moral physical mechanism, must itself be taken into account as a verifying experience, for justifying the final interpretation of ourselves and things around us. As developed in the religious experience which has found its highest expression in Hebrew and Christian Scripture, it gives therein the verification of facts to the theistic interpretation of the universe. But even in other forms, and in lesser degrees, a

The verification of the moral interpretation of the universe by the religions of the world.

s

mental experience of religious faith is a fact in the history of mankind so widespread and persistent, that it claims recognition as a legitimate factor in the solution of the universal problem; with as much reason as data of sense and cosmic faith receive recognition in the physical interpretation of nature and in common life. The misery of man when the divine centre is lost or obscured receives eloquent expression in the 'Pensées' of Pascal: the distress may be taken as part of the proof in experience that when religious faith and thought are dormant, an essential condition of harmony between the man and his surroundings is absent, and that his true ideal and chief end in the system of the universe is not recognised. The religious instinct, in its many forms, but especially in its Christian, has been the chief factor in the history of mankind. It is a motive in human conduct, in no way less notable than the cosmic faith which I believe that it is able to assimilate with itself, and in assimilating to humanise, by showing that the spiritual conception of the universe is more fully philosophical for man than the merely physical. If cosmic faith is the assurance that the material world will not in the end put to *intellectual* confusion those who rely on the universality of its natural order, this blended moral and religious faith not only guarantees the physical faith itself, but is the *absolute* assurance that the Supreme Power will not put to permanent *moral* confusion those who strive permanently to realise the ideals of truth and beauty and goodness; or who trust absolutely in infinite love, in and through which all things somehow work together for good to those who thus live. The God represented in the Ideal Man is thus for man the available revelation and guarantee of God or goodness on the throne of the universe.

LECTURE X.

WHAT IS GOD?

Simonides and Hiero.

IN the opening words of the present course, I alluded to "the prudent reserve of Simonides," who, according to the familiar story, being asked by Hiero, *What God was?* desired a day to think out the question, and then two days more, after that continually enlarging the time needed for finding the answer, but without ever being able to bring in a definition of God. During the months, since these opening words were spoken, Hiero's question has been pressing itself upon us in many forms. Are we now readier with an answer than Simonides was?

This course of lectures deals exclusively with the way in which man ought finally to interpret the universe.

The design of the present course of lectures, as I explained at the outset, does not comprehend discussion of special problems of religious thought. Some of these I hope to deal with next winter. At present I am concerned with the previous question of the credibility of *any* theological conception of existence. I am asking how the universe should finally be regarded by man? Must it be under the conception of mathematical quantity, or of physical causation only, as with Spinoza and Hume; or may it with reason be regarded as essentially supernatural reality, in analogy with man as a moral agent, and his higher experience? We have been thinking out the question, whether the general theistic problem, which involves the special problems and difficulties of religion, can be determined, or whether, on the contrary, it cannot enter within man's intellectual horizon. Is the modern physical conception of the universe the highest that is attainable; or is this conception—valid as far as it is verified by facts and reasonings that rest on cosmic faith—inadequate when measured by man as a moral being? Is the monotheistic interpretation of the universe the really reasonable one finally, under the more comprehensive faith, which sustains not only discursive reason in relation to data of sensuous perception, but reason in relation to all the data of moral and spiritual as well as sensuous experience?

I have accordingly tried to present for your consideration, in a philosophic temper, the chief ways in which the universe is looked at, by those who seek to satisfy themselves about the Power that is supremely and finally at work in it. The constructive conceptions of Universal Materialism, Panegoism, and Pantheism, were tried provisionally in succession; and I asked your candid consideration of what seemed unsatisfying,

Non-theistic interpretations of the universe.

because inadequate, in each, while not overlooking the partial truth which gives to each what strength it has. If you would convince another who really loves truth, of defect in conception, you must try to see the side at which things are looked at by him; for on that side his view of them is probably true: by seeing a truth, common to him and to you, he may more readily recognise with you what is wanting in his own conception. In the same spirit we next tried provisionally the destructive or agnostic way of looking at theism and theology, more or less adopted by some in this generation. Here all final conceptions of the universe other than a negative one disappear, and with them, when the agnosticism is bold enough, faith in everything that appears in experience, whether sensuous or spiritual; so that all supposed human knowledge, or interpretation of experience, subsides into the total darkness of universal nescience.

The correlation of cosmic or physical, and religious or theistic faith.

But the mental state in which one doubts about everything is a state in which man cannot live. Even animal life in man includes perceptions of some things, and faith in some of their physical meanings. We cannot live without eating and drinking, and we cannot eat or drink without faith in the nutriment, or in the agreeable sensations, which we believe the visible food to signify, when it is only seen, and before it is tasted. We are daily living in the movement which we call an experience of what is actual. How deep can we go in interpreting the meaning of experience?

Ought we to put a fully theistic meaning at last upon data of experience; or may we, must we, be contented to interpret it under the attenuated religious presupposition (if it may be called religious) of a wholly physical or non-moral order, with its physical or non-moral religion? Does God, or the final principle, mean only the ultimatély inexplicable natural order; or does God mean ever-active moral reason and purpose, at the root of an always divinely sustained physical order, in which God is Supreme? Is the universe to be finally interpreted in and through what is found in man—man at his highest or best—man with his ineradicable conviction of moral responsibility, and his religious consciousness that even the natural universe must be a manifestation of what he has to think of as the perfect reason of the ideal personality? Is the progressive evolution in space and time finally interpretable in the light of faith in the moral responsibility of man, which can rest on no fulcrum short of the centre of the universe, the throne of the Eternal living God? Or must it finally be interpreted in the darkness of an ultimately inexplicable, and possibly illusory, natural order, without a rational centre,—a sham cosmos in which there can be no absolute faith? Must it be this, and only this, although negation of spiritual faith is the crucifixion of that in man which seeks a sufficient response in perfect reason and goodness at the heart of things? Is there anything in the constitution of external nature, or of human understanding, that forbids man to interpret the universe finally as the revelation of a Power that, so far as he has to do with what is real, is in analogy with what is highest and best in himself; in harmony with his moral and religious ideals;—so that the ideal man may be taken practically as the representative or symbol of the true centre of the infinite reality iń which man finds himself, and with which he is connected in his whole living experience ? Is not intellectual and moral relief best found under this conception ?

A way open for a practical answer to Hiero's question ?

It is in this way of looking at the universe that I have sought for a practical answer to Hiero's question, an answer which might even have been offered by Simonides. It means that the question *may* be answered so far as it concerns the moral experience of man, while it is still infinitely unanswerable. It means that the deepest and truest thought man can have about the outside world, is that in which the natural universe is conceived as the immediate manifestation of the divine or infinite Person, in moral relation .to imperfect persons, who, in and through their experience of what is, are undergoing intellectual and spiritual education in really divine surroundings—the education in part consisting in struggles to master by obeying the physical nature with which they are continually in contact and collision, and which, in the light of their inner consciousness, is seen to be a revelation of the divine. It may thus be said that man may know God, and also that God cannot be known. And this blended knowledge and ignorance, real knowledge of that which yet passes knowledge, seems to be the final issue of human inquiry as to the co-existence of the three existences postulated in common experience. Nature or the outward world; each man in his own supernatural personality; and the Divine Supernature, on which Nature and Man depend—all these are in part, or practically, knowable: they can be known, that is to say, as far as human action in the universe needs the knowledge, as far, that is to say, as they enter into human experience, physical and spiritual. But reality as at the divine centre is only thus far cognisable, unless man can comprehend infinite experience in infinite reason. Perfect knowledge postulates an experience that is boundless in space and boundless in duration, and an intuition of reason which, transcending space and duration altogether, would be the intellectual vision of all as the omnipresent Eternal.

Physical science is reached by a leap in the dark, in the faith that the presence of physical order and purpose in nature will not suffer the physical inquirer to be put to confusion. Religion, too, is a leap in the dark, yet in hopeful faith in the constant agency of perfect moral reason, as the root not only of the physical order, but as the highest conception man can have of the universal principle of existence. So the moral or religious faith includes and justifies the physical. The Macrocosm, when looked at as

The scientific and the religious leaps in the dark, in faith and hope.

perfect or infinite microcosm, is found more human, more in harmony, that is to say, with the complete *homo mensura* principle of interpretation, than when looked at agnostically, as a finally unintelligible and wholly incalculable complex phenomenon presented to the senses,—which in the end may put us all to confusion. For the future history of *such* a universe may in the end contradict the presuppositions without which even physical science must dissolve in nescience, deprived of the witness of humanity to the conviction that we are living and moving and having our natural as well as our moral being in God. Is not man's most reconciling final relation to the infinite universe of reality, that of a person with a Perfect Person; an imperfect and fallible moral being with the Perfect Moral Being? Is not this idea needed even in order to justify confidence in that narrower intercourse with what is real, in which the physical interpreter hears the divine voice expressed, in terms of physical law, in the beneficent discoveries of the natural sciences and the advance of civilisation?

Revelations of God in and through man not excluded from our data by Lord Gifford's Deed.

I have presumed to include the revelation of the supernatural which one finds in moral and religious experience—not excluding as its most signal records those contained in Hebrew and Christian literature— as part of the material of a comprehensive Natural Theology — this notwithstanding the interdict which words in Lord Gifford's Deed may appear to put, especially upon the Hebrew and Christian books. But

I cannot suppose that the desire therein expressed, that Gifford lecturers should treat "the science of Infinite Being" without reference to any "supposed supernatural revelation," can be meant to exclude a reference in the name of reason to records of moral and religious experience which human beings are said to have gone through in Palestine or anywhere else. This remarkable experience, preserved in the Bible of Christianity, or in the catholic traditions of Christendom, whatever else it may be, is at least part of the history of mankind. It presents religious thoughts and faith to which men who once lived on this planet gave expression. If a bar is to exclude the student of natural theology from this recorded religious experience of mankind, and if he must be confined to the phenomena of external nature, in the way an astronomer or a chemist confines himself, so that the theology may be in the narrow sense "natural" and "scientific," he is deprived of the most significant facts which help to determine man's relation to the final problem of existence. As well say that the astronomer must form astronomical science without reference to the special revelations of astronomical law that are presented in the movements of the solar system, as that the philosophical theologian must deal with the ultimate problem of the universe without reference to the spiritual experience of persons signally inspired by the religious interpretation of life. A fruitful and not an abstract inquiry is surely what is wanted.

That God seemed to be mentally experienced in the way prophets and apostles say that they experienced God, is a recorded fact in the history of what has happened in the minds of persons who lived on this planet; whatever weight may be given to the recorded experience, or whatever explanation may be got through it, of the system of the universe.

A "God" compre-hensible in the tem-porally condi-tioned ex-perience of man cannot be God.

But is the God conceived only after the analogy of what is highest in man an adequate conception of the Infinite Reality? Does not the very spiritual experience of religiously inspired men bear witness to the truth, that the God who *can* be comprehended by man cannot be the Infinite God? It may be asked whether it is reasonable to suppose that the idea of God as Infinite Man is a solution of the final problem; and this only because it corresponds to what is highest in the implicates of the experience of an ephemeral race of living beings, on one of the lesser planets of the solar system? To conclude that a final conception of Being which thus lets itself down to man may be a solution of the final problem looks like arrogant assumption, the issue of sectarian narrowness, which makes the insignificant sect called mankind the measure of the Infinite Reality.

The human idea of God verified by man's ex-perience of the con-

It would be so, if this human finality were taken as adequate to the absolute reality. But the human finality is not offered as the conception of God taken from the divine centre—only as the conception of God necessarily taken at a human standpoint away from sequences of its rejection. the centre. It is only offered as the best conception possible at the intermediate position, where man may nevertheless find what is even eternally true for that position;—the real knowledge of an intelligence that cannot become omniscient, or know the actual contents of time independently of their conditions of time and change. It may be that which, when held intelligently by man, alone puts *him* in absolute rational harmony with the universe, and its acceptance then becomes the condition of success in the endeavour to live according to the deepest and truest *human* relation to what is real. That the religious conception of the universe works well, when rightly accepted and acted on, may be one example of the relation of means and ends on a supreme scale. Can rejection be justified, if this unfits the sceptic, as a complete human being, for his surroundings, or obscures the best ideal of man's office in the universe?

I have said that much in the records of the religious Supposed superconsciousness of the Divine Being. experience of mankind, in the various religions of the world, as well as the theory of human knowledge implied in these lectures, teaches the lesson that God is infinitely incognisable, while practically knowable in the spiritual interpretation of the universe which our moral and religious experience seems to justify. But one may ask, What kind of Spirit or Mind is this? Are we to imagine the divine intellectual life as a succession of changing acts like those of the inner life in man; or instead as one unchanging intuition of all that is, has been, and is yet to be; or as something different from, because superconsciously transcending, either of these representations? It is suggested that we must suppose God superconscious. But superconsciousness is something that, divorced from what is highest in man, is for us below, while nominally above, all intellect, feeling, and will. The very attempt to conceive a "Mind" of this sort lands the human mind in contradictions. It is suggested "that there may be in the infinite universe something grander and greater than consciousness. There may be species of existence, modes of being innameable by us, which are yet infinitely superior to consciousness, more to be desired than consciousness; and this chapter of greater chances may be even open to *us* in a future state. The division of the sphere of existence roundly into two parts—the conscious and the unconscious — is misleading: the second segment of the sphere, to wit, the unconscious, containing vastly more than the first; while also *its* separate divisions and modes may be wholly different from each other, though all confounded under one name—the unconscious. To divide existence into the conscious and unconscious provinces is as if we were to divide animals into men and not-men, where the second expresses a far greater sum of life than the first, though without reference to any of its differential features. So the word 'unconscious,' or 'not-conscious,'

strictly speaking, expresses no more than the absence
of consciousness, while the sphere of the unconscious
may embrace modes of being amongst which some
greater than consciousness may have place.   There
may be behind the phenomenal curtain something
grander than consciousness, though of course in-
describable. Philosophers, mystics, poets, prophets, and
revealers are all as impotent as the men of science to
say what this may be, though they have been for ever
putting their souls on the stretch to describe this
great and unexplored continent between consciousness
and annihilation.   To know and tell this would be to
know and tell all."   All this seems to suppose that
the superconscious God would be God in reality, and
not God as reached in and through the highest ideal
of man.   But the attempt so to think of God seems
to land those who make it in a lower idea than that
held when we think of Deity as infinitely magnified
man.   Known yet unknown,—known for the ends of
our moral and religious life,—unknown because incapable of perfect intellectual comprehension — the
one signal example of how human knowledge may be
real while the reality that is known passes out of
knowledge.

This abates the claims of transcendent idealism, which, *Solvitur ambulando.*
dissatisfied with a physical and theological knowledge
that is only in part, professes to interpret all from the
divine centre in what is therefore bound to be a virtual
omniscience, while in fact it supplies only a critical

analysis, or a dialectical synthesis, of abstract necessities of reason, instead of solving those mysteries of experience in time, from which philosophy draws its human interest. To the absolute idealist who finds inadequacy in a final conception of the universe that is determined, on the *homo mensura* principle, by what is highest in man, one can only say that its refutation is in his own hands. *Solvitur ambulando.* Let him produce the omniscience which the humbler philosophy method is blamed for not producing. Let him rid the life of all its mysteries, not by restating them in new language, but by solving them — thus superseding moral faith by perfect rational insight of the infinite universe. Let him actually show us what the universe presented in duration is as seen at its divine centre. The sight would supersede adverse criticism of the intermediate position with which I am satisfied.

The ultimate incomprehensibility of God by man sustains devotional reverence —Illustrations.

The mystery of an unknown and yet known God is the fountain of true reverential devotion, which instinctively feels that all sensuous and spiritual representations must be inadequate to infinite Being. This is the expressed voice of religious consciousness, when it is sufficiently awakened. The visible and invisible images of Catholicism, and not less the invisible mental representations of popular Protestantism, when presented as adequate to God, are rejected by the true worshipper. His language is:—

"Thou shalt not make unto thee any graven image,

or any likeness of any thing that is in heaven above, or that is in the earth beneath, or that is in the water under the earth : thou shalt not bow down thyself to them, nor serve them."

" Canst thou by searching find out God ? canst thou find out the Almighty unto perfection ? "

" O Lord, how great are thy works ! and thy thoughts are very deep. . . . Great is our Lord : His understanding is infinite."

" God hath set the world in their heart, so that no man can find out the work that God maketh from the beginning to the end. Then I beheld all the work of God, that a man cannot find out the work that is done under the sun : because though a man labour to seek it out, yet he shall not find it ; yea farther, though a wise man think to know it, yet shall he not be able to find it."

" To whom then will ye liken God ? or what likeness will ye compare unto Him ? There is no searching of His understanding. As the heavens are higher than the earth, so are my ways higher than your ways, and my thoughts than your thoughts."

" O the depth of the riches both of the wisdom and knowledge of God ! how unsearchable are His judg-ments, and His ways past finding out."

" I know in part. Now abideth faith, hope, love, these three, and the greatest of these is love."

Acknowledgment of the incomprehensibility of God, when men try to conceive Deity in absolute infinity, *Christian agnosti-cism.*

T

and not merely in and through what is highest and best in themselves, is an agnosticism that is implied in the language of the great thinkers of the Catholic Church. It is reiterated in the teaching of Origen and Augustine. Chrysostom speaks of God as transcending all apprehension of human knowledge; the universe of experience as from its divine centre is incomprehensible to even the highest order of finite intelligence. With Gregory of Nazianzen God alone is, in a unique sense, unknown. The pseudo-Dionysius supposes that God is infinitely above our knowledge, superconscious, above substance, above mind or spirit, above life. In the hyperbolical language of other Christian thinkers, God in His infinity is more than unknown: He is not unknown merely in the way in which the finite things that are outside the experience of an individual man are to him unknown : He is transcendently above human apprehension as such: He is without substance, and without actual existence.

Religious philosophy must therefore be in the end "abrupt," or at its highest, take the form of faith, not of perfectly intelligible unity.

Theology is therefore concerned with what is in part really cognisable, yet in its infinity incognisable. It is concerned with ideas of infinity which cannot be excluded, because they are finally presupposed in all natural or physical, and still more in all supernatural or spiritual experience ; yet these characteristic ideas cannot be completed in human understanding, because, however much enlarged, they must in us fall short, as fragments only of the infinite Reality,—if without absurdity one may speak of a "fragment" of infinity, or suppose that what transcends quantity can nevertheless be expressed in terms of greater or less quantity.

> " Our little systems have their day ;
> They have their day, and cease to be :
> They are but broken lights of Thee,
> And Thou, O Lord, art more than they.
>
> We have but faith : we cannot know,
> For knowledge is of things we see ;
> And yet we trust it comes from Thee,
> A beam in darkness : let it grow."

This unique character of man's highest possible knowledge of God, or of the final meaning of the universe, in which reason becomes moral faith, may have been in Bacon's view when he warns us that "perfection or completeness in divinity is not to be sought. For he that will reduce a knowledge into an art [or science] will make it round and uniform; but in divinity many things must be left abrupt. As the apostle saith, 'we know in part'; and to have the form of a total [as science requires] where there is but matter for a part, cannot be without supplies by supposition and presumption." It is man's constant need, in physical as in religious science, for what Bacon calls "supplies by supposition and presumption" that at last makes all human knowledge of real existence a *faith* or *trust* rather than perfect rational insight; so that faith or trust is man's highest form of reason, alike at last in natural and in supernatural science. But

Man's need for "supplies by supposition and presumption " in his interpretation of the universe.

here *reason* must be distinguished from *reasoning*, with which it is often confounded in a way that makes the word ambiguous. All fruitful reasoning presupposes reason, or rational trust in the reasonable, and nothing can be reasonably accepted that is inconsistent with the faith that we are living and thinking in a universe in which active moral Reason is supreme. Omniscience, as far as we can suppose what that means, seems to involve not only infinite rational relations, but infinite data of sense; thus superseding those "supplies by supposition and presumption" only, which Bacon finds indispensable for the intelligence of man. Omniscience seems to dispense with hypotheses, and even with reasoning. Intuitive, not discursive, thought is our ideal of infinite intelligence. Human knowledge, on the other hand, is advanced through the intervention of what is supposed to be already known — that is to say, by means of applied reasoning in discursive thought. But this resort for intellectual advancement must not be confounded with reason as that which *finally* authenticates conclusions, or interpretations of what is experienced: this, for distinction' sake, may be called faith, or moral trust.

Reasoning, as distinguished from finally constructive Reason, a symptom of finitude of intelli-   Mere argument, or reasoning as distinguished from the final reason, seems to be a mark of finitude in the intelligence that is obliged to employ it. To a mind that is able to comprehend all things, and all their relations, in one intellectual grasp, inferential thought must be a superfluity. We have illustration of this

in the mental experience even of men. Inventive gence and experience in the reasoner.
genius discerns in a flash of intellectual insight truth
to which a less comprehensive intellect needs to be
conducted by slow processes of syllogism and calcu-
lated comparison of instances. The dogmatic arguer,
who never thinks that his favourite ultimate premisses can need justification, or admit of criticism,
is a poor specimen of the reasoner; for reasoning is
worthy of respect only when it is used as a human
instrument for finding truth. In itself it only makes
patent what was latent in its premisses; the premisses
may be false; and the highest minds often see conclusions at once without the elaboration of reasoning.
It is told of a great mathematician that he could at
once recognise in the axioms and definitions of geometry truths which Euclid slowly evolves as conclusions in long trains of demonstration.

Again. The living mind that man has immediate Finite intelligence manifested in succes-sions of conscious acts and states, or under condition of dura-tion.
experience of is one in which conscious states are
succeeding one another in a continuous series, for
life as we have it is change. Our daily consciousness is a historical procession of invisible states of
blended thought, feeling, and volition. Can we suppose that anything like this is true of God? Is a
succession of ever-changing conscious acts taking place
continuously in the Infinite Being, contemporaneously
with our own conscious states and acts? and does
this divine succession consist of an infinite number of
such states, so that the divine succession of changing

thoughts is without beginning and without end? Must not this be more than an inadequate way of thinking about what we in much ignorance call "mind" in God? One need not take for granted that an eternal succession of changes is in itself a self-contradictory conception, as some have done in arguing for the existence of God. I do not know what an *eternal succession* of changes—either sensible phenomena or invisible conscious states—really means. Yet it is part of the mystery involved also in the future immortality of a finite conscious person; which we can only represent to ourselves as an endless succession of *future* self-conscious states or acts: at least if the immortal life is conceived as continued for ever in analogy and identity with the personal life now experienced by each man. But the self-consciousness of God is an idea that contains other difficulties than those which in the end are found in all attempts to form an idea of an unending personal consciousness. The relation of time to eternity, in whatever way it is approached, is the mystery of mysteries. A conscious life that lasts for millions of years *is* supposable, though it transcends human imagination: a conscious life that has *no beginning, and no end*, passes the apprehension of human knowledge.

The insight gained in resuming the three   At the end thus far of our meditations, we find ourselves on the shore of the infinite ocean, which contains the mysteries in the presence of which human thought about God, and about the Ego and Matter too, in their final relation to God, at last disappears. We have reached it by the human road, which is as it were at the side: we could not find our way to its divine depth. In the end we may even appear to have returned to the place from which we started, in " the simple creed of childhood," with its three postulated existences; but now in our return we see them all, may I hope, in some new lights.

postulated existences, after making the reflective circle which we have traversed in this course.

As to this, I might say, with regard to the final problem of life or existence, what Philonous in Berkeley's 'Dialogue' says about *his* question, concerning the final meaning of Matter. "I do not pretend to be a setter up of new notions. My endeavours tend only to unite and place in a clearer light truth which was before shared between the vulgar and philosophers. You see the water of yonder fountain, how it is forced upwards in a round column and a certain height; at which it breaks, and falls back into the basin out of which it arose: its ascent as well as descent proceeding on the same uniform law or principle of gravitation. Just so, the principles which at first view lead to scepticism, pursued to a certain point bring men back to commonsense." "Atheism," as Bacon says, "is rather in the lip than in the heart of man," so that "depth in philosophy bringeth men's minds about to religion," if a little "inclineth them to atheism."

"Yonder fountain." Deep and shallow philosophy.

I have had this in view all through this Course— first sceptical of monist systems of philosophy, then

Philosophy consummated in God.

finally analytic of experience — over which we have travelled this winter. I have tried to approach with faithfulness to facts the deepest and truest principle that is within man's reach for the final interpretation of his experience. We have been led with Plato and Aristotle to see in God the apex and culmination of true philosophy. The theological interpretation of the universe is with the chief thinkers from Plato to Hegel its final interpretation,—the natural interpretation elevated in and by the supernatural, which last is itself enriched by every discovery of natural science. When nature is seen to be God acting, so that each discovery in natural science is also a contribution to natural theology, it seems evident that collision between advancing science and religious faith is not possible. So with the poet we can at the end—

> " Raise
> The song of thanks and praise
> . . . For those obstinate questionings
> Of sense and outward things,
> Fallings from us, vanishings ;
> Blank misgivings of a creature
> Moving about in worlds not realised."

For there are found in man—

> " High instincts, before which our mortal nature
> Did tremble like a guilty thing surprised ! "

And latent in man's spirit are—

> " Those first affections,
> Those shadowy recollections,
> Which, be they what they may,
> Are yet the fountain light of all our day,

Are yet a master light of all our seeing :
    Uphold us—cherish—and have the power to make
Our noisy years seem moments in the being
Of the Eternal Silence : truths that wake,
      To perish never.
      Hence in a season of calm weather,
        Though inland far we be,
Our souls have sight of that immortal sea
    Which brought us hither ;
      Can in a moment travel thither—
And see the children sport upon the shore,
And hear the mighty waters rolling evermore."

We pause now, although we have hardly passed the threshold in this Introductory Course. The foundation in reason of the theistic interpretation of the universe ; the intellectual difficulties in which thought may seem to be involved by religion ; the alternatives of finality or progressiveness in moral judgments and in religious thought ; and the final destiny of moral agents,—are subjects which take us beyond the intention of this Course into Theistic Studies reserved for another winter, if life and health should be given to me.

INDEX.

A

Absolute, 188.

Agnosticism—and Materialism, 76 —stated by Professor Huxley, 196 ff.—its legitimacy as a presupposition, 198—reverses the teaching of Bacon, Descartes, and Locke, 201 ff.—and Kant, 204, 205—thought out by Hume, 205—and moral experience, 217 —and faith, 218, 223 ff.—and science, 219 — Christian, 289, 290.

Anaxagoras, 77.

Anaximander, 74.

Anthropocentric conception of the universe in Hellenic and Hebrew thought, 76 ff.

Aristotle, 57, 77, 129, 296.

Asceticism, 78.

Atheism and the universe, 18 ff.

Augustine, 108, 290.

Automaton theory of man, 259 ff.

Aquinas, 79.

Astronomy and Theology, 83 ff.

B

Bacon, 67—and final causes, 79 ff., 155—and Agnosticism, 201 ff. 291, 292, 295.

Bayle, 164.

Berkeley, Bishop—on mind and organism, 119—149, 249 — on knowledge of God, 264 ff.— 295.

Biology and Theology, 87 ff.

Boyle, 218.

Brahminism, 147.

Bruno, 148.

Buddhism, 147, 188.

Burton, Hill, 218.

Butler, Bishop, 8, 20, 31.

C

Calvinism and Pantheism, 147.

Carlyle, Thomas, on Hume, 214.

Cartesianism, 109.

Catholicism, 288, 289.

Causality, 91 ff.—and immaterialism, 126 ff.—means more than change, 232 ff. — natural and divine, 235 ff. — natural and moral, 257 ff.—and conscience, 269 ff.

Chalmers, Thomas, on creation, 228 ff.

Chrysostom, 290.

Christianity—and Philosophy, 33, 34 — 77, 108, 152, 274—and Natural Theology, 282 ff.—and Agnosticism, 289, 290.

THE END.

PRINTED BY WILLIAM BLACKWOOD AND SONS.

Catalogue

of

Messrs Blackwood & Sons'

Publications

PHILOSOPHICAL CLASSICS FOR ENGLISH READERS.

EDITED BY WILLIAM KNIGHT, LL.D.,

Professor of Moral Philosophy in the University of St Andrews.

In crown 8vo Volumes, with Portraits, price 3s. 6d.

Contents of the Series.

DESCARTES, by Professor Mahaffy, Dublin.—BUTLER, by Rev. W. Lucas Collins, M.A.—BERKELEY, by Professor Campbell Fraser.—FICHTE, by Professor Adamson, Glasgow. — KANT, by Professor Wallace, Oxford.—HAMILTON, by Professor Veitch, Glasgow.—HEGEL, by the Master of Balliol.—LEIBNIZ, by J. Theodore Merz.—VICO, by Professor Flint, Edinburgh.—HOBBES, by Professor Croom Robertson.—HUME, by the Editor. — SPINOZA, by the Very Rev. Principal Caird, Glasgow.—BACON: Part I. The Life, by Professor Nichol.—BACON: Part II. Philosophy, by the same Author.—LOCKE, by Professor Campbell Fraser.

FOREIGN CLASSICS FOR ENGLISH READERS.

EDITED BY MRS OLIPHANT.

In crown 8vo, 2s. 6d.

Contents of the Series.

DANTE, by the Editor.—VOLTAIRE, by General Sir E. B. Hamley, K.C.B.—PASCAL, by Principal Tulloch.—PETRARCH, by Henry Reeve, C.B.—GOETHE, by A. Hayward, Q.C.—MOLIÈRE, by the Editor and F. Tarver, M.A.—MONTAIGNE, by Rev. W. L. Collins, M.A.—RABELAIS, by Sir Walter Besant.—CALDERON, by E. J. Hasell.—SAINT SIMON, by Clifton W. Collins, M.A.—CERVANTES, by the Editor. — CORNEILLE AND RACINE, by Henry M. Trollope. — MADAME DE SÉVIGNÉ, by Miss Thackeray.—LA FONTAINE, AND OTHER FRENCH FABULISTS, by Rev. W. Lucas Collins, M.A.—SCHILLER, by James Sime, M.A., Author of 'Lessing, his Life and Writings.'—TASSO, by E. J. Hasell. — ROUSSEAU, by Henry Grey Graham. — ALFRED DE MUSSET, by C. F. Oliphant.

ANCIENT CLASSICS FOR ENGLISH READERS.

EDITED BY THE REV. W. LUCAS COLLINS, M.A.

Complete in 28 Vols. crown 8vo, cloth, price 2s. 6d. each. And may also be had in 14 Volumes, strongly and neatly bound, with calf or vellum back, £3, 10s.

Contents of the Series.

HOMER: THE ILIAD, by the Editor.—HOMER: THE ODYSSEY, by the Editor.—HERODOTUS, by George C. Swayne, M.A.—XENOPHON, by Sir Alexander Grant, Bart., LL.D. — EURIPIDES, by W. B. Donne.—ARISTOPHANES, by the Editor.—PLATO, by Clifton W. Collins, M.A.—LUCIAN, by the Editor. — ÆSCHYLUS, by the Right Rev. the Bishop of Colombo. — SOPHOCLES, by Clifton W. Collins, M.A. — HESIOD AND THEOGNIS, by the Rev. J. Davies, M.A.—GREEK ANTHOLOGY, by Lord Neaves.—VIRGIL, by the Editor.—HORACE, by Sir Theodore Martin, K.C.B. — JUVENAL, by Edward Walford, M.A. — PLAUTUS AND TERENCE, by the Editor.—THE COMMENTARIES OF CÆSAR, by Anthony Trollope.—TACITUS, by W. B. Donne.—CICERO, by the Editor. — PLINY'S LETTERS, by the Rev. Alfred Church, M.A., and the Rev. W. J. Brodribb, M.A. — LIVY, by the Editor.—OVID, by the Rev. A. Church, M.A.—CATULLUS, TIBULLUS, AND PROPERTIUS, by the Rev. Jas. Davies, M.A. — DEMOSTHENES, by the Rev. W. J. Brodribb, M.A.—ARISTOTLE, by Sir Alexander Grant, Bart., LL.D.—THUCYDIDES, by the Editor. — LUCRETIUS, by W. H. Mallock, M.A.—PINDAR, by the Rev. F. D. Morice, M.A.

Saturday Review.—"It is difficult to estimate too highly the value of such a series as this in giving 'English readers' an insight, exact as far as it goes, into those olden times which are so remote, and yet to many of us so close."

CATALOGUE

OF

MESSRS BLACKWOOD & SONS'

PUBLICATIONS.

———◆———

ALISON.
History of Europe. By Sir ARCHIBALD ALISON, Bart., D.C.L.
1. From the Commencement of the French Revolution to
the Battle of Waterloo.
LIBRARY EDITION, 14 vols., with Portraits. Demy 8vo, £10, 10s.
ANOTHER EDITION, in 20 vols. crown 8vo, £6.
PEOPLE'S EDITION, 13 vols. crown 8vo, £2, 11s.

2. Continuation to the Accession of Louis Napoleon.
LIBRARY EDITION, 8 vols. 8vo, £6, 7s. 6d.
PEOPLE'S EDITION, 8 vols. crown 8vo, 34s.

Epitome of Alison's History of Europe. Thirtieth Thou-
sand, 7s. 6d.
Atlas to Alison's History of Europe. By A. Keith Johnston.
LIBRARY EDITION, demy 4to, £3, 3s.
PEOPLE'S EDITION, 31s. 6d.
Life of John Duke of Marlborough. With some Account of
his Contemporaries, and of the War of the Succession. Third Edition. 2 vols.
8vo. Portraits and Maps, 30s.
Essays : Historical, Political, and Miscellaneous. 3 vols.
demy 8vo, 45s.

ACROSS FRANCE IN A CARAVAN: BEING SOME ACCOUNT
OF A JOURNEY FROM BORDEAUX TO GENOA IN THE "ESCARGOT," taken in the Winter
1889-90. By the Author of 'A Day of my Life at Eton.' With fifty Illustrations
by John Wallace, after Sketches by the Author, and a Map. Cheap Edition,
demy 8vo, 7s. 6d.

ACTA SANCTORUM HIBERNIÆ; Ex Codice Salmanticensi.
Nunc primum integre edita opera CAROLI DE SMEDT et JOSEPHI DE BACKER, e
Soc. Jesu, Hagiographorum Bollandianorum ; Auctore et Sumptus Largiente
JOANNE PATRICIO MARCHIONE BOTHAE. In One handsome 4to Volume, bound in
half roxburghe, £2, 2s.; in paper cover, 31s. 6d.

ADOLPHUS. Some Memories of Paris. By F. ADOLPHUS.
Crown 8vo, 6s.

AIKMAN.
Manures and the Principles of Manuring. By C. M. AIKMAN,
D.Sc., F.R.S.E., &c., Professor of Chemistry, Glasgow Veterinary College ;
Examiner in Chemistry, University of Glasgow, &c. Crown 8vo, 6s. 6d.
Farmyard Manure : Its Nature, Composition, and Treatment.
Crown 8vo, 1s. 6d.

AIRD. Poetical Works of Thomas Aird. Fifth Edition, with
Memoir of the Author by the Rev. JARDINE WALLACE, and Portrait. Crown 8vo,
7s. 6d.

ALLARDYCE.

The City of Sunshine. By ALEXANDER ALLARDYCE, Author of
'Earlscourt,' &c. New Edition. Crown 8vo, 6s.

Balmoral : A Romance of the Queen's Country. New Edition.
Crown 8vo, 6s.

Memoir of the Honourable George Keith Elphinstone, K.B.,
Viscount Keith of Stonehaven, Marischal, Admiral of the Red. 8vo, with Portrait, Illustrations, and Maps, 21s.

ALMOND. Sermons by a Lay Head-master. By HELY HUTCHINSON ALMOND, M.A. Oxon., Head-Master of Loretto School. Crown 8vo, 5s.

ANCIENT CLASSICS FOR ENGLISH READERS. Edited
by Rev. W. LUCAS COLLINS, M.A. Price 2s. 6d. each. *For List of Vols., see p. 2.*

ANDERSON. Daniel in the Critics' Den. A Reply to Dean
Farrar's 'Book of Daniel.' By ROBERT ANDERSON, LL.D., Barrister-at-Law, Assistant Commissioner of Police of the Metropolis; Author of 'The Coming Prince,' 'Human Destiny,' &c. Post 8vo, 4s. 6d.

AYTOUN.

Lays of the Scottish Cavaliers, and other Poems. By W.
EDMONDSTOUNE AYTOUN, D.C.L., Professor of Rhetoric and Belles-Lettres in the University of Edinburgh. New Edition. Fcap. 8vo, 3s. 6d.
ANOTHER EDITION. Fcap. 8vo, 7s. 6d.
CHEAP EDITION. 1s. Cloth, 1s. 3d.

An Illustrated Edition of the Lays of the Scottish Cavaliers.
From designs by Sir NOEL PATON. Cheaper Edition. Small 4to, 10s. 6d.

Bothwell : a Poem. Third Edition. Fcap., 7s. 6d.

Poems and Ballads of Goethe. Translated by Professor
AYTOUN and Sir THEODORE MARTIN, K.C.B. Third Edition. Fcap., 6s.

The Ballads of Scotland. Edited by Professor AYTOUN.
Fourth Edition. 2 vols. fcap. 8vo, 12s.

Memoir of William E. Aytoun, D.C.L. By Sir THEODORE
MARTIN, K.C.B. With Portrait. Post 8vo, 12s.

BACH.

On Musical Education and Vocal Culture. By ALBERT B.
BACH. Fourth Edition. 8vo, 7s. 6d.

The Principles of Singing. A Practical Guide for Vocalists
and Teachers. With Course of Vocal Exercises. Second Edition. With Portrait of the Author. Crown 8vo, 6s.

The Art Ballad : Loewe and Schubert. With Musical Illustrations. With a Portrait of LOEWE. Third Edition. Small 4to, 5s.

BEDFORD & COLLINS. Annals of the Free Foresters, from
1856 to the Present Day. By W. K. R. BEDFORD, W. E. W. COLLINS, and other Contributors. With 55 Portraits and 59 other Illustrations. Demy 8vo, 21s. *net.*

BELLAIRS. Gossips with Girls and Maidens, Betrothed and
Free. By LADY BELLAIRS. New Edition. Crown 8vo, 3s. 6d. Cloth, extra gilt edges, 5s.

BELLESHEIM. History of the Catholic Church of Scotland.
From the Introduction of Christianity to the Present Day. By ALPHONS BELLESHEIM, D.D., Canon of Aix-la-Chapelle. Translated, with Notes and Additions, by D. OSWALD HUNTER BLAIR, O.S.B., Monk of Fort Augustus. Cheap Edition. Complete in 4 vols. demy 8vo, with Maps. Price 21s. net.

BENTINCK. Racing Life of Lord George Cavendish Bentinck,
M.P., and other Reminiscences. By JOHN KENT, Private Trainer to the Goodwood Stable. Edited by the Hon. FRANCIS LAWLEY. With Twenty-three full-page Plates, and Facsimile Letter. Third Edition. Demy 8vo, 25s.

BESANT. The Revolt of Man. By Sir WALTER BESANT.
Tenth Edition. Crown 8vo, 3s. 6d.

BEVERIDGE.

Culross and Tulliallan ; or, Perthshire on Forth. Its History
and Antiquities. With Elucidations of Scottish Life and Character from the
Burgh and Kirk-Session Records of that District. By DAVID BEVERIDGE. 2 vols.
8vo, with Illustrations, 42s.

Between the Ochils and the Forth ; or, From Stirling Bridge
to Aberdour. Crown 8vo, 6s.

BICKERDYKE. A Banished Beauty. By JOHN BICKERDYKE,
Author of ' Days in Thule, with Rod, Gun, and Camera,' 'The Book of the All-
Round Angler,' 'Curiosities of Ale and Beer,' &c. With Illustrations. Crown
8vo, 6s.

BIRCH.

Examples of Stables, Hunting-Boxes, Kennels, Racing Estab-
lishments, &c. By JOHN BIRCH, Architect, Author of 'Country Architecture,'
&c. With 30 Plates. Royal 8vo, 7s.

Examples of Labourers' Cottages, &c. With Plans for Im-
proving the Dwellings of the Poor in Large Towns. With 34 Plates. Royal 8vo, 7s.

Picturesque Lodges. A Series of Designs for Gate Lodges,
Park Entrances, Keepers', Gardeners', Bailiffs', Grooms', Upper and Under Servants' Lodges, and other Rural Residences. With 16 Plates. 4to, 12s. 6d.

BLACK. Heligoland and the Islands of the North Sea. By
WILLIAM GEORGE BLACK. Crown 8vo, 4s.

BLACKIE.

Lays and Legends of Ancient Greece. By JOHN STUART
BLACKIE, Emeritus Professor of Greek in the University of Edinburgh. Second
Edition. Fcap. 8vo, 5s.

The Wisdom of Goethe. Fcap. 8vo. Cloth, extra gilt, 6s.

Scottish Song : Its Wealth, Wisdom, and Social Significance.
Crown 8vo. With Music. 7s. 6d.

A Song of Heroes. Crown 8vo, 6s.

John Stuart Blackie : A Biography. By ANNA M. STODDART.
With 3 Plates. Third Edition. 2 vols. demy 8vo, 21s.
POPULAR EDITION. With Portrait. Crown 8vo, 6s.

BLACKMORE. The Maid of Sker. By R. D. BLACKMORE,
Author of 'Lorna Doone,' &c. New Edition. Crown 8vo, 6s. Cheaper Edition. Crown 8vo, 3s. 6d.

BLACKWOOD.

Blackwood's Magazine, from Commencement in 1817 to August
1896. Nos. 1 to 970, forming 159 Volumes.

Index to Blackwood's Magazine. Vols. 1 to 50. 8vo, 15s.

Tales from Blackwood. First Series. Price One Shilling each,
in Paper Cover. Sold separately at all Railway Bookstalls.
They may also be had bound in 12 vols., cloth, 18s. Half calf, richly gilt, 30s.
Or the 12 vols. in 6, roxburghe, 21s. Half red morocco, 28s.

Tales from Blackwood. Second Series. Complete in Twenty-
four Shilling Parts. Handsomely bound in 12 vols., cloth, 30s. In leather back,
roxburghe style, 37s. 6d. Half calf, gilt, 52s. 6d. Half morocco, 55s.

Tales from Blackwood. Third Series. Complete in Twelve
Shilling Parts. Handsomely bound in 6 vols., cloth, 15s.; and in 12 vols., cloth,
18s. The 6 vols. in roxburghe, 21s. Half calf, 25s. Half morocco, 28s.

Travel, Adventure, and Sport. From 'Blackwood's Magazine.'
Uniform with 'Tales from Blackwood.' In Twelve Parts, each price 1s. Handsomely bound in 6 vols., cloth, 15s. And in half calf, 25s.

BLACKWOOD.
New Educational Series. *See separate Catalogue.*
New Uniform Series of Novels (Copyright).
Crown 8vo, cloth. Price 3s. 6d. each. Now ready:—

THE MAID OF SKER. By R. D. Blackmore.
WENDERHOLME. By P. G. Hamerton.
THE STORY OF MARGRÉDEL. By D. Storrar Meldrum.
MISS MARJORIBANKS. By Mrs Oliphant.
THE PERPETUAL CURATE, and THE RECTOR. By the Same.
SALEM CHAPEL, and THE DOCTOR'S FAMILY. By the Same.
A SENSITIVE PLANT. By E. D. Gerard.
LADY LEE'S WIDOWHOOD. By General Sir E. B. Hamley.
KATIE STEWART, and other Stories. By Mrs Oliphant.
VALENTINE AND HIS BROTHER. By the Same.
SONS AND DAUGHTERS. By the Same.
MARMORNE. By P. G. Hamerton.

REATA. By E. D. Gerard.
BEGGAR MY NEIGHBOUR. By the Same.
THE WATERS OF HERCULES. By the Same.
FAIR TO SEE. By L. W. M. Lockhart.
MINE IS THINE. By the Same.
DOUBLES AND QUITS. By the Same.
ALTIORA PETO. By Laurence Oliphant.
PICCADILLY. By the Same. With Illustrations.
THE REVOLT OF MAN. By Walter Besant.
LADY BABY. By D. Gerard.
THE BLACKSMITH OF VOE. By Paul Cushing.
THE DILEMMA. By the Author of 'The Battle of Dorking.'
MY TRIVIAL LIFE AND MISFORTUNE. By A Plain Woman.
POOR NELLIE. By the Same.

Others in preparation.

Standard Novels. Uniform in size and binding. Each complete in one Volume.

FLORIN SERIES, Illustrated Boards. Bound in Cloth, 2s. 6d.

TOM CRINGLE'S LOG. By Michael Scott.
THE CRUISE OF THE MIDGE. By the Same.
CYRIL THORNTON. By Captain Hamilton.
ANNALS OF THE PARISH. By John Galt.
THE PROVOST, &c. By the Same.
SIR ANDREW WYLIE. By the Same.
THE ENTAIL. By the Same.
MISS MOLLY. By Beatrice May Butt.
REGINALD DALTON. By J. G. Lockhart.

PEN OWEN. By Dean Hook.
ADAM BLAIR. By J. G. Lockhart.
LADY LEE'S WIDOWHOOD. By General Sir E. B. Hamley.
SALEM CHAPEL. By Mrs Oliphant.
THE PERPETUAL CURATE. By the Same.
MISS MARJORIBANKS. By the Same.
JOHN: A Love Story. By the Same.

SHILLING SERIES, Illustrated Cover. Bound in Cloth, 1s. 6d.

THE RECTOR, and THE DOCTOR'S FAMILY. By Mrs Oliphant.
THE LIFE OF MANSIE WAUCH. By D. M. Moir.
PENINSULAR SCENES AND SKETCHES. By F. Hardman.

SIR FRIZZLE PUMPKIN, NIGHTS AT MESS, &c.
THE SUBALTERN.
LIFE IN THE FAR WEST. By G. F. Ruxton.
VALERIUS: A Roman Story. By J. G. Lockhart.

BON GAULTIER'S BOOK OF BALLADS. Fifteenth Edition. With Illustrations by Doyle, Leech, and Crowquill. Fcap. 8vo, 5s.

BRADDON. Thirty Years of Shikar. By Sir EDWARD BRADDON, K.C.M.G. With Illustrations by G. D. Giles, and Map of Oudh Forest Tracts and Nepal Terai. Demy 8vo, 18s.

BROUGHAM. Memoirs of the Life and Times of Henry Lord Brougham. Written by HIMSELF. 3 vols. 8vo, £2, 8s. The Volumes are sold separately, price 16s. each.

BROWN. The Forester: A Practical Treatise on the Planting and Tending of Forest-trees and the General Management of Woodlands. By JAMES BROWN, LL.D. Sixth Edition, Enlarged. Edited by JOHN NISBET, D.Œc., Author of 'British Forest Trees,' &c. In 2 vols. royal 8vo, with 350 Illustrations, 42s. net.

BROWN. Stray Sport. By J. MORAY BROWN, Author of 'Shikar Sketches,' 'Powder, Spur, and Spear,' 'The Days when we went Hog-Hunting.' 2 vols. post 8vo, with Fifty Illustrations, 21s.

BROWN. A Manual of Botany, Anatomical and Physiological. For the Use of Students. By ROBERT BROWN, M.A., Ph.D. Crown 8vo, with numerous Illustrations, 12s. 6d.

BRUCE.

In Clover and Heather. Poems by WALLACE BRUCE. New and Enlarged Edition. Crown 8vo, 3s. 6d.
A limited number of Copies of the First Edition, on large hand-made paper, 12s. 6d.

Here's a Hand. Addresses and Poems. Crown 8vo, 5s.
Large Paper Edition, limited to 100 copies, price 21s.

BUCHAN. Introductory Text-Book of Meteorology. By ALEXANDER BUCHAN, LL.D., F.R.S.E., Secretary of the Scottish Meteorological Society, &c. New Edition. Crown 8vo, with Coloured Charts and Engravings.
[*In preparation.*

BURBIDGE.

Domestic Floriculture, Window Gardening, and Floral Decorations. Being Practical Directions for the Propagation, Culture, and Arrangement of Plants and Flowers as Domestic Ornaments. By F. W. BURBIDGE. Second Edition. Crown 8vo, with numerous Illustrations, 7s. 6d.

Cultivated Plants: Their Propagation and Improvement. Including Natural and Artificial Hybridisation, Raising from Seed, Cuttings, and Layers, Grafting and Budding, as applied to the Families and Genera in Cultivation. Crown 8vo, with numerous Illustrations, 12s. 6d.

BURGESS. The Viking Path : A Tale of the White Christ. By J. J. HALDANE BURGESS, Author of 'Rasmie's Büddie,' 'Shetland Sketches,' &c. Crown 8vo, 6s.

BURKE. The Flowering of the Almond Tree, and other Poems. By CHRISTIAN BURKE. Pott 4to, 5s.

BURROWS.

Commentaries on the History of England, from the Earliest Times to 1865. By MONTAGU BURROWS, Chichele Professor of Modern History in the University of Oxford; Captain R.N.; F.S.A., &c.; "Officier de l'Instruction Publique," France. Crown 8vo, 7s. 6d.

The History of the Foreign Policy of Great Britain. Demy 8vo, 12s.

BURTON.

The History of Scotland : From Agricola's Invasion to the Extinction of the last Jacobite Insurrection. By JOHN HILL BURTON, D.C.L., Historiographer-Royal for Scotland. New and Enlarged Edition, 8 vols., and Index. Crown 8vo, £3, 3s.

History of the British Empire during the Reign of Queen Anne. In 3 vols. 8vo. 36s.

The Scot Abroad. Third Edition. Crown 8vo, 10s. 6d.

The Book-Hunter. New Edition. With Portrait. Crown 8vo, 7s. 6d.

BUTCHER. The Fortunes of Armenosa. A Historical Romance of Memphis and Old Cairo. By the Very Rev. Dean BUTCHER, D.D., F.S.A., Chaplain at Cairo. Crown 8vo, 6s.

BUTE. The Altus of St Columba. With a Prose Paraphrase and Notes. In paper cover, 2s. 6d.

BUTT.

Theatricals : An Interlude. By BEATRICE MAY BUTT. Crown 8vo, 6s.

Miss Molly. Cheap Edition, 2s.

Eugenie. Crown 8vo, 6s. 6d.

Elizabeth, and other Sketches. Crown 8vo, 6s.

Delicia. New Edition. Crown 8vo, 2s. 6d.

CAIRD. Sermons. By JOHN CAIRD, D.D., Principal of the University of Glasgow. Seventeenth Thousand. Fcap. 8vo, 5s.

CALDWELL. Schopenhauer's System in its Philosophical Significance (the Shaw Fellowship Lectures, 1893). By WILLIAM CALDWELL, M.A., D.Sc., Professor of Moral and Social Philosophy, Northwestern University, U.S.A.; formerly Assistant to the Professor of Logic and Metaphysics, Edin., and Examiner in Philosophy in the University of St Andrews. Demy 8vo, 10s. 6d. net.

CALLWELL. The Effect of Maritime Command on Land Campaigns since Waterloo. By Major C. E. CALLWELL, R.A. With Plans. Post 8vo, 6s. *net.*

CAMPBELL. Sermons Preached before the Queen at Balmoral. By the Rev. A. A. CAMPBELL, Minister of Crathie. Published by Command of Her Majesty. Crown 8vo, 4s. 6d.

CAMPBELL. Records of Argyll. Legends, Traditions, and Recollections of Argyllshire Highlanders, collected chiefly from the Gaelic. With Notes on the Antiquity of the Dress, Clan Colours, or Tartans of the Highlanders. By Lord ARCHIBALD CAMPBELL. Illustrated with Nineteen full-page Etchings. 4to, printed on hand-made paper, £3, 3s.

CAMPBELL. Critical Studies in St Luke's Gospel : Its Demonology and Ebionitism. By COLIN CAMPBELL, D.D., Minister of the Parish of Dundee, formerly Scholar and Fellow of Glasgow University. Author of the 'Three First Gospels in Greek, arranged in parallel columns.' Post 8vo, 7s. 6d.

CANTON. A Lost Epic, and other Poems. By WILLIAM CANTON. Crown 8vo, 5s.

CARSTAIRS.
Human Nature in Rural India. By R. CARSTAIRS. Crown 8vo, 6s.
British Work in India. Crown 8vo, 6s.

CAUVIN. A Treasury of the English and German Languages. Compiled from the best Authors and Lexicographers in both Languages. By JOSEPH CAUVIN, LL.D. and Ph.D., of the University of Göttingen, &c. Crown 8vo, 7s. 6d.

CHARTERIS. Canonicity ; or, Early Testimonies to the Existence and Use of the Books of the New Testament. Based on Kirchhoffer's 'Quellensammlung.' Edited by A. H. CHARTERIS, D.D., Professor of Biblical Criticism in the University of Edinburgh. [*New Edition in preparation.*

CHENNELLS. Recollections of an Egyptian Princess. By her English Governess (Miss E. CHENNELLS). Being a Record of Five Years' Residence at the Court of Ismael Pasha, Khédive. Second Edition. With Three Portraits. Post 8vo, 7s. 6d.

CHESNEY. The Dilemma. By General Sir GEORGE CHESNEY, K.C.B., M.P., Author of 'The Battle of Dorking,' &c. New Edition. Crown 8vo, 3s. 6d.

CHRISTISON. Life of Sir Robert Christison, Bart., M.D., D.C.L. Oxon., Professor of Medical Jurisprudence in the University of Edinburgh. Edited by his SONS. In 2 vols. 8vo. Vol. I.—Autobiography. 16s. Vol. II.—Memoirs. 16s.

CHURCH. Chapters in an Adventurous Life. Sir Richard Church in Italy and Greece. By E. M. CHURCH. With Photogravure Portrait. Demy 8vo, 10s. 6d.

CHURCH SERVICE SOCIETY.
A Book of Common Order : being Forms of Worship issued by the Church Service Society. Seventh Edition, carefully revised. In 1 vol. crown 8vo, cloth, 3s. 6d. ; French morocco, 5s. Also in 2 vols. crown 8vo, cloth, 4s. ; French morocco, 6s. 6d.
Daily Offices for Morning and Evening Prayer throughout the Week. Crown 8vo, 3s. 6d.
Order of Divine Service for Children. Issued by the Church Service Society. With Scottish Hymnal. Cloth, 3d.

CLOUSTON. Popular Tales and Fictions: their Migrations
and Transformations. By W. A. CLOUSTON, Editor of 'Arabian Poetry for Eng·
lish Readers,' &c. 2 vols. post 8vo, roxburghe binding, 25s.

COCHRAN. A Handy Text-Book of Military Law. Compiled
chiefly to assist Officers preparing for Examination; also for all Officers of the
Regular and Auxiliary Forces. Comprising also a Synopsis of part of the Army
Act. By Major F. COCHRAN, Hampshire Regiment Garrison Instructor, North
British District. Crown 8vo, 7s. 6d.

COLQUHOUN. The Moor and the Loch. Containing Minute
Instructions in all Highland Sports, with Wanderings over Crag and Corrie,
Flood and Fell. By JOHN COLQUHOUN. Cheap Edition. With Illustrations.
Demy 8vo, 10s. 6d.

COLVILE. Round the Black Man's Garden. By Lady Z. COL-
VILE, F.R.G.S. With 2 Maps and 50 Illustrations from Drawings by the
Author and from Photographs. Demy 8vo, 16s.

CONDER. The Bible and the East. By Lieut.-Col. C. R.
CONDER, R.E., LL.D., D.C.L., M.R.A.S., Author of 'Tent Work in Palestine,'
&c. With Illustrations and a Map. Crown 8vo, 5s.

CONSTITUTION AND LAW OF THE CHURCH OF
SCOTLAND. With an Introductory Note by the late Principal Tulloch. New
Edition, Revised and Enlarged. Crown 8vo, 3s. 6d.

COTTERILL. Suggested Reforms in Public Schools. By C. C.
COTTERILL, M.A. Crown 8vo, 3s. 6d.

COUNTY HISTORIES OF SCOTLAND. In demy 8vo vol-
umes of about 350 pp. each. With 2 Maps. Price 7s. 6d. net.
Fife and Kinross. By ÆNEAS J. G. MACKAY, LL.D., Sheriff
of these Counties.
Dumfries and Galloway. By Sir HERBERT MAXWELL, Bart.,
M.P. [*Others in preparation.*

CRANSTOUN.
The Elegies of Albius Tibullus. Translated into English
Verse, with Life of the Poet, and Illustrative Notes. By JAMES CRANSTOUN,
LL.D., Author of a Translation of 'Catullus.' Crown 8vo, 6s. 6d.
The Elegies of Sextus Propertius. Translated into English
Verse, with Life of the Poet, and Illustrative Notes. Crown 8vo, 7s. 6d.

CRAWFORD. Saracinesca. By F. MARION CRAWFORD, Author
of 'Mr Isaacs,' &c., &c. Eighth Edition. Crown 8vo, 6s.

CRAWFORD.
The Doctrine of Holy Scripture respecting the Atonement.
By the late THOMAS J. CRAWFORD, D.D., Professor of Divinity in the University
of Edinburgh. Fifth Edition. 8vo, 12s.
The Fatherhood of God, Considered in its General and Special
Aspects. Third Edition, Revised and Enlarged. 8vo, 9s.
The Preaching of the Cross, and other Sermons. 8vo, 7s. 6d.
The Mysteries of Christianity. Crown 8vo, 7s. 6d.

CROSS. Impressions of Dante, and of the New World; with a
Few Words on Bimetallism. By J. W. CROSS, Editor of 'George Eliot's Life, as
related in her Letters and Journals.' Post 8vo, 6s.

CUMBERLAND. Sport on the Pamirs and Turkistan Steppes.
By Major C. S. CUMBERLAND. With Map and Frontispiece. Demy 8vo, 10s. 6d.

CURSE OF INTELLECT. Third Edition. Fcap. 8vo, 2s. 6d. net.

CUSHING. The Blacksmith of Voe. By PAUL CUSHING, Author
of 'The Bull i' th' Thorn,' 'Cut with his own Diamond.' Cheap Edition. Crown
8vo, 3s. 6d.

DAVIES.

Norfolk Broads and Rivers; or, The Waterways, Lagoons, and Decoys of East Anglia. By G. CHRISTOPHER DAVIES. Illustrated with Seven full-page Plates. New and Cheaper Edition. Crown 8vo, 6s.

Our Home in Aveyron. Sketches of Peasant Life in Aveyron and the Lot. By G. CHRISTOPHER DAVIES and Mrs BROUGHALL. Illustrated with full-page Illustrations. 8vo, 15s. Cheap Edition, 7s. 6d.

DE LA WARR. An Eastern Cruise in the 'Edeline.' By the Countess DE LA WARR. In Illustrated Cover. 2s.

DESCARTES. The Method, Meditations, and Principles of Philosophy of Descartes. Translated from the Original French and Latin. With a New Introductory Essay, Historical and Critical, on the Cartesian Philosophy. By Professor VEITCH, LL.D., Glasgow University. Tenth Edition. 6s. 6d.

DOGS, OUR DOMESTICATED : Their Treatment in reference to Food, Diseases, Habits, Punishment, Accomplishments. By 'MAGENTA.' Crown 8vo, 2s. 6d.

DOUGLAS.

The Ethics of John Stuart Mill. By CHARLES DOUGLAS, M.A., D.Sc., Lecturer in Moral Philosophy, and Assistant to the Professor of Moral Philosophy in the University of Edinburgh. Crown 8vo, 7s. 6d. *net*.

John Stuart Mill: A Study of his Philosophy. Crown 8vo, 4s. 6d. net.

DOUGLAS. Chinese Stories. By ROBERT K. DOUGLAS. With numerous Illustrations by Parkinson, Forestier, and others. New and Cheaper Edition. Small demy 8vo, 5s.

DOUGLAS. Iras: A Mystery. By THEO. DOUGLAS, Author of 'A Bride Elect.' Crown 8vo, 3s. 6d.

DU CANE. The Odyssey of Homer, Books I.-XII. Translated into English Verse. By Sir CHARLES DU CANE, K.C.M.G. 8vo, 10s. 6d.

DUDGEON. History of the Edinburgh or Queen's Regiment Light Infantry Militia, now 3rd Battalion The Royal Scots; with an Account of the Origin and Progress of the Militia, and a Brief Sketch of the Old Royal Scots. By Major R. C. DUDGEON, Adjutant 3rd Battalion the Royal Scots. Post 8vo, with Illustrations, 10s. 6d.

DUNSMORE. Manual of the Law of Scotland as to the Relations between Agricultural Tenants and the Landlords, Servants, Merchants, and Bowers. By W. DUNSMORE. 8vo, 7s. 6d.

ELIOT.

George Eliot's Life, Related in Her Letters and Journals. Arranged and Edited by her husband, J. W. CROSS. With Portrait and other Illustrations. Third Edition. 3 vols. post 8vo, 42s.

George Eliot's Life. With Portrait and other Illustrations. New Edition, in one volume. Crown 8vo, 7s. 6d.

Works of George Eliot (Standard Edition). 21 volumes, crown 8vo. In buckram cloth, gilt top, 2s. 6d. per vol.; or in roxburghe binding, 3s. 6d. per vol.

ADAM BEDE. 2 vols.—THE MILL ON THE FLOSS. 2 vols.—FELIX HOLT, THE RADICAL. 2 vols.—ROMOLA. 2 vols.—SCENES OF CLERICAL LIFE. 2 vols.—MIDDLEMARCH. 3 vols.—DANIEL DERONDA. 3 vols.—SILAS MARNER. 1 vol.—JUBAL. 1 vol.—THE SPANISH GIPSY. 1 vol.—ESSAYS. 1 vol.—THEOPHRASTUS SUCH. 1 vol.

Life and Works of George Eliot (Cabinet Edition). 24 volumes, crown 8vo, price £6. Also to be had handsomely bound in half and full calf. The Volumes are sold separately, bound in cloth, price 5s. each.

ELIOT.

Novels by George Eliot. Cheap Edition.

Adam Bede. Illustrated. 3s. 6d., cloth.—The Mill on the Floss. Illustrated. 3s. 6d., cloth.—Scenes of Clerical Life. Illustrated. 3s., cloth.—Silas Marner: the Weaver of Raveloe. Illustrated. 2s. 6d., cloth.—Felix Holt, the Radical. Illustrated. 3s. 6d., cloth.—Romola. With Vignette. 3s. 6d., cloth.

Middlemarch. Crown 8vo, 7s. 6d.

Daniel Deronda. Crown 8vo, 7s. 6d.

Essays. New Edition. Crown 8vo, 5s.

Impressions of Theophrastus Such. New Edition. Crown 8vo, 5s.

The Spanish Gypsy. New Edition. Crown 8vo, 5s.

The Legend of Jubal, and other Poems, Old and New. New Edition. Crown 8vo, 5s.

Wise, Witty, and Tender Sayings, in Prose and Verse. Selected from the Works of GEORGE ELIOT. New Edition. Fcap. 8vo, 3s. 6d.

ENGLISH CHURCH AND THE ROMISH SCHISM. Crown 8vo, 2s. 6d.

ESSAYS ON SOCIAL SUBJECTS. Originally published in the 'Saturday Review.' New Edition. First and Second Series. 2 vols. crown 8vo, 6s. each.

FAITHS OF THE WORLD, The. A Concise History of the Great Religious Systems of the World. By various Authors. Crown 8vo, 5s.

FALKNER. The Lost Stradivarius. By J. MEADE FALKNER. Second Edition. Crown 8vo, 6s.

FERGUSON. Sir Samuel Ferguson in the Ireland of his Day. By LADY FERGUSON, Author of 'The Irish before the Conquest,' 'Life of William Reeves, D.D., Lord Bishop of Down, Connor, and Dromore,' &c., &c. With Two Portraits. 2 vols. post 8vo, 21s.

FERRIER.

Philosophical Works of the late James F. Ferrier, B.A. Oxon., Professor of Moral Philosophy and Political Economy, St Andrews. New Edition. Edited by Sir ALEXANDER GRANT, Bart., D.C.L., and Professor LUSHINGTON. 3 vols. crown 8vo, 34s. 6d.

Institutes of Metaphysic. Third Edition. 10s. 6d.

Lectures on the Early Greek Philosophy. 4th Edition. 10s. 6d.

Philosophical Remains, including the Lectures on Early Greek Philosophy. New Edition. 2 vols. 24s.

FLINT.

Historical Philosophy in France and French Belgium and Switzerland. By ROBERT FLINT, Corresponding Member of the Institute of France, Hon. Member of the Royal Society of Palermo, Professor in the University of Edinburgh, &c. 8vo, 21s.

Agnosticism. Being the Croall Lecture for 1887-88. *[In the press.*

Theism. Being the Baird Lecture for 1876. Ninth Edition, Revised. Crown 8vo, 7s. 6d

Anti-Theistic Theories. Being the Baird Lecture for 1877. Fifth Edition. Crown 8vo, 10s. 6d.

FOREIGN CLASSICS FOR ENGLISH READERS. Edited by Mrs OLIPHANT. Price 2s. 6d. *For List of Volumes, see page 2.*

FOSTER. The Fallen City, and other Poems. By WILL FOSTER. Crown 8vo, 6s.

FRANCILLON. Gods and Heroes; or, The Kingdom of Jupiter. By R. E. FRANCILLON. With 8 Illustrations. Crown 8vo, 5s.

FRANCIS. Among the Untrodden Ways. By M. E. FRANCIS (Mrs Francis Blundell), Author of 'In a North Country Village,' 'A Daughter of the Soil,' 'Frieze and Fustian,' &c. Crown 8vo, 3s. 6d.

FRASER.

Philosophy of Theism. Being the Gifford Lectures delivered before the University of Edinburgh in 1894-95. First Series. By ALEXANDER CAMPBELL FRASER, D.C.L. Oxford; Emeritus Professor of Logic and Metaphysics in the University of Edinburgh. Post 8vo, 7s. 6d. net.

Philosophy of Theism. Being the Gifford Lectures delivered before the University of Edinburgh in 1895-96. Second Series. Post 8vo, 7s. 6d. *net.*

FRASER. St Mary's of Old Montrose: A History of the Parish of Maryton. By the Rev. WILLIAM RUXTON FRASER, M.A., F.S.A. Scot., Emeritus Minister of Maryton; Author of 'History of the Parish and Burgh of Laurencekirk.' Crown 8vo, 3s. 6d.

FULLARTON.

Merlin: A Dramatic Poem. By RALPH MACLEOD FULLARTON. Crown 8vo, 5s.

Tanhäuser. Crown 8vo, 6s.

Lallan Sangs and German Lyrics. Crown 8vo, 5s.

GALT.

Novels by JOHN GALT. With General Introduction and Prefatory Notes by S. R. CROCKETT. The Text Revised and Edited by D. STORRAR MELDRUM, Author of 'The Story of Margrédel.' With Photogravure Illustrations from Drawings by John Wallace. Fcap. 8vo, 3s. net each vol.

ANNALS OF THE PARISH, and THE AYRSHIRE LEGATEES. 2 vols.—SIR ANDREW WYLIE. 2 vols.—THE ENTAIL; or, The Lairds of Grippy. 2 vols.—THE PROVOST, and THE LAST OF THE LAIRDS. 2 vols.

See also STANDARD NOVELS, *p. 6.*

GENERAL ASSEMBLY OF THE CHURCH OF SCOTLAND.

Scottish Hymnal, With Appendix Incorporated. Published for use in Churches by Authority of the General Assembly. 1. Large type, cloth, red edges, 2s. 6d.; French morocco, 4s. 2. Bourgeois type, limp cloth, 1s.; French morocco, 2s. 3. Nonpareil type, cloth, red edges, 6d.; French morocco, 1s. 4d. 4. Paper covers, 3d. 5. Sunday-School Edition, paper covers, 1d.; cloth, 2d. No. 1, bound with the Psalms and Paraphrases, French morocco, 8s. No. 2, bound with the Psalms and Paraphrases, cloth, 2s.; French morocco, 3s.

Prayers for Social and Family Worship. Prepared by a Special Committee of the General Assembly of the Church of Scotland. Entirely New Edition, Revised and Enlarged. Fcap. 8vo, red edges, 2s.

Prayers for Family Worship. A Selection of Four Weeks' Prayers. New Edition. Authorised by the General Assembly of the Church of Scotland. Fcap. 8vo, red edges, 1s. 6d.

One Hundred Prayers. Prepared by the Committee on Aids to Devotion. 16mo, cloth limp, 6d.

Morning and Evening Prayers for Affixing to Bibles. Prepared by the Committee on Aids to Devotion. 1d. for 6, or 1s. per 100.

GERARD.

Reata: What's in a Name. By E. D. GERARD. Cheap Edition. Crown 8vo, 3s. 6d.

Beggar my Neighbour. Cheap Edition. Crown 8vo, 3s. 6d.

The Waters of Hercules. Cheap Edition. Crown 8vo, 3s. 6d.

A Sensitive Plant. Crown 8vo, 3s. 6d.

GERARD.

A Foreigner. An Anglo-German Study. By E. GERARD.
Crown 8vo, 6s.

The Land beyond the Forest. Facts, Figures, and Fancies
from Transylvania. With Maps and Illustrations. 2 vols. post 8vo, 25s.

Bis: Some Tales Retold. Crown 8vo, 6s.

A Secret Mission. 2 vols. crown 8vo, 17s.

GERARD.

The Wrong Man. By DOROTHEA GERARD. Second Edition.
Crown 8vo, 6s.

Lady Baby. Cheap Edition. Crown 8vo, 3s. 6d.

Recha. Second Edition. Crown 8vo, 6s.

The Rich Miss Riddell. Second Edition. Crown 8vo, 6s.

GERARD. Stonyhurst Latin Grammar. By Rev. JOHN GERARD.
Second Edition. Fcap. 8vo, 3s.

GILL.

Free Trade: an Inquiry into the Nature of its Operation.
By RICHARD GILL. Crown 8vo, 7s. 6d.

Free Trade under Protection. Crown 8vo, 7s. 6d.

GORDON CUMMING.

At Home in Fiji. By C. F. GORDON CUMMING. Fourth
Edition, post 8vo. With Illustrations and Map. 7s. 6d.

A Lady's Cruise in a French Man-of-War. New and Cheaper
Edition. 8vo. With Illustrations and Map. 12s. 6d.

Fire-Fountains. The Kingdom of Hawaii: Its Volcanoes,
and the History of its Missions. With Map and Illustrations. 2 vols. 8vo, 25s.

Wanderings in China. New and Cheaper Edition. 8vo, with
Illustrations, 10s.

Granite Crags: The Yŏ-semité Region of California. Illustrated with 8 Engravings. New and Cheaper Edition. 8vo, 8s. 6d.

GRAHAM. Manual of the Elections (Scot.) (Corrupt and Illegal
Practices) Act, 1890. With Analysis, Relative Act of Sederunt, Appendix con-
taining the Corrupt Practices Acts of 1883 and 1885, and Copious Index. By J.
EDWARD GRAHAM, Advocate. 8vo, 4s. 6d.

GRAND.

A Domestic Experiment. By SARAH GRAND, Author of
'The Heavenly Twins,' 'Ideala: A Study from Life.' Crown 8vo, 6s.

Singularly Deluded. Crown 8vo, 6s.

GRANT. Bush-Life in Queensland. By A. C. GRANT. New
Edition. Crown 8vo, 6s.

GRANT. Life of Sir Hope Grant. With Selections from his
Correspondence. Edited by HENRY KNOLLYS, Colonel (H.P.) Royal Artillery,
his former A.D.C., Editor of 'Incidents in the Sepoy War;' Author of 'Sketches
of Life in Japan,' &c. With Portraits of Sir Hope Grant and other Illustrations. Maps and Plans. 2 vols. demy 8vo, 21s.

GRIER.

In Furthest Ind. The Narrative of Mr EDWARD CARLYON of
Ellswether, in the County of Northampton, and late of the Honourable East India
Company's Service, Gentleman. Wrote by his own hand in the year of grace 1697.
Edited, with a few Explanatory Notes, by SYDNEY C. GRIER. Post 8vo, 6s.

His Excellency's English Governess. Crown 8vo, 6s.

An Uncrowned King: A Romance of High Politics. Crown
8vo, 6s.

GUTHRIE-SMITH. Crispus: A Drama. By H. GUTHRIE-
SMITH. Fcap. 4to, 5s.

HAGGARD. Under Crescent and Star. By Lieut.-Col. ANDREW HAGGARD, D.S.O., Author of 'Dodo and I,' 'Tempest Torn,' &c. With a Portrait. Second Edition. Crown 8vo, 6s.

HALDANE. Subtropical Cultivations and Climates. A Handy Book for Planters, Colonists, and Settlers. By R. C. HALDANE. Post 8vo, 9s.

HAMERTON.

Wenderholme: A Story of Lancashire and Yorkshire Life. By P. G. HAMERTON, Author of 'A Painter's Camp.' New Edition. Crown 8vo, 3s. 6d.

Marmorne. New Edition. Crown 8vo, 3s. 6d.

HAMILTON.

Lectures on Metaphysics. By Sir WILLIAM HAMILTON, Bart., Professor of Logic and Metaphysics in the University of Edinburgh. Edited by the Rev. H. L. MANSEL, B.D., LL.D., Dean of St Paul's; and JOHN VEITCH, M.A., LL.D., Professor of Logic and Rhetoric, Glasgow. Seventh Edition. 2 vols. 8vo, 24s.

Lectures on Logic. Edited by the SAME. Third Edition, Revised. 2 vols., 24s.

Discussions on Philosophy and Literature, Education and University Reform. Third Edition. 8vo, 21s.

Memoir of Sir William Hamilton, Bart., Professor of Logic and Metaphysics in the University of Edinburgh. By Professor VEITCH, of the University of Glasgow. 8vo, with Portrait, 18s.

Sir William Hamilton: The Man and his Philosophy. Two Lectures delivered before the Edinburgh Philosophical Institution, January and February 1883. By Professor VEITCH. Crown 8vo, 2s.

HAMLEY.

The Operations of War Explained and Illustrated. By General Sir EDWARD BRUCE HAMLEY, K.C.B., K.C.M.G. Fifth Edition, Revised throughout. 4to, with numerous Illustrations, 30s.

National Defence; Articles and Speeches. Post 8vo, 6s.

Shakespeare's Funeral, and other Papers. Post 8vo, 7s. 6d.

Thomas Carlyle: An Essay. Second Edition. Crown 8vo, 2s. 6d.

On Outposts. Second Edition. 8vo, 2s.

Wellington's Career; A Military and Political Summary. Crown 8vo, 2s.

Lady Lee's Widowhood. New Edition. Crown 8vo, 3s. 6d. Cheaper Edition, 2s. 6d.

Our Poor Relations. A Philozoic Essay. With Illustrations, chiefly by Ernest Griset. Crown 8vo, cloth gilt, 3s. 6d.

The Life of General Sir Edward Bruce Hamley, K.C.B., K.C.M.G. By ALEXANDER INNES SHAND. With two Photogravure Portraits and other Illustrations. Cheaper Edition. With a Statement by Mr EDWARD HAMLEY. 2 vols. demy 8vo, 10s. 6d.

HARE. Down the Village Street: Scenes in a West Country Hamlet. By CHRISTOPHER HARE. Second Edition. Crown 8vo, 6s.

HARRADEN. In Varying Moods: Short Stories. By BEATRICE HARRADEN, Author of 'Ships that Pass in the Night.' Twelfth Edition. Crown 8vo, 3s. 6d.

HARRIS.

From Batum to Baghdad, *viâ* Tiflis, Tabriz, and Persian Kurdistan. By WALTER B. HARRIS, F.R.G.S., Author of 'The Land of an African Sultan; Travels in Morocco,' &c. With numerous Illustrations and 2 Maps. Demy 8vo, 12s.

HARRIS.
Tafilet. The Narrative of a Journey of Exploration to the
Atlas Mountains and the Oases of the North-West Sahara. With Illustrations
by Maurice Romberg from Sketches and Photographs by the Author, and Two
Maps. Demy 8vo, 12s.
A Journey through the Yemen, and some General Remarks
upon that Country. With 3 Maps and numerous Illustrations by Forestier and
Wallace from Sketches and Photographs taken by the Author. Demy 8vo, 16s.
Danovitch, and other Stories. Crown 8vo, 6s.

HAWKER. The Prose Works of Rev. R. S. HAWKER, Vicar of
Morwenstow. Including 'Footprints of Former Men in Far Cornwall.' Re-edited,
with Sketches never before published. With a Frontispiece. Crown 8vo, 3s. 6d.

HAY. The Works of the Right Rev. Dr George Hay, Bishop of
Edinburgh. Edited under the Supervision of the Right Rev. Bishop STRAIN.
With Memoir and Portrait of the Author. 5 vols. crown 8vo, bound in extra
cloth, £1, 1s. The following Volumes may be had separately—viz. :
The Devout Christian Instructed in the Law of Christ from the Written
Word. 2 vols., 8s.—The Pious Christian Instructed in the Nature and Practice
of the Principal Exercises of Piety. 1 vol., 3s.

HEATLEY.
The Horse-Owner's Safeguard. A Handy Medical Guide for
every Man who owns a Horse. By G. S. HEATLEY, M.R.C.V.S. Crown 8vo, 5s.
The Stock-Owner's Guide. A Handy Medical Treatise for
every Man who owns an Ox or a Cow. Crown 8vo, 4s. 6d.

HEDDERWICK. Lays of Middle Age; and other Poems. By
JAMES HEDDERWICK, LL.D., Author of 'Backward Glances.' Price 3s. 6d.

HEMANS.
The Poetical Works of Mrs Hemans. Copyright Editions.
Royal 8vo, 5s. The Same with Engravings, cloth, gilt edges, 7s. 6d.
Select Poems of Mrs Hemans. Fcap., cloth, gilt edges, 3s.

HERKLESS. Cardinal Beaton: Priest and Politician. By
JOHN HERKLESS, Professor of Church History, St Andrews. With a Portrait.
Post 8vo, 7s. 6d.

HEWISON. The Isle of Bute in the Olden Time. With Illus-
trations, Maps, and Plans. By JAMES KING HEWISON, M.A., F.S.A. (Scot.)
Minister of Rothesay. Vol. I., Celtic Saints and Heroes. Crown 4to, 15s. net.
Vol. II., The Royal Stewards and the Brandanes. Crown 4to, 15s. net.

HIBBEN. Inductive Logic. By JOHN GRIER HIBBEN, Ph.D.,
Assistant Professor of Logic in Princeton University, U.S.A. Crown 8vo,
3s. 6d. net.

HOME PRAYERS. By Ministers of the Church of Scotland
and Members of the Church Service Society. Second Edition. Fcap. 8vo, 3s.

HORNBY. Admiral of the Fleet Sir Geoffrey Phipps Hornby,
G.C.B. A Biography. By Mrs FRED. EGERTON. With Three Portraits. Demy
8vo, 16s.

HUTCHINSON. Hints on the Game of Golf. By HORACE G.
HUTCHINSON. Ninth Edition, Enlarged. Fcap. 8vo. cloth, 1s.

HYSLOP. The Elements of Ethics. By JAMES H. HYSLOP,
Ph.D., Instructor in Ethics, Columbia College, New York, Author of 'The
Elements of Logic.' Post 8vo, 7s. 6d. net.

IDDESLEIGH.
Lectures and Essays. By the late EARL of IDDESLEIGH,
G.C.B., D.C.L., &c. 8vo, 16s.
Life, Letters, and Diaries of Sir Stafford Northcote, First
Earl of Iddesleigh. By ANDREW LANG. With Three Portraits and a View of
Pynes. Third Edition. 2 vols. post 8vo, 31s. 6d.
POPULAR EDITION. With Portrait and View of Pynes. Post 8vo, 7s. 6d.

IGNOTUS. The Supremacy and Sufficiency of Jesus Christ, as set forth in the Epistle to the Hebrews. By IGNOTUS. Crown 8vo, 3s. 6d.

INDEX GEOGRAPHICUS : Being a List, alphabetically arranged, of the Principal Places on the Globe, with the Countries and Subdivisions of the Countries in which they are situated, and their Latitudes and Longitudes. Imperial 8vo, pp. 676, 21s.

JEAN JAMBON. Our Trip to Blunderland ; or, Grand Excursion to Blundertown and Back. By JEAN JAMBON. With Sixty Illustrations designed by CHARLES DOYLE, engraved by DALZIEL. Fourth Thousand. Cloth, gilt edges, 6s. 6d. Cheap Edition, cloth, 3s. 6d. Boards, 2s. 6d.

JEBB. A Strange Career. The Life and Adventures of JOHN GLADWYN JEBB. By his Widow. With an Introduction by H. RIDER HAGGARD, and an Electrogravure Portrait of Mr Jebb. Third Edition. Demy 8vo, 10s. 6d. CHEAP EDITION. With Illustrations by John Wallace. Crown 8vo, 3s. 6d.

Some Unconventional People. By Mrs GLADWYN JEBB, Author of 'Life and Adventures of J. G. Jebb.' With Illustrations. Crown 8vo, 3s. 6d.

JENNINGS. Mr Gladstone : A Study. By LOUIS J. JENNINGS, M.P., Author of 'Republican Government in the United States,' 'The Croker Memoirs,' &c. Popular Edition. Crown 8vo, 1s.

JERNINGHAM.

Reminiscences of an Attaché. By HUBERT E. H. JERNINGHAM. Second Edition. Crown 8vo, 5s.

Diane de Breteuille. A Love Story. Crown 8vo, 2s. 6d.

JOHNSTON.

The Chemistry of Common Life. By Professor J. F. W. JOHNSTON. New Edition, Revised. By ARTHUR HERBERT CHURCH, M.A. Oxon.; Author of 'Food : its Sources, Constituents, and Uses,' &c. With Maps and 102 Engravings. Crown 8vo, 7s. 6d.

Elements of Agricultural Chemistry. An entirely New Edition from the Edition by Sir CHARLES A. CAMERON, M.D., F.R.C.S.I., &c. Revised and brought down to date by C. M. AIKMAN, M.A., B.Sc., F.R.S.E., Professor of Chemistry, Glasgow Veterinary College. 17th Edition. Crown 8vo, 6s. 6d.

Catechism of Agricultural Chemistry. An entirely New Edition from the Edition by Sir CHARLES A. CAMERON. Revised and Enlarged by C. M. AIKMAN, M.A., &c. 95th Thousand. With numerous Illustrations. Crown 8vo, 1s.

JOHNSTON. Agricultural Holdings (Scotland) Acts, 1883 and 1889 ; and the Ground Game Act, 1880. With Notes, and Summary of Procedure, &c. By CHRISTOPHER N. JOHNSTON, M.A., Advocate. Demy 8vo, 5s.

JOKAI. Timar's Two Worlds. By MAURUS JOKAI. Authorised Translation by Mrs HEGAN KENNARD. Cheap Edition. Crown 8vo, 6s.

KEBBEL. The Old and the New : English Country Life. By T. E. KEBBEL, M.A., Author of 'The Agricultural Labourers,' 'Essays in History and Politics,' 'Life of Lord Beaconsfield.' Crown 8vo, 5s.

KERR. St Andrews in 1645-46. By D. R. KERR. Crown 8vo, 2s. 6d.

KINGLAKE.

History of the Invasion of the Crimea. By A. W. KINGLAKE. New Edition, Abridged by Lt.-Colonel Sir GEORGE S. CLARKE, K.C.M.G., R.E. With Maps and Plans. [*In preparation.*

History of the Invasion of the Crimea. By A. W. KINGLAKE. Cabinet Edition, Revised. With an Index to the Complete Work. Illustrated with Maps and Plans. Complete in 9 vols., crown 8vo, at 6s. each.

KINGLAKE.
History of the Invasion of the Crimea. Demy 8vo. Vol. VI.
Winter Troubles. With a Map, 16s. Vols. VII. and VIII. From the Morrow of
Inkerman to the Death of Lord Raglan. With an Index to the Whole Work.
With Maps and Plans. 28s.
Eothen. A New Edition, uniform with the Cabinet Edition
of the 'History of the Invasion of the Crimea.' 6s.
CHEAPER EDITION. With Portrait and Biographical Sketch of the Author.
Crown 8vo, 3s. 6d.

KIRBY. In Haunts of Wild Game: A Hunter-Naturalist's
Wanderings from Kahlamba to Libombo. By FREDERICK VAUGHAN KIRBY,
F.Z.S. (Maqaqamba). With numerous Illustrations by Charles Whymper, and a
Map. Large demy 8vo, 25s.

KLEIN. Among the Gods. Scenes of India, with Legends by
the Way. By AUGUSTA KLEIN. With 22 Full-page Illustrations. Demy 8vo, 15s.

KNEIPP. My Water-Cure. As Tested through more than
Thirty Years, and Described for the Healing of Diseases and the Preservation of
Health. By SEBASTIAN KNEIPP, Parish Priest of Wörishofen (Bavaria). With a
Portrait and other Illustrations. Authorised English Translation from the
Thirtieth German Edition, by A. de F. Cheap Edition. With an Appendix, con-
taining the Latest Developments of Pfarrer Kneipp's System, and a Preface by
E. Gerard. Crown 8vo, 3s. 6d.

KNOLLYS. The Elements of Field-Artillery. Designed for
the Use of Infantry and Cavalry Officers. By HENRY KNOLLYS, Colonel Royal
Artillery; Author of 'From Sedan to Saarbrück,' Editor of 'Incidents in the
Sepoy War,' &c. With Engravings. Crown 8vo, 7s. 6d.

LANG. Life, Letters, and Diaries of Sir Stafford Northcote,
First Earl of Iddesleigh. By ANDREW LANG. With Three Portraits and a View
of Pynes. Third Edition. 2 vols. post 8vo, 31s. 6d.
POPULAR EDITION. With Portrait and View of Pynes. Post 8vo, 7s. 6d.

LEES. A Handbook of the Sheriff and Justice of Peace Small
Debt Courts. With Notes, References, and Forms. By J. M. LEES, Advocate,
Sheriff of Stirling, Dumbarton, and Clackmannan. 8vo, 7s. 6d.

LINDSAY.
Recent Advances in Theistic Philosophy of Religion. By Rev.
JAMES LINDSAY, M.A., B.D., B.Sc., F.R.S.E., F.G.S., Minister of the Parish of
St Andrew's, Kilmarnock. Demy 8vo, 9s.
The Progressiveness of Modern Christian Thought. Crown
8vo, 6s.
Essays, Literary and Philosophical. Crown 8vo, 3s. 6d.

LOCKHART.
Doubles and Quits. By LAURENCE W. M. LOCKHART. New
Edition. Crown 8vo, 3s. 6d.
Fair to See. New Edition. Crown 8vo, 3s. 6d.
Mine is Thine. New Edition. Crown 8vo, 3s. 6d.

LOCKHART.
The Church of Scotland in the Thirteenth Century. The
Life and Times of David de Bernham of St Andrews (Bishop), A.D. 1239 to 1253.
With List of Churches dedicated by him, and Dates. By WILLIAM LOCKHART,
A.M., D.D., F.S.A. Scot., Minister of Colinton Parish. 2d Edition. 8vo, 6s.
Dies Tristes: Sermons for Seasons of Sorrow. Crown 8vo, 6s.

LORIMER.
The Institutes of Law: A Treatise of the Principles of Juris-
prudence as determined by Nature. By the late JAMES LORIMER, Professor of
Public Law and of the Law of Nature and Nations in the University of Edin-
burgh. New Edition, Revised and much Enlarged. 8vo, 18s.
The Institutes of the Law of Nations. A Treatise of the
Jural Relation of Separate Political Communities. In 2 vols. 8vo. Volume I.,
price 16s. Volume II., price 20s.

LUGARD. The Rise of our East African Empire : Early Efforts
in Uganda and Nyasaland. By F. D. LUGARD, Captain Norfolk Regiment.
With 130 Illustrations from Drawings and Photographs under the personal
superintendence of the Author, and 14 specially prepared Maps. In 2 vols. large
demy 8vo, 42s.

M'CHESNEY.
Miriam Cromwell, Royalist : A Romance of the Great Rebel-
lion. By DORA GREENWELL M'CHESNEY. Crown 8vo, 6s.
Kathleen Clare : Her Book, 1637-41. Edited by DORA GREEN-
WELL M'CHESNEY. With Frontispiece, and five full-page Illustrations by James
A. Shearman. Crown 8vo, 6s.

M'COMBIE. Cattle and Cattle-Breeders. By WILLIAM M'COMBIE,
Tillyfour. New Edition, Enlarged, with Memoir of the Author by JAMES
MACDONALD, F.R.S.E., Secretary Highland and Agricultural Society of Scotland.
Crown 8vo, 3s. 6d.

M'CRIE.
Works of the Rev. Thomas M'Crie, D.D. Uniform Edition.
4 vols. crown 8vo, 24s.
Life of John Knox. Crown 8vo, 6s. Another Edition, 3s. 6d.
Life of Andrew Melville. Crown 8vo, 6s.
History of the Progress and Suppression of the Reformation
in Italy in the Sixteenth Century. Crown 8vo, 4s.
History of the Progress and Suppression of the Reformation
in Spain in the Sixteenth Century. Crown 8vo, 3s. 6d.

M'CRIE. The Public Worship of Presbyterian Scotland. Histori-
cally treated. With copious Notes, Appendices, and Index. The Fourteenth
Series of the Cunningham Lectures. By the Rev. CHARLES G. M'CRIE, D.D.
Demy 8vo, 10s. 6d.

MACDONALD. A Manual of the Criminal Law (Scotland) Procedure Act, 1887. By NORMAN DORAN MACDONALD. Revised by the LORD
JUSTICE-CLERK. 8vo, 10s. 6d.

MACDONALD AND SINCLAIR. History of Polled Aberdeen
and Angus Cattle. Giving an Account of the Origin, Improvement, and Characteristics of the Breed. By JAMES MACDONALD and JAMES SINCLAIR. Illustrated
with numerous Animal Portraits. Post 8vo, 12s. 6d.

MACDOUGALL AND DODDS. A Manual of the Local Govern-
ment (Scotland) Act, 1894. With Introduction, Explanatory Notes, and Copious
Index. By J. PATTEN MACDOUGALL, Legal Secretary to the Lord Advocate, and
J. M. DODDS. Tenth Thousand, Revised. Crown 8vo, 2s. 6d. net.

MACINTYRE. Hindu - Koh : Wanderings and Wild Sports on
and beyond the Himalayas. By Major-General DONALD MACINTYRE, V.C., late
Prince of Wales' Own Goorkhas, F.R.G.S. *Dedicated to H.R.H. The Prince of
Wales.* New and Cheaper Edition, Revised, with numerous Illustrations. Post
8vo, 3s. 6d.

MACKAY.
A Manual of Modern Geography ; Mathematical, Physical,
and Political. By the Rev. ALEXANDER MACKAY, LL.D., F.R.G.S. 11th
Thousand, Revised to the present time. Crown 8vo, pp. 688, 7s. 6d.
Elements of Modern Geography. 55th Thousand, Revised to
the present time. Crown 8vo, pp. 300, 3s.
The Intermediate Geography. Intended as an Intermediate
Book between the Author's 'Outlines of Geography' and 'Elements of Geo-
graphy.' Eighteenth Edition, Revised. Fcap. 8vo, pp. 238, 2s.
Outlines of Modern Geography. 191st Thousand, Revised to
the present time. Fcap. 8vo, pp. 128, 1s.
Elements of Physiography. New Edition. Rewritten and
Enlarged. With numerous Illustrations. Crown 8vo.   [*In the press.*

MACKENZIE. Studies in Roman Law. With Comparative Views of the Laws of France, England, and Scotland. By Lord MACKENZIE, one of the Judges of the Court of Session in Scotland. Sixth Edition, Edited by JOHN KIRKPATRICK, M.A., LL.B., Advocate, Professor of History in the University of Edinburgh. 8vo, 12s.

MACPHERSON. Glimpses of Church and Social Life in the Highlands in Olden Times. By ALEXANDER MACPHERSON, F.S.A. Scot. With 6 Photogravure Portraits and other full-page Illustrations. Small 4to, 25s.

M'PHERSON. Golf and Golfers. Past and Present. By J. GORDON M'PHERSON, Ph.D., F.R.S.E. With an Introduction by the Right Hon. A. J. BALFOUR, and a Portrait of the Author. Fcap. 8vo, 1s. 6d.

MACRAE. A Handbook of Deer-Stalking. By ALEXANDER MACRAE, late Forester to Lord Henry Bentinck. With Introduction by Horatio Ross, Esq. Fcap. 8vo, with 2 Photographs from Life. 3s. 6d.

MAIN. Three Hundred English Sonnets. Chosen and Edited by DAVID M. MAIN. New Edition. Fcap. 8vo, 3s. 6d.

MAIR. A Digest of Laws and Decisions, Ecclesiastical and Civil, relating to the Constitution, Practice, and Affairs of the Church of Scotland. With Notes and Forms of Procedure. By the Rev. WILLIAM MAIR, D.D., Minister of the Parish of Earlston. New Edition, Revised. Crown 8vo, 9s. net.

MARCHMONT AND THE HUMES OF POLWARTH. By One of their Descendants. With numerous Portraits and other Illustrations. Crown 4to, 21s. net.

MARSHMAN. History of India. From the Earliest Period to the present time. By JOHN CLARK MARSHMAN, C.S.I. Third and Cheaper Edition. Post 8vo, with Map, 6s.

MARTIN.

The Æneid of Virgil. Books I.-VI. Translated by Sir THEODORE MARTIN, K.C.B. Post 8vo, 6s.

Goethe's Faust. Part I. Translated into English Verse. Second Edition, crown 8vo, 6s. Ninth Edition, fcap. 8vo, 3s. 6d.

Goethe's Faust. Part II. Translated into English Verse. Second Edition, Revised. Fcap. 8vo, 6s.

The Works of Horace. Translated into English Verse, with Life and Notes. 2 vols. New Edition. Crown 8vo, 21s.

Poems and Ballads of Heinrich Heine. Done into English Verse. Third Edition. Small crown 8vo, 5s.

The Song of the Bell, and other Translations from Schiller, Goethe, Uhland, and Others. Crown 8vo, 7s. 6d.

Madonna Pia: A Tragedy; and Three Other Dramas. Crown 8vo, 7s. 6d.

Catullus. With Life and Notes. Second Edition, Revised and Corrected. Post 8vo, 7s. 6d.

The 'Vita Nuova' of Dante. Translated, with an Introduction and Notes. Third Edition. Small crown 8vo, 5s.

Aladdin: A Dramatic Poem. By ADAM OEHLENSCHLAEGER. Fcap. 8vo, 5s.

Correggio: A Tragedy. By OEHLENSCHLAEGER. With Notes. Fcap. 8vo, 3s.

MARTIN. On some of Shakespeare's Female Characters. By HELENA FAUCIT, Lady MARTIN. Dedicated by permission to Her Most Gracious Majesty the Queen. Fifth Edition. With a Portrait by Lehmann. Demy 8vo, 7s. 6d.

MARWICK. Observations on the Law and Practice in regard to Municipal Elections and the Conduct of the Business of Town Councils and Commissioners of Police in Scotland. By Sir JAMES D. MARWICK, LL.D., Town-Clerk of Glasgow. Royal 8vo, 30s.

MATHESON.
Can the Old Faith Live with the New ? or, The Problem of Evolution and Revelation. By the Rev. GEORGE MATHESON, D.D. Third Edition. Crown 8vo, 7s. 6d.
The Psalmist and the Scientist; or, Modern Value of the Religious Sentiment. Third Edition. Crown 8vo, 5s.
Spiritual Development of St Paul. Third Edition. Cr. 8vo, 5s.
The Distinctive Messages of the Old Religions. Second Edition. Crown 8vo, 5s.
Sacred Songs. New and Cheaper Edition. Crown 8vo, 2s. 6d.

MAURICE. The Balance of Military Power in Europe. An Examination of the War Resources of Great Britain and the Continental States. By Colonel MAURICE, R.A., Professor of Military Art and History at the Royal Staff College. Crown 8vo, with a Map, 6s.

MAXWELL.
A Duke of Britain. A Romance of the Fourth Century. By Sir HERBERT MAXWELL, Bart., M.P., F.S.A., &c., Author of 'Passages in the Life of Sir Lucian Elphin.' Fourth Edition. Crown 8vo, 6s.
Life and Times of the Rt. Hon. William Henry Smith, M.P. With Portraits and numerous Illustrations by Herbert Railton, G. L. Seymour, and Others. 2 vols. demy 8vo, 25s.
POPULAR EDITION. With a Portrait and other Illustrations. Crown 8vo, 3s. 6d.
Scottish Land-Names : Their Origin and Meaning. Being the Rhind Lectures in Archæology for 1893. Post 8vo, 6s.
Meridiana : Noontide Essays. Post 8vo, 7s. 6d.
Post Meridiana : Afternoon Essays. Post 8vo, 6s.
Dumfries and Galloway. Being one of the Volumes of the County Histories of Scotland. With Two Maps. Demy 8vo, 7s. 6d. *net.*

MELDRUM.
The Story of Margrédel : Being a Fireside History of a Fifeshire Family. By D. STORRAR MELDRUM. Cheap Edition. Crown 8vo, 3s. 6d.
Grey Mantle and Gold Fringe. Crown 8vo, 6s.

MERZ. A History of European Thought in the Nineteenth Century. By JOHN THEODORE MERZ. Vol. I., post 8vo. [*Immediately.*

MICHEL. A Critical Inquiry into the Scottish Language. With the view of Illustrating the Rise and Progress of Civilisation in Scotland. By FRANCISQUE-MICHEL, F.S.A. Lond. and Scot., Correspondant de l'Institut de France, &c. 4to, printed on hand-made paper, and bound in roxburghe, 66s.

MICHIE.
The Larch : Being a Practical Treatise on its Culture and General Management. By CHRISTOPHER Y. MICHIE, Forester, Cullen House. Crown 8vo, with Illustrations. New and Cheaper Edition, Enlarged, 5s.
The Practice of Forestry. Crown 8vo, with Illustrations. 6s.

MIDDLETON. The Story of Alastair Bhan Comyn; or, The Tragedy of Dunphail. A Tale of Tradition and Romance. By the Lady MIDDLETON. Square 8vo, 10s. Cheaper Edition, 5s.

MILLER. The Story of Mr H——, the Herbalist. By HUGH MILLER, F.R.S.E., late H.M. Geological Survey, Author of 'Landscape Geology.' With a Photogravure Frontispiece. Crown 8vo, 2s. 6d.

MINTO.
A Manual of English Prose Literature, Biographical and Critical : designed mainly to show Characteristics of Style. By W. MINTO, M.A., Hon. LL.D. of St Andrews ; Professor of Logic in the University of Aberdeen. Third Edition, Revised. Crown 8vo, 7s. 6d.
Characteristics of English Poets, from Chaucer to Shirley. New Edition, Revised. Crown 8vo, 7s. 6d.
Plain Principles of Prose Composition. Crown 8vo, 1s. 6d.

MINTO.

The Literature of the Georgian Era. Edited, with a Biographical Introduction, by Professor KNIGHT, St Andrews. Post 8vo, 6s.

MOIR. Life of Mansie Wauch, Tailor in Dalkeith. By D. M.
MOIR. With CRUIKSHANK'S Illustrations. Cheaper Edition. Crown 8vo, 2s. 6d.
Another Edition, without Illustrations, fcap. 8vo, 1s. 6d.

MOLE. For the Sake of a Slandered Woman. By MARION
MOLE. Fcap. 8vo, 2s. 6d. net.

MOMERIE.

Defects of Modern Christianity, and other Sermons. By
ALFRED WILLIAMS MOMERIE, M.A., D.Sc., LL.D. Fifth Edition. Crown
8vo, 5s.

The Basis of Religion. Being an Examination of Natural
Religion. Third Edition. Crown 8vo, 2s. 6d.

The Origin of Evil, and other Sermons. Eighth Edition,
Enlarged. Crown 8vo, 5s.

Personality. The Beginning and End of Metaphysics, and
a Necessary Assumption in all Positive Philosophy. Fifth Edition, Revised.
Crown 8vo, 3s.

Agnosticism. Fourth Edition, Revised. Crown 8vo, 5s.

Preaching and Hearing ; and other Sermons. Fourth Edition,
Enlarged. Crown 8vo, 5s.

Belief in God. Third Edition. Crown 8vo, 3s.

Inspiration ; and other Sermons. Second Edition, Enlarged.
Crown 8vo, 5s.

Church and Creed. Third Edition. Crown 8vo, 4s. 6d.

The Future of Religion, and other Essays. Second Edition.
Crown 8vo, 3s. 6d.

MONCREIFF.

The Provost-Marshal. A Romance of the Middle Shires. By
the Hon. FREDERICK MONCREIFF. Crown 8vo, 6s.

The X Jewel. A Romance of the Days of James VI. Crown
8vo, 6s.

MONTAGUE. Military Topography. Illustrated by Practical
Examples of a Practical Subject. By Major-General W. E. MONTAGUE, C.B.,
P.S.C., late Garrison Instructor Intelligence Department, Author of 'Campaign-
ing in South Africa.' With Forty-one Diagrams. Crown 8vo, 5s.

MONTALEMBERT. Memoir of Count de Montalembert. A
Chapter of Recent French History. By Mrs OLIPHANT, Author of the 'Life of
Edward Irving,' &c. 2 vols. crown 8vo, £1, 4s.

MORISON.

Doorside Ditties. By JEANIE MORISON. With a Frontispiece. Crown 8vo, 3s. 6d.

Æolus. A Romance in Lyrics. Crown 8vo, 3s.

There as Here. Crown 8vo, 3s.
₊ *A limited impression on hand-made paper, bound in vellum, 7s. 6d.*

Selections from Poems. Crown 8vo, 4s. 6d.

Sordello. An Outline Analysis of Mr Browning's Poem.
Crown 8vo, 3s.

Of "Fifine at the Fair," "Christmas Eve and Easter Day,"
and other of Mr Browning's Poems. Crown 8vo, 3s.

The Purpose of the Ages. Crown 8vo, 9s.

Gordon : An Our-day Idyll. Crown 8vo, 3s.

Saint Isadora, and other Poems. Crown 8vo, 1s. 6d.

Snatches of Song. Paper, 1s. 6d. ; cloth, 3s.

Pontius Pilate. Paper, 1s. 6d. ; cloth, 3s.

MORISON.
 Mill o' Forres. Crown 8vo, 1s.
 Ane Booke of Ballades. Fcap. 4to, 1s.

MOZLEY. Essays from 'Blackwood.' By the late ANNE
 MOZLEY, Author of 'Essays on Social Subjects'; Editor of 'The Letters and
 Correspondence of Cardinal Newman,' 'Letters of the Rev. J. B. Mozley,' &c.
 With a Memoir by her Sister, FANNY MOZLEY. Post 8vo, 7s. 6d.

MUNRO. The Lost Pibroch, and other Sheiling Stories. By
 NEIL MUNRO. Crown 8vo, 6s.

MUNRO. Rambles and Studies in Bosnia - Herzegovina and
 Dalmatia. With an Account of the Proceedings of the Congress of Archæolo-
 gists and Anthropologists held at Sarajevo in 1894. By ROBERT MUNRO, M.A.,
 M.D., F.R.S.E., Author of 'The Lake-Dwellings of Europe,' &c. With numerous
 Illustrations. Demy 8vo, 12s. 6d. net.

MUNRO. On Valuation of Property. By WILLIAM MUNRO,
 M.A., Her Majesty's Assessor of Railways and Canals for Scotland. Second
 Edition, Revised and Enlarged. 8vo, 3s. 6d.

MURDOCH. Manual of the Law of Insolvency and Bankruptcy:
 Comprehending a Summary of the Law of Insolvency, Notour Bankruptcy,
 Composition - Contracts, Trust - Deeds, Cessios, and Sequestrations; and the
 Winding-up of Joint-Stock Companies in Scotland; with Annotations on the
 various Insolvency and Bankruptcy Statutes; and with Forms of Procedure
 applicable to these Subjects. By JAMES MURDOCH, Member of the Faculty of
 Procurators in Glasgow. Fifth Edition, Revised and Enlarged. 8vo, 12s. net.

MY TRIVIAL LIFE AND MISFORTUNE: A Gossip with
 no Plot in Particular. By A PLAIN WOMAN. Cheap Edition. Crown 8vo, 3s. 6d.
 By the SAME AUTHOR.
 POOR NELLIE. Cheap Edition. Crown 8vo, 3s. 6d.

MY WEATHER - WISE COMPANION. Presented by B. T.
 Fcap. 8vo, 1s. net.

NAPIER. The Construction of the Wonderful Canon of Loga-
 rithms. By JOHN NAPIER of Merchiston. Translated, with Notes, and a
 Catalogue of Napier's Works, by WILLIAM RAE MACDONALD. Small 4to, 15s.
 A few large-paper copies on Whatman paper, 30s.

NEAVES. Songs and Verses, Social and Scientific. By An Old
 Contributor to 'Maga.' By the Hon. Lord NEAVES. Fifth Edition. Fcap.
 8vo, 4s.

NICHOLSON.
 A Manual of Zoology, for the Use of Students. With a
 General Introduction on the Principles of Zoology. By HENRY ALLEYNE
 NICHOLSON, M.D., D.Sc., F.L.S., F.G.S., Regius Professor of Natural History in
 the University of Aberdeen. Seventh Edition, Rewritten and Enlarged. Post
 8vo, pp. 956, with 555 Engravings on Wood, 18s.

 Text-Book of Zoology, for Junior Students. Fifth Edition,
 Rewritten and Enlarged. Crown 8vo, with 358 Engravings on Wood, 10s. 6d.

 Introductory Text-Book of Zoology, for the Use of Junior
 Classes. Sixth Edition, Revised and Enlarged, with 166 Engravings, 3s.

 Outlines of Natural History, for Beginners: being Descriptions of a Progressive Series of Zoological Types. Third Edition, with
 Engravings, 1s. 6d.

 A Manual of Palæontology, for the Use of Students. With a
 General Introduction on the Principles of Palæontology. By Professor H.
 ALLEYNE NICHOLSON and RICHARD LYDEKKER, B.A. Third Edition, entirely
 Rewritten and greatly Enlarged. 2 vols. 8vo, £3, 3s.

 The Ancient Life-History of the Earth. An Outline of the
 Principles and Leading Facts of Palæontological Science. Crown 8vo, with 276
 Engravings, 10s. 6d.

NICHOLSON.

On the "Tabulate Corals" of the Palæozoic Period, with Critical Descriptions of Illustrative Species. Illustrated with 15 Lithographed Plates and numerous Engravings. Super-royal 8vo, 21s.

Synopsis of the Classification of the Animal Kingdom. 8vo, with 106 Illustrations, 6s.

On the Structure and Affinities of the Genus Monticulipora and its Sub-Genera, with Critical Descriptions of Illustrative Species. Illustrated with numerous Engravings on Wood and Lithographed Plates. Super-royal 8vo, 18s.

NICHOLSON.

Thoth. A Romance. By JOSEPH SHIELD NICHOLSON, M.A., D.Sc., Professor of Commercial and Political Economy and Mercantile Law in the University of Edinburgh. Third Edition. Crown 8vo, 4s. 6d.

A Dreamer of Dreams. A Modern Romance. Second Edition. Crown 8vo, 6s.

NICOLSON AND MURE. A Handbook to the Local Government (Scotland) Act, 1889. With Introduction, Explanatory Notes, and Index. By J. BADENACH NICOLSON, Advocate, Counsel to the Scotch Education Department, and W. J. MURE, Advocate, Legal Secretary to the Lord Advocate for Scotland. Ninth Reprint. 8vo, 5s.

OLIPHANT.

Masollam : A Problem of the Period. A Novel. By LAURENCE OLIPHANT. 3 vols. post 8vo, 25s. 6d.

Scientific Religion ; or, Higher Possibilities of Life and Practice through the Operation of Natural Forces. Second Edition. 8vo, 16s.

Altiora Peto. Cheap Edition. Crown 8vo, boards, 2s. 6d. ; cloth, 3s. 6d. Illustrated Edition. Crown 8vo, cloth, 6s.

Piccadilly. With Illustrations by Richard Doyle. New Edition, 3s. 6d. Cheap Edition, boards, 2s. 6d.

Traits and Travesties ; Social and Political. Post 8vo, 10s. 6d.

Episodes in a Life of Adventure ; or, Moss from a Rolling Stone. Cheaper Edition. Post 8vo, 3s. 6d.

Haifa : Life in Modern Palestine. Second Edition. 8vo, 7s. 6d.

The Land of Gilead. With Excursions in the Lebanon. With Illustrations and Maps. Demy 8vo, 21s.

Memoir of the Life of Laurence Oliphant, and of Alice Oliphant, his Wife. By Mrs M. O. W. OLIPHANT. Seventh Edition. 2 vols. post 8vo, with Portraits. 21s.
POPULAR EDITION. With a New Preface. Post 8vo, with Portraits. 7s. 6d.

OLIPHANT.

Who was Lost and is Found. By Mrs OLIPHANT. Second Edition. Crown 8vo, 6s.

Miss Marjoribanks. New Edition. Crown 8vo, 3s. 6d.

The Perpetual Curate, and The Rector. New Edition. Crown 8vo, 3s. 6d.

Salem Chapel, and The Doctor's Family. New Edition. Crown 8vo, 3s. 6d.

Katie Stewart, and other Stories. New Edition. Crown 8vo, cloth, 3s. 6d.

Katie Stewart. Illustrated boards, 2s. 6d.

Valentine and his Brother. New Edition. Crown 8vo, 3s. 6d.

Sons and Daughters. Crown 8vo, 3s. 6d.

Two Stories of the Seen and the Unseen. The Open Door —Old Lady Mary. Paper covers, 1s.

OLIPHANT. Notes of a Pilgrimage to Jerusalem and the Holy
Land. By F. R. OLIPHANT. Crown 8vo, 3s. 6d.

OSWALD. By Fell and Fjord; or, Scenes and Studies in Iceland. By E. J. OSWALD. Post 8vo, with Illustrations. 7s. 6d.

PAGE.

Introductory Text-Book of Geology. By DAVID PAGE, LL.D.,
Professor of Geology in the Durham University of Physical Science, Newcastle.
With Engravings and Glossarial Index. New Edition. Revised by Professor
LAPWORTH of Mason Science College, Birmingham. [*In preparation.*

Advanced Text-Book of Geology, Descriptive and Industrial.
With Engravings, and Glossary of Scientific Terms. New Edition. Revised by
Professor LAPWORTH. [*In preparation.*

Introductory Text-Book of Physical Geography. With Sketch-
Maps and Illustrations. Edited by Professor LAPWORTH, LL.D., F.G.S., &c.,
Mason Science College, Birmingham. Thirteenth Edition, Revised and Enlarged.
2s. 6d.

Advanced Text-Book of Physical Geography. Third Edition.
Revised and Enlarged by Professor LAPWORTH. With Engravings. 5s.

PATON.

Spindrift. By Sir J. NOEL PATON. Fcap., cloth, 5s.

Poems by a Painter. Fcap., cloth, 5s.

PATON. Body and Soul. A Romance in Transcendental Pathology. By FREDERICK NOEL PATON. Third Edition. Crown 8vo, 1s.

PATRICK. The Apology of Origen in Reply to Celsus. A
Chapter in the History of Apologetics. By the Rev. J. PATRICK, D.D. Post 8vo,
7s. 6d.

PAUL. History of the Royal Company of Archers, the Queen's
Body-Guard for Scotland. By JAMES BALFOUR PAUL, Advocate of the Scottish
Bar. Crown 4to, with Portraits and other Illustrations. £2, 2s.

PEILE. Lawn Tennis as a Game of Skill. By Lieut.-Col. S. C.
F. PEILE, B.S.C. Revised Edition, with new Scoring Rules. Fcap. 8vo, cloth, 1s.

PETTIGREW. The Handy Book of Bees, and their Profitable
Management. By A. PETTIGREW. Fifth Edition, Enlarged, with Engravings.
Crown 8vo, 3s. 6d.

PFLEIDERER. Philosophy and Development of Religion.
Being the Edinburgh Gifford Lectures for 1894. By OTTO PFLEIDERER, D.D.
Professor of Theology at Berlin University. In 2 vols. post 8vo, 15s. net.

PHILOSOPHICAL CLASSICS FOR ENGLISH READERS.
Edited by WILLIAM KNIGHT, LL.D., Professor of Moral Philosophy, University
of St Andrews. In crown 8vo volumes, with Portraits, price 3s. 6d.
[*For List of Volumes, see page 2.*

POLLARD. A Study in Municipal Government: The Corporation of Berlin. By JAMES POLLARD, C.A., Chairman of the Edinburgh Public
Health Committee, and Secretary of the Edinburgh Chamber of Commerce.
Second Edition, Revised. Crown 8vo, 3s. 6d.

POLLOK. The Course of Time: A Poem. By ROBERT POLLOK,
A.M. Cottage Edition, 32mo, 8d. The Same, cloth, gilt edges, 1s. 6d. Another
Edition, with Illustrations by Birket Foster and others, fcap., cloth, 3s. 6d., or
with edges gilt, 4s.

PORT ROYAL LOGIC. Translated from the French; with
Introduction, Notes, and Appendix. By THOMAS SPENCER BAYNES, LL.D., Professor in the University of St Andrews. Tenth Edition, 12mo, 4s.

POTTS AND DARNELL.

Aditus Faciliores: An Easy Latin Construing Book, with
Complete Vocabulary By A. W. POTTS, M.A., LL.D., and the Rev. C. DARNELL,
M.A., Head-Master of Cargilfield Preparatory School Edinburgh. Tenth Edition,
fcap. 8vo, 3s. 6d.

POTTS AND DARNELL.
Aditus Faciliores Graeci. An Easy Greek Construing Book,
with Complete Vocabulary. Fifth Edition, Revised. Fcap. 8vo, 3s.

POTTS. School Sermons. By the late ALEXANDER WM. POTTS,
LL.D., First Head-Master of Fettes College. With a Memoir and Portrait.
Crown 8vo, 7s. 6d.

PRINGLE. The Live Stock of the Farm. By ROBERT O.
PRINGLE. Third Edition. Revised and Edited by JAMES MACDONALD. Crown
8vo, 7s. 6d.

PRYDE. Pleasant Memories of a Busy Life. By DAVID PRYDE,
M.A., LL.D., Author of 'Highways of Literature,' 'Great Men in European History,' 'Biographical Outlines of English Literature,' &c. With a Mezzotint Portrait. Post 8vo, 6s.

PUBLIC GENERAL STATUTES AFFECTING SCOTLAND
from 1707 to 1847, with Chronological Table and Index. 3 vols. large 8vo, £3, 3s.

PUBLIC GENERAL STATUTES AFFECTING SCOTLAND,
COLLECTION OF. Published Annually, with General Index.

RAE. The Syrian Church in India. By GEORGE MILNE RAE,
M.A., D.D., Fellow of the University of Madras; late Professor in the Madras
Christian College. With 6 full-page Illustrations. Post 8vo, 10s. 6d.

RAMSAY. Scotland and Scotsmen in the Eighteenth Century.
Edited from the MSS. of JOHN RAMSAY, Esq. of Ochtertyre, by ALEXANDER
ALLARDYCE, Author of 'Memoir of Admiral Lord Keith, K.B.,' &c. 2 vols.
8vo, 31s. 6d.

RANKIN.
A Handbook of the Church of Scotland. By JAMES RANKIN,
D.D., Minister of Muthill; Author of 'Character Studies in the Old Testament,'
&c. An entirely New and much Enlarged Edition. Crown 8vo, with 2 Maps,
7s. 6d.

The First Saints. Post 8vo, 7s. 6d.

The Creed in Scotland. An Exposition of the Apostles
Creed. With Extracts from Archbishop Hamilton's Catechism of 1552, John
Calvin's Catechism of 1556, and a Catena of Ancient Latin and other Hymns.
Post 8vo, 7s. 6d.

The Worthy Communicant. A Guide to the Devout Obser-
vance of the Lord's Supper. Limp cloth, 1s. 3d.

The Young Churchman. Lessons on the Creed, the Com-
mandments, the Means of Grace, and the Church. Limp cloth, 1s. 3d.

First Communion Lessons. 25th Edition. Paper Cover, 2d.

RANKINE. A Hero of the Dark Continent. Memoir of Rev.
Wm. Affleck Scott, M.A., M.B., C.M., Church of Scotland Missionary at Blantyre,
British Central Africa. By W. HENRY RANKINE, B.D., Minister at St Boswells.
With a Portrait and other Illustrations. Crown 8vo, 5s.

RECORDS OF THE TERCENTENARY FESTIVAL OF THE
UNIVERSITY OF EDINBURGH. Celebrated in April 1884. Published under
the Sanction of the Senatus Academicus. Large 4to, £2, 12s. 6d.

ROBERTSON. The Early Religion of Israel. As set forth by
Biblical Writers and Modern Critical Historians. Being the Baird Lecture for
1888-89. By JAMES ROBERTSON, D.D., Professor of Oriental Languages in the
University of Glasgow. Fourth Edition. Crown 8vo, 10s. 6d.

ROBERTSON.
Orellana, and other Poems. By J. LOGIE ROBERTSON,
M.A. Fcap. 8vo. Printed on hand-made paper. 6s.

A History of English Literature. For Secondary Schools.
With an Introduction by Professor MASSON, Edinburgh University. Cr. 8vo, 3s.

ROBERTSON.
English Verse for Junior Classes. In Two Parts. Part I.—
Chaucer to Coleridge. Part II.—Nineteenth Century Poets. Crown 8vo, each
1s. 6d. net.

ROBERTSON. Our Holiday among the Hills. By JAMES and
JANET LOGIE ROBERTSON. Fcap. 8vo, 3s. 6d.

ROBERTSON. Essays and Sermons. By the late W. ROBERT-
SON, B.D., Minister of the Parish of Sprouston. With a Memoir and Portrait.
Crown 8vo, 5s. 6d.

RODGER. Aberdeen Doctors at Home and Abroad. The Story
of a Medical School. By ELLA HILL BURTON RODGER. Demy 8vo, 10s. 6d.

ROSCOE. Rambles with a Fishing-Rod. By E. S. ROSCOE.
Crown 8vo, 4s. 6d.

ROSS AND SOMERVILLE. Beggars on Horseback : A Riding
Tour in North Wales. By MARTIN ROSS and E. Œ. SOMERVILLE. With Illustrations by E. Œ. SOMERVILLE. Crown 8vo, 3s. 6d.

RUTLAND.
Notes of an Irish Tour in 1846. By the DUKE OF RUTLAND,
G.C.B. (Lord JOHN MANNERS). New Edition. Crown 8vo, 2s. 6d.
Correspondence between the Right Honble. William Pitt
and Charles Duke of Rutland, Lord - Lieutenant of Ireland, 1781-1787. With
Introductory Note by JOHN DUKE OF RUTLAND. 8vo, 7s. 6d.

RUTLAND.
Gems of German Poetry. Translated by the DUCHESS OF
RUTLAND (Lady JOHN MANNERS). [*New Edition in preparation.*
Impressions of Bad-Homburg. Comprising a Short Account
of the Women's Associations of Germany under the Red Cross. Crown 8vo, 1s. 6d.
Some Personal Recollections of the Later Years of the Earl
of Beaconsfield, K.G. Sixth Edition. 6d.
Employment of Women in the Public Service. 6d.
Some of the Advantages of Easily Accessible Reading and
Recreation Rooms and Free Libraries. With Remarks on Starting and Main-
taining them. Second Edition. Crown 8vo, 1s.
A Sequel to Rich Men's Dwellings, and other Occasional
Papers. Crown 8vo, 2s. 6d.
Encouraging Experiences of Reading and Recreation Rooms,
Aims of Guilds, Nottingham Social Guide, Existing Institutions, &c., &c.
Crown 8vo, 1s.

SAINTSBURY. The Flourishing of Romance and the Rise of
Allegory (12th and 13th Centuries). By GEORGE SAINTSBURY, M.A., Professor of
Rhetoric and English Literature in Edinburgh University. Being the first vol-
ume issued of "PERIODS OF EUROPEAN LITERATURE." Edited by Professor
SAINTSBURY. Crown 8vo, 3s. 6d.

SALMON. Songs of a Heart's Surrender, and other Verse.
By ARTHUR L. SALMON. Fcap. 8vo, 2s.

SCHEFFEL. The Trumpeter. A Romance of the Rhine. By
JOSEPH VICTOR VON SCHEFFEL. Translated from the Two Hundredth German
Edition by JESSIE BECK and LOUISA LORIMER. With an Introduction by Sir
THEODORE MARTIN, K.C.B. Long 8vo, 3s. 6d.

SCHILLER. Wallenstein. A Dramatic Poem. By FRIEDRICH
VON SCHILLER. Translated by C. G. N. LOCKHART. Fcap. 8vo, 7s. 6d.

SCOTT. Tom Cringle's Log. By MICHAEL SCOTT. New Edition.
With 19 Full-page Illustrations. Crown 8vo, 3s. 6d.

SCOUGAL. Prisons and their Inmates; or, Scenes from a
Silent World. By FRANCIS SCOUGAL. Crown 8vo, boards, 2s.

SELKIRK. Poems. By J. B. SELKIRK, Author of 'Ethics and Æsthetics of Modern Poetry,' 'Bible Truths with Shakespearian Parallels,' &c. Crown 8vo, printed on antique paper, 6s.

SELLAR'S Manual of the Acts relating to Education in Scotland. By J. EDWARD GRAHAM, B.A. Oxon., Advocate. Ninth Edition. Demy 8vo, 12s. 6d.

SETH.

Scottish Philosophy. A Comparison of the Scottish and German Answers to Hume. Balfour Philosophical Lectures, University of Edinburgh. By ANDREW SETH, LL.D., Professor of Logic and Metaphysics in Edinburgh University. Second Edition. Crown 8vo, 5s.

Hegelianism and Personality. Balfour Philosophical Lectures. Second Series. Second Edition. Crown 8vo, 5s.

SETH. A Study of Ethical Principles. By JAMES SETH, M.A., Professor of Philosophy in Cornell University, U.S.A. Second Edition, Revised. Post 8vo, 10s. 6d. net.

SHADWELL. The Life of Colin Campbell, Lord Clyde. Illustrated by Extracts from his Diary and Correspondence. By Lieutenant-General SHADWELL, C.B. With Portrait, Maps, and Plans. 2 vols. 8vo, 36s.

SHAND.

The Life of General Sir Edward Bruce Hamley, K.C.B., K.C.M.G. By ALEX. INNES SHAND, Author of 'Kilcarra,' 'Against Time,' &c. With two Photogravure Portraits and other Illustrations. Cheaper Edition, with a Statement by Mr Edward Hamley. 2 vols. demy 8vo, 10s. 6d.

Half a Century; or, Changes in Men and Manners. Second Edition. 8vo, 12s. 6d.

Letters from the West of Ireland. Reprinted from the 'Times.' Crown 8vo, 5s.

SHARPE. Letters from and to Charles Kirkpatrick Sharpe. Edited by ALEXANDER ALLARDYCE, Author of 'Memoir of Admiral Lord Keith, K.B.,' &c. With a Memoir by the Rev. W. K. R. BEDFORD. In 2 vols. 8vo. Illustrated with Etchings and other Engravings. £2, 12s. 6d.

SIM. Margaret Sim's Cookery. With an Introduction by L. B. WALFORD, Author of 'Mr Smith: A Part of his Life,' &c. Crown 8vo, 5s.

SIMPSON. The Wild Rabbit in a New Aspect; or, Rabbit-Warrens that Pay. A book for Landowners, Sportsmen, Land Agents, Farmers, Gamekeepers, and Allotment Holders. A Record of Recent Experiments conducted on the Estate of the Right Hon. the Earl of Wharncliffe at Wortley Hall. By J. SIMPSON. Second Edition, Enlarged. Small crown 8vo, 5s.

SKELTON.

The Table-Talk of Shirley. By JOHN SKELTON, Advocate, C.B., LL.D., Author of 'The Essays of Shirley.' With a Frontispiece. Sixth Edition, Revised and Enlarged. Post 8vo, 7s. 6d.

The Table-Talk of Shirley. Second Series. Summers and Winters at Balmawhapple. With Illustrations. Two Volumes. Post 8vo, 10s. net.

Maitland of Lethington; and the Scotland of Mary Stuart. A History. Limited Edition, with Portraits. Demy 8vo, 2 vols, 28s. net.

The Handbook of Public Health. A Complete Edition of the Public Health and other Sanitary Acts relating to Scotland. Annotated, and with the Rules, Instructions, and Decisions of the Board of Supervision brought up to date with relative forms. Second Edition. With Introduction, containing the Administration of the Public Health Act in Counties. 8vo, 8s. 6d.

The Local Government (Scotland) Act in Relation to Public Health. A Handy Guide for County and District Councillors, Medical Officers, Sanitary Inspectors, and Members of Parochial Boards. Second Edition. With a new Preface on appointment of Sanitary Officers. Crown 8vo, 2s.

SKRINE. Columba: A Drama. By JOHN HUNTLEY SKRINE,
Warden of Glenalmond; Author of 'A Memory of Edward Thring.' Fcap. 4to, 6s.

SMITH.
Thorndale; or, The Conflict of Opinions. By WILLIAM SMITH,
Author of 'A Discourse on Ethics,' &c. New Edition. Crown 8vo, 10s. 6d.
Gravenhurst; or, Thoughts on Good and Evil. Second Edition. With Memoir and Portrait of the Author. Crown 8vo, 8s.
The Story of William and Lucy Smith. Edited by GEORGE
MERRIAM. Large post 8vo, 12s. 6d.

SMITH. Memoir of the Families of M'Combie and Thoms,
originally M'Intosh and M'Thomas. Compiled from History and Tradition. By
WILLIAM M'COMBIE SMITH. With Illustrations. 8vo, 7s. 6d.

SMITH. Greek Testament Lessons for Colleges, Schools, and
Private Students, consisting chiefly of the Sermon on the Mount and the Parables
of our Lord. With Notes and Essays. By the Rev. J. HUNTER SMITH, M.A.,
King Edward's School, Birmingham. Crown 8vo, 6s.

SMITH. The Secretary for Scotland. Being a Statement of the
Powers and Duties of the new Scottish Office. With a Short Historical Intro-
duction, and numerous references to important Administrative Documents. By
W. C. SMITH, LL.B., Advocate. 8vo, 6s.

"SON OF THE MARSHES, A."
From Spring to Fall; or, When Life Stirs. By "A SON OF
THE MARSHES." Cheap Uniform Edition. Crown 8vo, 3s. 6d.
Within an Hour of London Town: Among Wild Birds and
their Haunts. Edited by J. A. OWEN. Cheap Uniform Edition. Crown 8vo,
3s. 6d.
With the Woodlanders and by the Tide. Cheap Uniform
Edition. Crown 8vo, 3s. 6d.
On Surrey Hills. Cheap Uniform Edition. Crown 8vo, 3s. 6d.
Annals of a Fishing Village. Cheap Uniform Edition. Crown
8vo, 3s. 6d.

SORLEY. The Ethics of Naturalism. Being the Shaw Fellow-
ship Lectures, 1884. By W. R. SORLEY, M.A., Fellow of Trinity College, Cambridge, Professor of Moral Philosophy in the University of Aberdeen. Crown
8vo, 6s.

SPEEDY. Sport in the Highlands and Lowlands of Scotland
with Rod and Gun. By TOM SPEEDY. Second Edition, Revised and Enlarged.
With Illustrations by Lieut.-General Hope Crealocke, C.B., C.M.G., and others.
8vo, 15s.

SPROTT. The Worship and Offices of the Church of Scotland.
By GEORGE W. SPROTT, D.D., Minister of North Berwick. Crown 8vo, 6s.

STATISTICAL ACCOUNT OF SCOTLAND. Complete, with
Index. 15 vols. 8vo, £16, 16s.

STEPHENS.
The Book of the Farm; detailing the Labours of the Farmer,
Farm-Steward, Ploughman, Shepherd, Hedger, Farm-Labourer, Field-Worker,
and Cattle-man. Illustrated with numerous Portraits of Animals and Engravings
of Implements, and Plans of Farm Buildings. Fourth Edition. Revised, and
in great part Rewritten by JAMES MACDONALD, F.R.S.E., Secretary Highland
and Agricultural Society of Scotland. Complete in Six Divisional Volumes,
bound in cloth, each 10s. 6d., or handsomely bound, in 3 volumes, with leather
back and gilt top, £3, 3s.
Catechism of Practical Agriculture. 22d Thousand. Revised
by JAMES MACDONALD, F.R.S.E. With numerous Illustrations. Crown 8vo, 1s.
The Book of Farm Implements and Machines. By J. SLIGHT
and R. SCOTT BURN, Engineers. Edited by HENRY STEPHENS. Large 8vo, £2, 2s.

STEVENSON. British Fungi. (Hymenomycetes.) By Rev. JOHN STEVENSON, Author of 'Mycologia Scotica,' Hon. Sec. Cryptogamic Society of Scotland. Vols. I. and II., post 8vo, with Illustrations, price 12s. 6d. net each.

STEWART. Advice to Purchasers of Horses. By JOHN STEWART, V.S. New Edition. 2s. 6d.

STEWART. Boethius: An Essay. By HUGH FRASER STEWART, M.A., Trinity College, Cambridge. Crown 8vo, 7s. 6d.

STODDART. Angling Songs. By THOMAS TOD STODDART. New Edition, with a Memoir by ANNA M. STODDART. Crown 8vo, 7s. 6d.

STODDART.

John Stuart Blackie: A Biography. By ANNA M. STODDART. With 3 Plates. Third Edition. 2 vols. demy 8vo, 21s.
POPULAR EDITION, with Portrait. Crown 8vo, 6s.

Sir Philip Sidney: Servant of God. Illustrated by MARGARET L. HUGGINS. With a New Portrait of Sir Philip Sidney. Small 4to, with a specially designed Cover. 5s.

STORMONTH.

Dictionary of the English Language, Pronouncing, Etymological, and Explanatory. By the Rev. JAMES STORMONTH. Revised by the Rev. P. H. PHELP. Library Edition. New and Cheaper Edition, with Supplement. Imperial 8vo, handsomely bound in half morocco, 18s. net.

Etymological and Pronouncing Dictionary of the English Language. Including a very Copious Selection of Scientific Terms. For use in Schools and Colleges, and as a Book of General Reference. The Pronunciation carefully revised by the Rev. P. H. PHELP, M.A. Cantab. Thirteenth Edition, with Supplement. Crown 8vo, pp. 800. 7s. 6d.

The School Etymological Dictionary and Word-Book. New Edition, Revised. [*In preparation.*]

STORY.

Nero; A Historical Play. By W. W. STORY, Author of 'Roba di Roma.' Fcap. 8vo, 6s.

Vallombrosa. Post 8vo, 5s.

Poems. 2 vols., 7s. 6d.

Fiammetta. A Summer Idyl. Crown 8vo, 7s. 6d.

Conversations in a Studio. 2 vols. crown 8vo, 12s. 6d.

Excursions in Art and Letters. Crown 8vo, 7s. 6d.

A Poet's Portfolio: Later Readings. 18mo, 3s. 6d.

STRACHEY. Talk at a Country House. Fact and Fiction. By Sir EDWARD STRACHEY, Bart. With a Portrait of the Author. Crown 8vo, 4s. 6d. net.

STURGIS. Little Comedies, Old and New. By JULIAN STURGIS. Crown 8vo, 7s. 6d.

SUTHERLAND. Handbook of Hardy Herbaceous and Alpine Flowers, for General Garden Decoration. Containing Descriptions of upwards of 1000 Species of Ornamental Hardy Perennial and Alpine Plants; along with Concise and Plain Instructions for their Propagation and Culture. By WILLIAM SUTHERLAND, Landscape Gardener; formerly Manager of the Herbaceous Department at Kew. Crown 8vo, 7s. 6d.

TAYLOR. The Story of my Life. By the late Colonel MEADOWS TAYLOR, Author of 'The Confessions of a Thug,' &c., &c. Edited by his Daughter. New and Cheaper Edition, being the Fourth. Crown 8vo, 6s.

THOMSON.
 The Diversions of a Prime Minister. By Basil Thomson.
 With a Map, numerous Illustrations by J. W. Cawston and others, and Repro-
 ductions of Rare Plates from Early Voyages of Sixteenth and Seventeenth Cen-
 turies. Small demy 8vo, 15s.
 South Sea Yarns. With 10 Full-page Illustrations. Cheaper
 Edition. Crown 8vo, 3s. 6d.

THOMSON.
 Handy Book of the Flower-Garden : Being Practical Direc-
 tions for the Propagation, Culture, and Arrangement of Plants in Flower-
 Gardens all the year round. With Engraved Plans. By DAVID THOMSON,
 Gardener to his Grace the Duke of Buccleuch, K.T., at Drumlanrig. Fourth
 and Cheaper Edition. Crown 8vo, 5s.
 The Handy Book of Fruit-Culture under Glass : Being a
 series of Elaborate Practical Treatises on the Cultivation and Forcing of Pines,
 Vines, Peaches, Figs, Melons, Strawberries, and Cucumbers. With Engravings
 of Hothouses, &c. Second Edition, Revised and Enlarged. Crown 8vo, 7s. 6d.

THOMSON. A Practical Treatise on the Cultivation of the
 Grape Vine. By WILLIAM THOMSON, Tweed Vineyards. Tenth Edition. 8vo, 5s.

THOMSON. Cookery for the Sick and Convalescent. With
 Directions for the Preparation of Poultices, Fomentations, &c. By BARBARA
 THOMSON. Fcap. 8vo, 1s. 6d.

THORBURN. Asiatic Neighbours. By S. S. THORBURN, Bengal
 Civil Service, Author of 'Bannú; or, Our Afghan Frontier,' 'David Leslie :
 A Story of the Afghan Frontier,' 'Musalmans and Money-Lenders in the Pan-
 jab.' With Two Maps. Demy 8vo, 10s. 6d. net.

THORNTON. Opposites. A Series of Essays on the Unpopular
 Sides of Popular Questions. By LEWIS THORNTON. 8vo, 12s. 6d.

TRANSACTIONS OF THE HIGHLAND AND AGRICUL-
 TURAL SOCIETY OF SCOTLAND. Published annually, price 5s.

TRAVERS.
 Mona Maclean, Medical Student. A Novel. By GRAHAM
 TRAVERS. Eleventh Edition. Crown 8vo, 6s.
 Fellow Travellers. Third Edition. Crown 8vo, 6s.

TRYON. Life of Admiral Sir George Tryon. By Rear-Admiral
 C. C. PENROSE FITZGERALD. With Portrait and numerous Illustrations. Demy
 8vo, 18s.

TULLOCH.
 Rational Theology and Christian Philosophy in England in
 the Seventeenth Century. By JOHN TULLOCH, D.D., Principal of St Mary's Col-
 lege in the University of St Andrews, and one of her Majesty's Chaplains in
 Ordinary in Scotland. Second Edition. 2 vols. 8vo, 16s.
 Modern Theories in Philosophy and Religion. 8vo, 15s.
 Luther, and other Leaders of the Reformation. Third Edi-
 tion, Enlarged. Crown 8vo, 3s. 6d.
 Memoir of Principal Tulloch, D.D., LL.D. By Mrs OLIPHANT,
 Author of 'Life of Edward Irving.' Third and Cheaper Edition. 8vo, with
 Portrait, 7s. 6d.

TWEEDIE. The Arabian Horse : His Country and People.
 By Major-General W. TWEEDIE, C.S.I., Bengal Staff Corps; for many years
 H.B.M.'s Consul-General, Baghdad, and Political Resident for the Government
 of India in Turkish Arabia. In one vol. royal 4to, with Seven Coloured Plates
 and other Illustrations, and a Map of the Country. Price £3, 3s. net.

TYLER. The Whence and the Whither of Man. A Brief History of his Origin and Development through Conformity to Environment. The Morse Lectures of 1895. By JOHN M. TYLER, Professor of Biology, Amherst College, U.S.A. Post 8vo, 6s. net.

VEITCH.
Memoir of John Veitch, LL.D., Professor of Logic and Rhetoric, University of Glasgow. By MARY R. L. BRYCE. With Portrait and 3 Photogravure Plates. Demy 8vo, 7s. 6d.
Border Essays. By JOHN VEITCH, LL.D., Professor of Logic and Rhetoric, University of Glasgow. Crown 8vo, 4s. 6d. *net.*
The History and Poetry of the Scottish Border : their Main Features and Relations. New and Enlarged Edition. 2 vols. demy 8vo, 16s.
Institutes of Logic. Post 8vo, 12s. 6d.
The Feeling for Nature in Scottish Poetry. From the Earliest Times to the Present Day. 2 vols. fcap. 8vo, in roxburghe binding, 15s.
Merlin and other Poems. Fcap. 8vo, 4s. 6d.
Knowing and Being. Essays in Philosophy. First Series. Crown 8vo, 5s.
Dualism and Monism ; and other Essays. Essays in Philosophy. Second Series. With an Introduction by R. M. Wenley. Crown 8vo, 4s. 6d. net.

VIRGIL. The Æneid of Virgil. Translated in English Blank Verse by G. K. RICKARDS, M.A., and Lord RAVENSWORTH. 2 vols. fcap. 8vo, 10s.

WACE. Christianity and Agnosticism. Reviews of some Recent Attacks on the Christian Faith. By HENRY WACE, D.D., Principal of King's College, London ; Preacher of Lincoln's Inn ; Chaplain to the Queen. Second Edition. Post 8vo, 10s. 6d. net.

WADDELL. An Old Kirk Chronicle : Being a History of Auldhame, Tyninghame, and Whitekirk, in East Lothian. From Session Records, 1615 to 1850. By Rev. P. HATELY WADDELL, B.D., Minister of the United Parish. Small Paper Edition, 200 Copies. Price £1. Large Paper Edition, 50 Copies. Price £1, 10s.

WALFORD. Four Biographies from 'Blackwood' : Jane Taylor, Hannah More, Elizabeth Fry, Mary Somerville. By L. B. WALFORD. Crown 8vo, 5s.

WARREN'S (SAMUEL) WORKS :—
Diary of a Late Physician. Cloth, 2s. 6d. ; boards, 2s.
Ten Thousand A-Year. Cloth, 3s. 6d. ; boards, 2s. 6d.
Now and Then. The Lily and the Bee. Intellectual and Moral Development of the Present Age. 4s. 6d.
Essays : Critical, Imaginative, and Juridical. 5s.

WENLEY.
Socrates and Christ : A Study in the Philosophy of Religion. By R. M. WENLEY, M.A., D.Sc., D.Phil., Professor of Philosophy in the University of Michigan, U.S.A. Crown 8vo, 6s.
Aspects of Pessimism. Crown 8vo, 6s.

WHITE.
The Eighteen Christian Centuries. By the Rev. JAMES WHITE. Seventh Edition. Post 8vo, with Index, 6s.
History of France, from the Earliest Times. Sixth Thousand. Post 8vo, with Index, 6s.

WHITE.
Archæological Sketches in Scotland—Kintyre and Knapdale.
By Colonel T. P. WHITE, R.E., of the Ordnance Survey. With numerous Illustrations. 2 vols. folio, £4, 4s. Vol. I., Kintyre, sold separately, £2, 2s.
The Ordnance Survey of the United Kingdom. A Popular
Account. Crown 8vo, 5s.

WILLIAMSON. The Horticultural Handbook and Exhibitor's
Guide. A Treatise on Cultivating, Exhibiting, and Judging Plants, Flowers, Fruits, and Vegetables. By W. WILLIAMSON, Gardener. Revised by MALCOLM DUNN, Gardener to his Grace the Duke of Buccleuch and Queensberry, Dalkeith Park. New and Cheaper Edition, enlarged. Crown 8vo, paper cover, 2s. ; cloth, 2s. 6d.

WILLIAMSON. Poems of Nature and Life. By DAVID R.
WILLIAMSON, Minister of Kirkmaiden. Fcap. 8vo, 3s.

WILLS. Behind an Eastern Veil. A Plain Tale of Events
occurring in the Experience of a Lady who had a unique opportunity of observing the Inner Life of Ladies of the Upper Class in Persia. By C. J. WILLS, Author of ' In the Land of the Lion and Sun,' ' Persia as it is,' &c., &c. Cheaper Edition. Demy 8vo, 5s.

WILSON.
Works of Professor Wilson. Edited by his Son-in-Law,
Professor FERRIER. 12 vols. crown 8vo, £2, 8s.
Christopher in his Sporting-Jacket. 2 vols., 8s.
Isle of Palms, City of the Plague, and other Poems. 4s.
Lights and Shadows of Scottish Life, and other Tales. 4s.
Essays, Critical and Imaginative. 4 vols., 16s.
The Noctes Ambrosianæ. 4 vols., 16s.
Homer and his Translators, and the Greek Drama. Crown
8vo, 4s.

WORSLEY.
Poems and Translations. By PHILIP STANHOPE WORSLEY,
M.A. Edited by EDWARD WORSLEY. Second Edition, Enlarged. Fcap. 8vo, 6s.
Homer's Odyssey. Translated into English Verse in the
Spenserian Stanza. By P. S. Worsley. New and Cheaper Edition. Post 8vo, 7s. 6d. net.
Homer's Iliad. Translated by P. S. Worsley and Prof. Con-
ington. 2 vols. crown 8vo, 21s.

YATE. England and Russia Face to Face in Asia. A Record of
Travel with the Afghan Boundary Commission. By Captain A. C. YATE, Bombay Staff Corps. 8vo, with Maps and Illustrations, 21s.

YATE. Northern Afghanistan ; or, Letters from the Afghan
Boundary Commission. By Major C. E. YATE, C.S.I., C.M.G., Bombay Staff Corps, F.R.G.S. 8vo, with Maps, 18s.

YULE. Fortification : For the use of Officers in the Army, and
Readers of Military History. By Colonel YULE, Bengal Engineers. 8vo, with Numerous Illustrations, 10s.

www.ingramcontent.com/pod-product-compliance
Lightning Source LLC
Chambersburg PA
CBHW031145120726
47905CB00006B/1821